TAKING FLIGHT

CARIBBEAN
STUDIES
SERIES

Anton L. Allahar and Natasha Barnes
Series Editors

TAKING FLIGHT

Caribbean Women Writing from Abroad

JENNIFER DONAHUE

University Press of Mississippi / Jackson

The University Press of Mississippi is the scholarly publishing agency of the Mississippi Institutions of Higher Learning: Alcorn State University, Delta State University, Jackson State University, Mississippi State University, Mississippi University for Women, Mississippi Valley State University, University of Mississippi, and University of Southern Mississippi.

www.upress.state.ms.us

Designed by Peter D. Halverson

The University Press of Mississippi is a member of the Association of University Presses.

Copyright © 2020 by University Press of Mississippi
All rights reserved

Portions of chapter 5 first appeared as an article in *ariel*, volume 50, issue 2–3, April–July 2019, pages 59–80, copyright © 2019 Johns Hopkins University Press and the University of Calgary.

First printing 2020

∞

Library of Congress Cataloging-in-Publication Data

Names: Donahue, Jennifer Lynn, author.
Title: Taking flight : Caribbean women writing from abroad / Jennifer Donahue.
Other titles: Caribbean studies series (Jackson, Miss.)
Description: Jackson : University Press of Mississippi, 2020. | Series: Caribbean studies series | Includes bibliographical references and index.
Identifiers: LCCN 2020011793 (print) | LCCN 2020011794 (ebook) | ISBN 9781496828637 (hardback) | ISBN 9781496828705 (trade paperback) | ISBN 9781496828712 (epub) | ISBN 9781496828729 (epub) | ISBN 9781496828736 (pdf) | ISBN 9781496828743 (pdf)
Subjects: LCSH: Caribbean literature—History and criticism. | Caribbean literature—Women authors. | Psychic trauma in literature. | BISAC: LITERARY CRITICISM / Caribbean & Latin American
Classification: LCC PN849.C3 D66 2020 (print) | LCC PN849.C3 (ebook) | DDC 809/.8928709729—dc23
LC record available at https://lccn.loc.gov/2020011793
LC ebook record available at https://lccn.loc.gov/2020011794

British Library Cataloging-in-Publication Data available

CONTENTS

ACKNOWLEDGMENTS

vii

INTRODUCTION

3

CHAPTER ONE

THE IMMIGRANT EXPERIENCE
Trauma, Folklore, and Migration in
Danticat's *Breath, Eyes, Memory* and *Krik? Krak!*

13

CHAPTER TWO

DIVIDED ALLEGIANCES AND ALTERNATIVE HISTORIES
Michelle Cliff's and Margaret Cezair-Thompson's
Focus on Psychological Exile

36

CHAPTER THREE

TRAVERSING THE TRIANGULAR ROAD
Retrieving the Past and Reconsidering Cultural Identity in
Praisesong for the Widow and *Small Island*

60

CHAPTER FOUR

REDEFINING BEAUTY
Elizabeth Nunez's and Pauline Melville's Exploration of
Illness, Migration, and Transformation

84

CHAPTER FIVE
CONSUMING THE CARIBBEAN
Sexuality, Social Norms, and Belonging in *Here Comes the Sun* and *Land of Love and Drowning*
107

EPILOGUE
133

NOTES
135

BIBLIOGRAPHY
144

INDEX
153

ACKNOWLEDGMENTS

I am indebted to everyone who has supported me on this intellectual and introspective journey; your encouragement has made the writing of this manuscript possible. Thank you to my mentors at the University of Maryland and Florida State University. My study has benefited immensely from the critical input of Merle Collins, Laura Rosenthal, Candace Ward, Maxine Montgomery, and Martin Munro, among others. My deep gratitude goes to my colleagues at the University of Arizona. I have been especially blessed with supportive colleagues in the Africana Studies Program; thank you for believing in this project. This book has been shaped by your feedback and I am very appreciative of your continued support. I want to particularly express my gratitude to my dean in the College of Humanities, Alain-Philippe Durand, and my director, Praise Zenenga, for guiding, challenging, and critiquing my work. I am also grateful to my early interlocutors who helped me hone my arguments. I delivered papers related to this book at the Caribbean Studies Association, Modern Language Association, College English Association, and American Comparative Literature Association conferences; suggestions and queries from attendees guided the development of this work. Thanks are due to the staff at the University Press of Mississippi, particularly Vijay Shah, Lisa McMurtray, Valerie Jones, and the anonymous readers who were instrumental in shaping this project. I am extremely grateful to my students in classes on Caribbean literature who have shared their insights and prompted me to question my conclusions. Thank you to my family for encouraging my curiosity and cheering me on at every turn. Finally, I would like to thank my partner, Thomas, for believing in me more than I believe in myself. Your abiding love has been instrumental in this and all that I do. May we all favor acceptance over anger, seek to dissolve the forces that divide us, shun silence in favor of truth, and find peace.

TAKING FLIGHT

INTRODUCTION

> Conceived of as defective or deficient from male norms and as potentially diseased, women have long been embodiments of shame in our culture, and, indeed, the female socialization process can be viewed as a prolonged immersion in shame.
>
> —J. BROOKS BOUSON

On October 15, 2017, actress Alyssa Milano tweeted, "If you've been sexually harassed or assaulted write 'me too' as a reply to this tweet." Milano's call to action reignited Tarana Burke's movement, a campaign founded long before the advent of social media. Like Burke, authors such as Edwidge Danticat, Michelle Cliff, and Margaret Cezair-Thompson have shed light on the magnitude and impact of sexual assault and abuse. Their work, and the work of the other Caribbean women authors that this project examines, frames sexual violence as a systemic issue warranting immediate attention. Caribbean women have been saying #Metoo for hundreds of years. More recently, truth tellers including Tiphanie Yanique and Nicole Dennis-Benn have utilized the medium of fiction to break the pervasive silence surrounding abuse and exploitation. Collectively, the works under study illustrate the deep-rooted consequences of gender, sexual, and race-based trauma and trace the steps that women take to find safer ground from oppression.

In these works, culturally sanctioned violence affects the ability of female characters to be at home in their bodies or in the spaces they inhabit. The protagonists, recipients of the socialization process that J. Brooks Bouson mentions, endure various forms of trauma and migrate to ease the resulting sense of shame.[1] Following protracted decision-making processes, the women leave home. In each case, the determination to move, oftentimes out of the Caribbean region, comes with great difficulty. Importantly, the choice to reject the site of trauma is rooted in self-protection in that characters embrace the unknown in the hope of having their physical and emotional needs met. As the texts discussed demonstrate, there is a clear link between trauma, shame, and migration, with trauma serving as a precursor to the protagonists' emigration. The works continue the legacy of narrating black women's long-standing contestation of systems of oppression, reference historical trauma, and draw attention to the historical racialization and sexualization of black women's bodies.

Taking Flight takes a closer look at the immigrant experience in contemporary Caribbean women's writing and considers the effects of restrictive social mores. One of the aims of this book is to better understand the complex relationship between social norms and trauma. This approach is based on a close reading of literary representations of Caribbean women with particular attention to how female bodies are policed, how moral, racial, and sexual codes are linked, and how the enforcement of social norms can function as a form of trauma. My argument defines trauma as a "powerful indicator of oppressive cultural institutions and practices" and hinges on the idea that body and sexual politics operate as sources of trauma in the works under study (Vickroy 4). The characters navigate oppressive and repressive systems in spaces that are built on exclusion, violence, and abuse. The difficulty of creating home in that space is compounded by national cultures that privilege shame and secrecy. In the works, gender and sexual norms function as a source of trauma as well as a significant factor in Caribbean women's decision to relocate.

Scholars including Erica Johnson, Patricia Moran, and Melissa Harris-Perry have observed the link between femininity and shame. Although the characters' reactions to social control vary, shame and silence predominate; the upshot is that migration is often rendered attractive. The silence surrounding trauma is influenced by cultural values and ideologies. It is therefore necessary to consider the relationship between trauma, shame, and sexual politics. I duly enquire into how shame works as a social regulator that frequently leads to withdrawal or avoidant behaviors in those who violate socially sanctioned mores. While shame often functions as a sociocultural reinforcer of behavior in the texts under study, and thus shapes women's experiences as citizens, it is important to attend to how dissociation, a common response to trauma that disrupts the "usually integrated functions of consciousness, memory, identity, or sensitivity to the environment," serves as a literary trope as well as a coping mechanism (Alayarian 151). In several of the works, this psychological defense mechanism precedes migration.

Central to this book, then, is an attempt to position flight as a counter to disempowerment and to consider how flight, whether through dissociation or migration, operates as a form of resistance.

CARIBBEAN WOMEN'S WRITING

Taking Flight examines a selection of Caribbean women's writing published since 1984. While psychological reactions to trauma have attracted scholarly attention since the late nineteenth century, the American Psychological Association did not formally recognize dissociative disorders and post-traumatic stress disorder until 1980. This selection of texts, published after the release of the DSM-III (*Diagnostic and Statistical Manual of Mental Disorders*) in 1980, narrates the effects of trauma after the condition gained increased visibility. One of the larger goals of this book is to expand understandings of trauma beyond war and sexual violence. Central to my argument is the belief that diversifying the clinical definition of trauma will shed light on other forms of oppression such as racism, sexism, and homophobia.

In focusing on Caribbean women's writing, the book draws attention to the fact that Caribbean women writers continue to be underpublished and underrepresented within Caribbean studies. While prior to the 1970s Caribbean literature was dominated by male-authored, bildungsroman-type tales, the growth of Caribbean women's writing has expanded the field to tackle subjects that were formerly seen as taboo.[2] Early Caribbean literature by authors such as V. S. Naipaul, Earl Lovelace, and Claude McKay often features a male character leaving the islands for the metropole, but these texts present a largely one-dimensional portrait of that experience. By addressing migration and exile from a female perspective, the authors supplement the narratives advanced by their male counterparts. Contemporary works authored by women tend to consider psychological exile[3] as an important but not necessarily requisite part of the migratory experience and employ the trope of flight to foreground the emotional difficulties that can accompany migration. While in the masculine or "traditional" bildungsroman the male character coming of age is often paired with a quest for education or self-improvement, in Caribbean women's writing this negotiation is frequently associated with trauma and the subsequent migration of the female protagonist. Though, as Carine Mardorossian observes, the exiled (usually male) writer is often seen as more objective because of his alienation, the gendering of exile largely ignores the concerns of women (16). Perhaps in response, authors such as Elizabeth Nunez, Paule Marshall, and Andrea Levy reinscribe the traditionalist genre of the bildungsroman to center the experiences of Caribbean women.

The authors featured primarily reside outside the region and represent diverse experiences. Addressing the work of female migrant authors is not intended to diminish the male migratory experience, suggest that Afro-Caribbean males do not experience trauma, situate men as inherently more stable, or position these works as culturally or geographically representative of the Caribbean region or of all Caribbean women. Instead, this book seeks to complicate the relationship between gender, trauma, and mobility in Caribbean women's writing and to shed light on the sociocultural forces that disproportionately affect women. Admittedly, the term "Caribbean women" can collapse difference and create a false sense of similarity. Chandra Mohanty, among others, has expressed concern that viewing literature solely through a gendered lens can result in "an assumption of women as an always already constituted group, one that has been labeled powerless, exploited, sexually harassed, and so on" (23). Following this, I utilize the term "Caribbean women" with the understanding that Caribbean women are not a homogenous group; instead, Caribbean women's literature and the voices of Caribbean women reflect distinct racial, cultural, and socioeconomic positions.

As scholars such as Donald Hill have explained, transnationalism refers to the ties linking people across borders and is the result of "globalization whereby a group of people, with their own special culture and folklore, are spread out over several countries or continents and continue to act as a unit" (8).[4] Hill is invoked here to highlight the role of folklore in homemaking. Folklore is central to the characters' journeys through personal unburdening and historical unlearning. In many of the texts explored in this book, home is a contested and problematic space and folklore provides comfort in unfamiliar environments. In works such as Danticat's *Breath, Eyes, Memory* and *Krik? Krak!*, home is far from ideal and it is the process of escape that allows the protagonists to place themselves in new material realities. The works address issues of identity and belonging and foreground the relationship between violence and citizenship. In her study of the relationship between mother and motherland, Simone Alexander claims that the absence of an ideal homeland "intensifies the imagining and the inventing of home spaces or homelands" (10). The authors of this selection of texts write in order to carve out more ideal places for their characters, but flight is not without adverse effects. The titles of works such as *The Migration of Ghosts* and *Small Island*, for instance, suggest that migration and exile, like trauma, are haunting influences that do not immediately vanish following departure. Characters continue to grapple with feelings of shame and disembodiment and face prejudice and exclusion in their new environments. The title of Pauline Melville's *The Migration of Ghosts*, in particular, positions migrants as already deceased and warns of the danger of becoming a ghost of yourself abroad. What the narratives illustrate is that migration does not inherently equal escape; there is no guarantee that the new location that migrants arrive to will offer a substantial improvement over their previous conditions. Collectively, the works point to migration as an essential component in the process that negotiates lived experience and idealized portraits of home.

Reading flight as a process provoked by conditions that adversely affect personal wellbeing foregrounds the impetus for migration. Migration is far from an easy process for most of the characters but offers the protagonists the ability to reinvent themselves much in the same way that the experience affords the authors a means of creative genesis. As a result of their own migration, writers such as Cliff and Dennis-Benn are perhaps better able to critique their homelands from a distance. Although migration can be understood as bitter and frustrating, the selected texts counter that view with a rich portrait of cultural hybridity. While the process can mean displacement for many, it offers an avenue for liberation for some. Cezair-Thompson's *The True History of Paradise* and Marshall's *Praisesong for the Widow*, for example, situate the protagonists as recipients of ancestral knowledge to counter the dominant historical narrative.

The authors discussed herein craft characters who are often forced to leave home in order to escape personal and political violence. The women in these works constantly reconfigure and reinvent themselves, often in ways that incorporate a multitude of historic and cultural influences. This is seen in texts such as Nunez's *Boundaries* and *Anna In-Between* wherein Anna Sinclair reconstructs home amidst her mother's illness. In many of the texts, the transformative process is not simply one of coming of age or embracing cultural reconnection, but of coming to terms with one's role as a postcolonial subject, woman, and daughter, among a host of other identities. Because, as Beth Tobin points out, "most postcolonial work on the Caribbean is so focused on what the colonizers did that the islands' inhabitants never register as fully human subjects," it is important to center the experiences of Caribbean women (147). Through its interdisciplinary approach and female-centric reading of Caribbean literature, *Taking Flight* intervenes in a series of conversations about the narration of individual and collective trauma.

TRAUMA, SHAME, AND SOCIAL NORMS

This project joins Caribbean studies and trauma studies to assert that the perpetuation of repressive social mores[5] is often linked with trauma in contemporary Caribbean women's literature. Social norms serve as a catalyst for forms of trauma as varied as the distress related to Clare Savage's negotiation of her biracial identity in Cliff's *Abeng* and Susan Hay's struggle with anorexia nervosa in Melville's "The Sparkling Bitch." It is worth noting that the term "trauma" can be traced to the Greek word for "wound." For Sigmund Freud, this wound is one that is inflicted on the mind rather than on the body (quoted in Caruth 3). Cathy Caruth describes trauma[6] as painfully disruptive experiences that are like "a wound that cries out, that addresses us in the attempt to tell us of a reality or truth that is not otherwise available" (4).

Focusing on the narration of various forms of trauma highlights how literature reflects the relationship between trauma, shame, and social norms. *Taking Flight* reads the body as a medium for the transmission of cultural meanings with emphasis on the control and surveillance of women's bodies. Germane to my discussion of social norms is the function of sexual politics, or the "moral, sexual, symbolic, cultural and political codes in which individuals, families and the nation are linked" (Wieringa and Sívori 14). In examining the connection between Caribbean women's sexuality and their political realities, I understand gender and sexual norms as being socially constructed and read the trauma associated with repressive gender/sexual norms as having significant consequences for Caribbean women's physical and emotional health.

In each of the texts, social mores operate as a form of social control that shapes behavior and conveys cultural meanings. The works respond to and reflect the expectations that govern Caribbean women's lives. Michelle Balaev's work is helpful in understanding the social dimension of trauma. Balaev finds that if the "self is conceived as both a product of culture and individual idiosyncratic tendencies and behaviours, then it follows that the meaning of trauma is found between the poles of the individual and the society" (155). Although the protagonists experience shame for a variety of reasons, shame, rooted in misrecognition and the fear of negative evaluation, is intertwined with trauma and is a wound in and of itself. In fact, psychotherapist Aida Alayarian indicates that shame is the "most direct psychological defense against overwhelming traumatic experiences" (153). The driving forces behind women's trauma in the works under study are the conventions that favor silence and invisibility over the narration of truth.

The fear of exposure and evaluation, in several of the works, drives female characters to internalize harmful beliefs about their identities and their bodies and to seek refuge far from home.

Shame, as numerous scholars have noted, is a common effect of sexual abuse but can also have an impact on those who do not conform to social norms. As a result of the gender socialization process, particular types of expression are viewed as socially acceptable while others can provoke censure. The resulting sense of shame, for characters who cannot or do not follow proscribed norms, is interpreted as evidence of personal failure. In *Sister Citizen*, Harris-Perry summarizes shame as the sentiment that assumes that "the room is straight and that the self is off-kilter. Shame urges us to internalize the crooked room" (105). In the works under study, shame occurs when characters experience abuse or break a social boundary. The social element is key; shame, the tension between the perceived and ideal selves, rises when characters feel the need to withdraw from a real or imagined audience capable of judging them.

In a number of the texts, the psychological consequences of trauma are most visible through the characters' subsequent use of dissociation,[7] and it is through migration and dissociation that the women preserve selfhood. The trope of the split personality often appears in Caribbean and postcolonial women's writing and plays a central role in works including *Breath, Eyes, Memory*. For Danticat's protagonist, dissociation, often referred to as "doubling" in Caribbean literature, works as a survival strategy that allows the mind to break from the physical body during traumatic occurrences. To be clear, not all responses to trauma are pathological, nor is there necessarily a causal link between trauma and dissociation. For some of the women in this collection of texts, though, dissociation serves as a haven during or following a traumatic event. In several of the works, dissociation operates as a form of imaginative flight and is a key component in the process of migration. While dissociation often affords emotional healing for the protagonists, it is not a replacement for but instead prefigures emigration. That is, the practice of dissociation prepares characters to distance themselves from the location of trauma because they have the space to process their experiences. As my readings of novels such as Danticat's *Krik? Krak!* and Marshall's *Praisesong for the Widow* demonstrate, the dissociative state works as a protective space that bridges a painful location and another new and potentially frightening one.

Central to the characters' search for identity is the attempt to regain control of their bodies and to cast off shame in favor of recognition. In works including Yanique's *Land of Love and Drowning*, trauma changes how characters understand themselves and illustrates the indelible effect of trauma on their psyches. For the characters, dissociation and migration share the common goals of safety and affirmation. As Danticat observes, "There is a lot of flight imagery in the myths of people who have been enslaved. As soon as you try to put limits on people, their imagination takes flight. Even madness, psychosis, is a kind of flight" (Alexandre and Howard 162). Danticat's claim speaks to the range of emotional responses to trauma and positions dissociation as a process that allows characters to parse the feelings and memories associated with trauma. For the protagonists in these prose works, dissociation and migration serve as means of distancing themselves from the physical reminders of pain. In each of the works under study, trauma functions as the catalyst for physical or psychic flight; put simply, trauma, perhaps driven by the tension between the real and imagined homeland, works as the activating event that propels migration.

MIGRATION

In turning to literature to explore the complexity of migration, I apply Nikos Papastergiadis's understanding of migration as a process that initiates mutual transformation.[8] Papastergiadis asserts that "migrants are often transformed by their journey, and their presence is a catalyst to new transformations in the spaces they enter" (10). This observation regarding the regenerative property of flight rings true in each of the works as the authors employ the trope of flight to bring their protagonists to a space of change. In Caribbean fiction, the motif of flight is frequently associated with restrictive conditions, and characters often migrate to gain independence. That is, flight is directly related to issues of confinement and indeed may be influenced by rigid gender and sexual norms. Through fiction, migrant authors such as Cliff and Dennis-Benn narrate the difficulties of leaving home and respond to repressive conditions, including racism, sexism, and homophobia. By writing and rewriting history, they reproduce the struggles of migration and counter romanticized portraits of the process. This book is as much an examination of the motif of flight in Caribbean women's literature as it is a celebration of women's voices and a commentary on the conditions that necessitate the need to find expression.

In the works discussed in each chapter, flight serves as a recurring response to oppressive conditions and offers Caribbean women a means of coming to terms with questions of place and identity. It is physical and emotional hardship that functions as the inertia that prompts migration. The relationship between migration and personal identity is detailed in Mimi Sheller and John Urry's *Tourism Mobilities*. Sheller and Urry point out that "many Caribbean novelists and writers maintain that to become truly Caribbean you must first go elsewhere; migration, exile, and return have become the grounds for forging a pan-Caribbean identity" (14–15). As a region marked by out-migrations, the Caribbean proves a rich space for negotiations of place and home. In an increasingly globalized society, Caribbean women's literature, and in particular the writing of Caribbean migrant authors, speaks to the realities of the contemporary immigrant experience and brings awareness to the link between trauma and migration.

Caribbean women's literature provides excellent insight into the factors that play into migration and points to the necessity of narrating the migratory experience. While Avey's flight in Marshall's *Praisesong for the Widow* is voluntary, one should not lose sight of the fact that the common thread joining the texts is that hardship is the force that initiates migration. The negotiation of identity following departure is central to the narratives, and the characters' moves away from home affect their conceptions of citizenship and belonging. In texts including *The True History of Paradise*, home is a space of danger and alienation; Jean Landing has little choice but to flee for safety, and the act of flying serves as a space of suspension that bridges her new home and her homeland. Supporting this is Susan Friedman's observation that "safety might reside neither in home nor homeland but only in flight" (200). In a number of the works, the psychic bruises of trauma surface after characters leave their homes; their struggles in their new homelands render visible the invisible wounds caused by continued invalidation, suppression, and alienation and signal the embodied experience of emotional trauma. To stress, once threats to safety and self are removed, the signifiers of trauma, namely self-harming behavior and withdrawal from society, come to the fore. In essence, characters perceive themselves as defective or deficient, and this self-concept persists in their new location; trauma, then, migrates offsite and poses a sustained challenge to their wellbeing.

Although the women frequently reject the site of trauma, the shame associated with trauma initially turns inward and manifests as a repudiation of the self. Whether coping with violence, abuse, racism, homophobia, or exploitation, the protagonists' violations of social convention are met with resistance and condemnation. Their transgressions, rooted in deference to or defiance of a status quo informed by racist and homophobic misogyny, result in the internalization of shame. In response, they must come to accept themselves in new places. In the works, women navigate threats to health and identity, are condemned for their actions, endure a sustained trial, and emerge transformed because they have regained a degree of control over their bodies and their environments. Instead of falling in line, they forge new paths and reclaim their futures.

This study is ordered around thematic discussions of trauma and migration. Chapters explore how diverse forms of trauma are related to the characters' responses to societal pressures and focus on trauma stemming from the social control of sexuality, the navigation of racial identity, and the distress that follows migration, disease, and the violation of gender and sexual norms. The works, many of which are semi-autobiographical projects, are set in or authored by writers from Haiti, Jamaica, Barbados, Guyana, and the Virgin Islands. The first chapter examines physical and psychic fragmentation in Danticat's *Breath, Eyes, Memory* and *Krik? Krak!* In Danticat's work, folklore and flight intersect to highlight the relationship between dissociation, flight, and transformation. The second chapter examines psychological transnationalism in novels by Cliff and Cezair-Thompson. As the works illustrate, psychological exile is an essential part of the migratory experience; growing up with divided allegiances, each cognizant of their difference at every turn, the protagonists Jean and Clare are primed for flight. The chapter that follows reads transnational identity as based on cultural heritage rather than physical location. In *Praisesong for the Widow* and *Small Island*, Marshall and Levy utilize the historical novel to reify the importance of cultural connection.

The fourth chapter turns to works by Melville and Nunez to explore how breast cancer and anorexia nervosa offer physical and emotional renewal for the protagonists. In *The Migration of Ghosts, Boundaries,* and *Anna In-Between*, Melville and Nunez use their characters to question body-image ideals. The final chapter analyzes how Yanique's *Land of Love and Drowning* and Dennis-Benn's *Here Comes the Sun* critique the surveillance of women's bodies. In highlighting the multigenerational impact of incest, sex work, and commercial land development, the authors foreground resistance to exploitative practices. Overall, this book sheds light on the impact of viewing women's bodies as defective or deficient and explores the consequences of the gendered socialization process. The narratives suggest that the experiences of Caribbean women are a microcosm for pervasive inequality worldwide. *Taking Flight* illustrates that when women's bodies are regulated, shame and silence can result while unearned political, gender, and racial power remains unchallenged.

CHAPTER ONE

THE IMMIGRANT EXPERIENCE
Trauma, Folklore, and Migration in Danticat's
Breath, Eyes, Memory and *Krik? Krak!*

> I come from a place where breath, eyes, and memory are one, a place from which you carry your past like the hair on your head. Where women return to their children as butterflies or as tears in the eyes of the statues that their daughters pray to. My mother was as brave as the stars at dawn. She too was from this place. My mother was like that women who could never bleed and then could never stop bleeding, the one who gave in to her pain, to live as a butterfly.
> —EDWIDGE DANTICAT, *Breath, Eyes, Memory*

In an interview with Sandy Alexandre and Ravi Howard, author Edwidge Danticat remarks that her favorite kind of butterfly is the monarch because it "flies 3,000 miles each winter, from colder climates to warmer ones. The butterfly that leaves the cold climate is not the same one that returns the following spring" (113). Much like the monarch butterfly that Danticat describes, the female characters in her texts *Breath, Eyes, Memory* (1994) and *Krik? Krak!* (1995) survive myriad forms of trauma, take flight, and are forever changed. In *Breath, Eyes, Memory*, her debut novel, Danticat gives voice to the impact of sexual trauma and the possibility of emotional liberation. In two stories from the short story collection *Krik? Krak!*, "Nineteen Thirty-Seven" and "Caroline's Wedding," characters navigate life after losing a parental figure and turn to folklore to connect with their deceased loved ones. Each of the two works position the navigation of trauma as central to the protagonists' emotional growth. This chapter uses Danticat's insight regarding the migration of monarch butterflies to explore the link between trauma, folklore,[1] and migration.

Danticat's work illustrates the transformative nature of flight and features Haitian and Haitian American characters who learn how to reconcile the effects of traumatic events. In both works, flight comes as a result of hardship. In *Breath, Eyes, Memory*, sexual trauma is the catalyst to virginity testing and dissociation.[2] It is through the practice of dissociation that the protagonist, Sophie, copes with inherited and personal trauma. Dissociation allows Sophie to imaginatively travel during traumatic events. The practice enables her to endure being tested by her mother, facilitates sexual intimacy with her husband, and prepares her to return to Haiti twice—first to grapple with the impact of her own trauma and later to bury her mother. In "Nineteen Thirty-Seven," strife comes as a result of political oppression. The story, set during Rafael Trujillo's reign, details one woman's flight across the Haitian border and another's imprisonment for being a suspected soucouyant.[3] Another short story from *Krik? Krak!*, "Caroline's Wedding," explores the pain of migration through the metaphor of Caroline's severed forearm, a birth defect likely caused by an injection that her mother received when she was imprisoned after an immigration raid. Overall, the works showcase women in various states of imprisonment, with flight, whether imagined or literal, serving as the vehicle for escape.

Despite their separation from home, the characters maintain cultural ties through folklore. For Danticat, a Haitian American author who migrated to the United States at the age of twelve, folklore offers a way to retain a connection to Haiti. The folktales that the author incorporates evidence the connection between folklore and Haitian gender, sexual, and social norms. For instance, it is oral lore that instructs Sophie on the dangers of physical intimacy in *Breath, Eyes, Memory*. In "Caroline's Wedding," a tale warns sisters Caroline and Grace of the incestuous threat that their deceased father poses. In "Nineteen Thirty-Seven," entrenched beliefs result in the imprisonment of women believed to be shapeshifters. In short, folklore functions as a social tool as well as a cultural touchstone. As Danticat's work illustrates, folklore is an essential part of Haitian culture and is central to the immigrant experience. In *Breath, Eyes, Memory* and *Krik? Krak!*, Danticat fuses print and oral cultures and positions folklore as a tool for communicating values, solidifying relationships, and navigating trauma.

TRAUMA AND MIGRATION

Breath, Eyes, Memory begins with the reunion of Sophie Caco and her mother, Martine. Martine, who was raped as a young woman in Haiti, left her homeland within a year of giving birth to Sophie. Martine's flight to the United States, motivated by her need to escape the nightmares that led her to attempt suicide multiple times, left Sophie in the care of Atie, Martine's older sister. As a child, Sophie questions where her mother and father are. She reflects, "One time I asked her [Tante Atie] how it was that I was born with a mother and no father. She told me the story of a little girl who was born out of the petals of roses, water from the stream, and a chunk of the sky" (Danticat, *Breath, Eyes, Memory* 45).[4] This response, along with the message that "if you see a lot of trouble in your life, it is because you were chosen to carry part of the sky on your head," glosses over the realities of trauma and employs folklore to make sense of strife (*BEM* 24). Rather than recognize or explain the absence of Sophie's father, Atie invokes the language of nature to reframe Sophie's conception and birth. Here, oral lore is used to comfort a child who is trying to understand her origins. Atie does not detail Sophie's origin story, but instead uses the story of an unnamed girl's birth to respond to Sophie's query. While Atie's use of folklore reimagines Sophie's conception, it also erases Martine's trauma. In both instances, nature is called upon to explain difficult situations. According to Atie, it is women who bear great burdens. It is women who are "chosen" to suffer but who, like Martine, exhibit strength during times of immense grief.

In Danticat's novel, the primary source of women's suffering is rooted in a lack of control over their bodies and the environments they find themselves in. In the days before Sophie departs Haiti for life in New York City with her mother, Atie tells Sophie that "when we were children we had no control over anything. Not even this body" (*BEM* 19). Later, Martine offers insight into Sophie's conception. She discloses, "A man grabbed me from the side of the road, pulled me into a cane field, and put you in my body.... I did not know this man. I never saw his face. He had it covered when he did this to me. But now when I look at your face I think it is true what they say. A child out of wedlock always looks like its father" (*BEM* 59). Atie and Martine's reflections raise the issue of consent, or lack thereof. Martine's trauma is amplified by the fact that she never saw her abuser's face; she cannot connect her pain with her perpetrator. The lack of control during Martine's rape, referenced via the euphemism "this," is multilayered. In that moment, Martine lost her virginity, lost control of her procreative rights, and lost the ability to discern the identity of her rapist. Because the unidentified man chose to cover his face, Martine lives in a perpetual state of fear; her rapist could be anyone and could return at any moment and she would not be able to identify him. The fact that Sophie resembles her father prompts Martine to constantly relive her rape every time she looks at her daughter's face.

Importantly, the space of New York City illuminates the abuse that was repressed in Haiti; it is in New York that Sophie becomes the inheritor of her mother's trauma. In the months following their reunion, Sophie gains an intimate understanding of how trauma shapes her mother's wellbeing. She wakes her mother from the nightmares that visit her in her sleep. Later, Sophie comes to understand that Martine's "nightmares had somehow become [her] own, so much so that [she] would wake up some mornings wondering if [they] hadn't both spent the night dreaming about the same thing: a man with no face, pounding a life into a helpless young girl" (*BEM* 196). Offering further insight into her mother's sexual assault, Sophie joins a description of the Tonton Macoutes, a paramilitary force formed by François Duvalier, with a depiction of her father. "Ordinary criminals walked naked in the night. They slicked their bodies with oil so they could slip through most fingers. But the *Macoutes*, they did not hide. When they entered a house, they asked to be fed, demanded the woman of the house, and forced her into her own bedroom. . . . My father might have been a *Macoute*," Sophie relates (*BEM* 137). She continues, "He was a stranger who, when my mother was eighteen years old, grabbed her on her way back from school. He dragged her into the cane fields, and pinned her down to the ground. . . . He kept pounding her until she was too stunned to make a sound. When he was done, he made her keep her face in the dirt, threatening to shoot her if she looked up" (*BEM* 137–38). In this passage, the author renders the political personal. Through Sophie, readers glean additional details surrounding Martine's rape. It is Sophie, instead of Martine or Atie, who narrates the traumatic moments of her conception. Sophie's account, perhaps the most graphic description, is haunting in its imagery and links pain with control. Martine's rape, which she reads as the ultimate loss of control, informs her decision to leave Haiti, to diligently guard her daughter's virginity, and to commit suicide.

Danticat utilizes Sophie and Martine's reunion to highlight the relationship between trauma and migration. To be clear, it is trauma that propels Martine's immigration to the United States. In the shared space of trauma, New York City, Sophie learns the intimate details of her mother's pain. Later, Sophie confronts her inherited and personal trauma at a cane field, a historical site of oppression and the location of Martine's rape. Although the process of migration was painful for Sophie because she left Atie, the only mother she had ever known, it is through migration that trauma is replicated. As the following section details, it is in the space of her mother's home that Sophie endures abuse. Sophie's arrival intensifies Martine's nightmares and brings Martine to subject her daughter to the same form of testing that she underwent. As Martine and Sophie's reunion illustrates, the effects of abuse are pervasive and long-lasting. Throughout the course of the narrative, Sophie confronts her mother's abuser and the legacy of virginity testing that her mother propagated. Despite Sophie's attempts to assert agency and leave the trauma of her childhood behind, the inherited trauma of her mother's rape and the trauma of her virginity testing follows her to her home with her husband, Joseph. It is not until she revisits Haiti that she begins to address the pain of sexual trauma.

PURITY AND LIBERATION

Central to Sophie's personal trauma is the practice of virginity testing. In the weeks before Martine begins testing Sophie, she explains the practice to her daughter: "When I was a girl, my mother used to test us to see if we were virgins. She would put her fingers in our very private parts and see if it would go inside. . . . The way my mother was raised, a mother is supposed to do that to her daughter until the daughter is married. It is her responsibility to keep her pure" (*BEM* 58). Here and throughout, testing is compared to a virginity cult that privileges chastity. In *Breath, Eyes, Memory*, the practice of virginity testing is intimately connected with patriarchal values. Evidencing this is Sophie's memory of being told that "our men, they insist that their women are virgins and have their ten fingers" (*BEM* 150). Tante Atie reflects, "They train you to find a husband. . . . They poke at your panties in the middle of the night, to see if you are still whole. They listen when you pee, to find out if you're peeing too loud. If you pee loud, it means you've got big spaces between your legs" (*BEM* 135). In both cases, women are evaluated on the basis of their utility to men. The unnamed "they," the women who continue the practice of virginity testing, are positioned as relentless in their protection of purity and resort to the violation of personal space to maintain their daughters' chastity; in the process, the young women are reduced to vessels ready to serve a future husband. The practice of virginity testing, somewhat normalized via the term "our men," serves as preparation for a successful marriage.

For the women who continue this practice, it is their own reputations, perhaps more than those of their daughters, that are at stake. Granmè Ifé, Sophie's grandmother, explains the connection between testing and self-interest: "If a child dies, you do not die. But if your child is disgraced, you are disgraced.... If I give a soiled daughter to her husband, he can shame my family, speak evil of me, even bring her back to me" (BEM 155–56). It is precisely because of this conditioning and her own rape that Martine is hypervigilant against threats to Sophie's virginity. After Joseph enters Sophie's life, Martine tests her daughter weekly to ensure that she is "still *whole*" (BEM 85). When Sophie later confronts Martine about why she tested her, Martine discloses that she did it only because her mother did it to her. "I have no greater excuse. I realize standing here that the two greatest pains of my life are very much related. The one good thing about my being raped was that it made the testing stop. The testing and the rape. I live both every day," Martine relates (BEM 172–73). The impact of Haitian gender and sexual norms are evident when Martine connects the two forms of sexual trauma. It is not until Sophie leaves home that Martine realizes that her pain is linked with her daughter's. Here and throughout, Danticat points to the unspeakability of sexual and gender-based trauma and the practices that uphold patriarchal power.

In *Breath, Eyes, Memory* the practice of virginity testing is intimately connected with the tradition of storytelling. Sophie is introduced to the tale of the Marasas, or inseparable lovers, when Martine tests her for the first time. As Mireille Rosello observes, the tale is "embedded into an episode of sexual violence" (120). More specifically, Martine tries to distract her daughter from the pain and humiliation of testing with the tale of the lovers who were "the same person, duplicated in two.... When they laughed, they even laughed the same and when they cried, their tears were identical" (BEM 83). Here, the folktale of the Marasas, a tale built on the Haitian Kreyòl word for "twin," serves two functions—it attempts to make the practice easier for mother as well as daughter and also reflects Martine's hope for the relationship. Unlike Sophie, Martine wishes for a relationship like that of the Marasas, the identical lovers. Martine's hope for a lifetime with her daughter is shattered by Joseph's arrival. After Joseph enters Sophie's life, Martine, perhaps threatened by a competitor for Sophie's heart, becomes obsessed with her daughter's virginity. With Joseph in her daughter's life, Martine loses the hope that, like in the story, Sophie can become her mother's Marasa by eschewing a romantic relationship with a man.

Interestingly, Sophie begins to double while hearing the tale of the Marasas; during testing, she learns how to distract herself via dissociation.

Martine tells Sophie "stories while she was doing it, weaving elaborate tales to keep [her] mind off the finger. . . . There were many stories about our ancestors having *doubled*. It was said that most of our presidents had actually been split in two: part flesh and part shadow. That was the only way they could murder and rape so many people and still go home to play with their children and make love to their wives" (*BEM* 155). In this passage, doubling is positioned as a counter to splitting and functions as a practice that allows political figures to segment their personal and professional lives. In order to make the testing stop, to preserve herself before she splits in two, Sophie decides to remove her hymen and fail her mother's test. While Martine's testing abruptly concludes as a result of sexual assault, Sophie's ends, not as a result of sexual intercourse, but from self-immolation; it is the act of deflowering herself that enables Sophie to find refuge from the harmful practice of testing. Punctuating the scene where Sophie removes her hymen is the story of a woman who desperately wanted to stop bleeding. "If she wanted to stop bleeding, she would have to give up her right to be a human being. She could choose what to be, a plan or an animal, but she could no longer be a woman," Danticat writes (*BEM* 86). The woman pleads to the goddess Erzulie to make her a butterfly. That cry precedes the description of Sophie's flesh "ripp[ing] apart as [she] pressed the pestle into it" (*BEM* 87). Sophie's act of liberation, which she understands as like "breaking manacles," leaves her with stitches between her legs (*BEM* 128).

Sophie later turns to dissociation to emotionally remove herself from traumatic memories and events. Although Sophie initially begins doubling to cope with the practice of testing, she later dissociates when sexually intimate with Joseph. Sophie describes the singular scene of intimacy in the text: "He reached over and pulled my body towards his. I closed my eyes and thought of the *Marasas*, the *doubling*. I was lying there on that bed and my clothes were being peeled off my body, but really I was somewhere else" (*BEM* 202). What is striking in this scene is that Sophie doubles to console her mother. She thinks not of a faraway place, but of the source of so much of her pain. While intimate with Joseph, she imagines herself in bed with Martine; "I was holding her and fighting off that man, keeping those images out of her head. I was telling her that it was all right," she explains (*BEM* 202–3). This visitation becomes a nightly practice, motivated by her impulse to protect her mother, whereby "from my place as a shadow on the wall, I would look after her and wake her up as soon as the nightmares started, just like I did when I was home" (*BEM* 203). Ultimately, Sophie's use of dissociation prepares her for her journey to Haiti to confront the trauma that haunts her. Put simply, dissociation operates as a form of figurative flight that precedes migration and primes the protagonist for her return home.

NAVIGATING TRAUMA

In Danticat's work, it is the women who are willing to confront their history of abuse who begin to find closure. For Sophie, removal from her mother's home is the first step in navigating trauma. After leaving her mother's house, the place of her abuse, personal and inherited trauma follows her to her home with Joseph. Sophie quickly realizes that the legacy of trauma greatly complicates her ability to be sexually intimate with her husband. She recognizes the impact of trauma on her marriage and abruptly leaves for Haiti with her daughter in tow. Removing herself from New York City, the place where abuse converged for her, and returning to Haiti begins the process of emotional liberation. Sophie's trip to Haiti proves central in her confrontation of lived and inherited trauma. It is not the return alone that allows Sophie to confront her past; instead, it is the reunion of mother and daughter in Haiti that brings healing in the face of traumatic events.

Sophie's emotional growth is exemplified by her grandmother's proclamation that "the daughter is never fully a woman until her mother has passed on before her" (*BEM* 234). This line, and the text as a whole, positions death as a necessary component of maturation and identity development. While the homeland for Martine and Sophie "remains the place of ancestors," it is largely constructed as a place of ghosts, a location Martine notes is "still very painful" for her because it evokes memories of her rape (Rodriguez 51, *BEM* 78). Despite its painful associations for Martine, Haiti serves as a neutral space that fosters reconciliation and reconnection for Sophie and Martine. Martine attempts to forget and to erase her past, but Sophie needs to remember. Sophie's return to Haiti triggers memories that come to the forefront; hardship, although painful, propels the protagonist's emotional growth. By confronting inherited trauma and the legacy of testing that has traumatized generations of Haitian women, Sophie can more fully come to terms with her history of sexual abuse.

Although place figures prominently in *Breath, Eyes, Memory*, the people who surround the protagonist are equally important to her efforts to recover her identity and achieve closure. Evidencing the fact that Sophie's identity is shaped by migration away from relatives is the conversation between Tante Atie and Sophie when Sophie leaves Haiti for the first time. When

Tante Atie asks Sophie, "Do you see what you are leaving?' Sophie responds, "I know I am leaving you" (*BEM* 34). For Sophie, the experience of leaving people transcends that of leaving country; for her, separation from loved ones engenders feelings of dislocation. Even more significant in this line, though, is the association between Atie and Haiti, as the spelling and pronunciation suggest that Atie has become Haiti, or Ayiti. By linking Atie and her homeland, Danticat develops the trope of particular people coming to embody particular places. Sophie's efforts to reunite place and people at the conclusion of the novel, then, can be read as symbolic of the relationship between community and emotional liberation.

As previously mentioned, Sophie inherits a legacy of rape as well as a practice to cope with its emotional effects—dissociation. This shared sense of trauma, connected with Haiti as its place of genesis, becomes increasingly embedded in Sophie's psyche when she moves to the United States, the place where Martine and Sophie struggle with the effects of sexual violence and the legacy of rape. Reconciliation with Martine at the conclusion of the text is central to Sophie's emotional catharsis; Sophie notes that after the reunion she finally has her mother's "approval' and is now 'safe" (*BEM* 200). What is ambiguous, though, is whether Sophie is physically or emotionally "safe." Danticat reinforces the role of the maternal in Haitian culture in that Sophie must obtain her mother's approval (for her husband, her daughter, her life choices, etc.). Through multiple trips to Haiti, Sophie reconnects with her cultural past and her family. She reflects on the importance of this process: "I knew my hurt and hers were links in a long chain and if she hurt me, it was because she was hurt, too. It was up to me to avoid my turn in the fire. It was up to me to make sure that my daughter never slept with ghosts, never lived with nightmares, and never had her name burnt in the flames" (*BEM* 207).

Sophie's journey of reconnection culminates in a healing catharsis following her mother's death. After she negotiates inherited trauma and works through the pain of sexual abuse that she experienced at the hands of her mother, she is able to unite her disparate selves into an identity that recognizes her heritage as well as her future. Sophie regains her identity as a woman, wife, and mother through this cathartic process; she moves from being her "mother's daughter and Tante Atie's child" to a liberated young woman (*BEM* 49). In this line, Danticat draws the distinction between the terms "daughter" and "child," with "daughter" denoting a biological relation and "child" suggesting more of an emotional connection. As this explanation of relations implies, Sophie is emotionally closer with her Aunt Atie, who raised her for twelve years, than with the mother who left her shortly after giving birth. Danticat, interestingly, assigns a stronger emotional connection to the term "child" than to "daughter," with the former carrying more weight than the latter. After leaving the nurturing space that Aunt Atie fostered, Sophie feels emotionally and culturally dislocated in New York City. Indicative of this is Sophie's remark that "it was as though I had disappeared" when she moved to New York (*BEM* 40). It is thus important to recognize that Martine and Sophie live as part of a marginalized community where they exist "in-between." For the protagonist and her mother, Haiti is not a place of abject exile, nor is the United States an unproblematic safe space. In *Breath, Eyes, Memory*, the conflict at the center of the text is mediated through the reconciliation of place and personal identity.

While Sophie begins to navigate the healing process after she returns to Haiti, her relationship with Joseph aids in her development of a more integrated sense of self. Notably, it is when Sophie meets Joseph that she begins to question her beliefs. During one of their initial discussions, Joseph asks Sophie what she is going to study in college. After Sophie notes that she thinks she is going to become a doctor, Joseph presses her, "What would Sophie like to do?" (*BEM* 72). As a result of this questioning, Sophie realizes that she had "never really dared to dream on [her] own" (*BEM* 72). This realization is the initial step in her first act of liberation, an act that exiles her from her mother's home—the tearing of her hymen with a mortar and pestle in the effort to stop the practice of testing that her mother subjects her to. By having Sophie inherit her mother's pain and experience the impact of sexual trauma via testing, Danticat highlights the character's deep-rooted sense of shame about her body. If "shame about the body is a cultural inheritance of women," as J. Brooks Bouson argues, then Danticat's novel, by contrast, suggests that the cycle can be broken (1).

As the physical embodiment of shame for her mother, and thus a representative of the effects of sexual abuse, Sophie transforms shame into power as she translates her mother's trauma into a story that honors her strength. While Sophie "speaks" the truth largely via action when she runs through a cane field, the environment of Martine's rape, Danticat gives voice to trauma and shame throughout the text. Because of the novel's reach and the attention that it has garnered, Danticat includes an afterward in the most recent edition. Therein, she pens a letter to Sophie. The author states, "I felt blessed to have shared your secrets, your mother's, your aunt's, your grandmother's secrets, mysteries deeply embedded in you, in them, much like the wiry vetiver clinging to the side of these hills" (*BEM* 235). Although this line suggests a sense of connected shame, as Bouson alludes to, Danticat addresses the tendency to take Sophie's story of abuse as representative of all Haitian women. Danticat writes, "Of course, not all Haitian mothers are like your mother. Not all Haitian daughters are tested, as you have been" (*BEM* 236). The author concludes the afterword with this simple wish: "May these words bring wings to your feet" (*BEM* 236). The need to amend the text implies that a fictional character has, for some readers, come to represent a collective. As the final line suggests, literature can emancipate and uplift as much as it can shape conceptions of other people and other places.

IDENTITY AND HOME

Much in the same way that migration occasions a reconsideration of identity, Joseph introduces Sophie to the benefits of accepting her hybrid identity. In perhaps the most explicit discussion of cultural hybridity, Joseph explains that he is "'not American' but rather 'African-American'"; this distinction shows Sophie that the integration of identities can be an antidote to assimilation (*BEM* 72). Illustrating the impact of cultural transnationalism on homemaking is the fact that when Sophie returns to her home with Joseph after "clearing her head" in Haiti, she nonchalantly calls Haiti "home" (*BEM* 184). The use of this moniker stresses her simultaneous incorporation into Haitian and American societies. Importantly, Sophie recognizes her identity as wife and mother in Providence, Rhode Island, at the same time that she considers Haiti "home." As her movement back and forth between the United States and Haiti suggests, Sophie easily crosses between these culturally distinct realities and identities. Rather than remaining separate spaces, the two homes blend together as evidenced by the flexible use of the referent "home."

Travel between the United States and Haiti enables the protagonist to come to a fuller realization of her place in the world. She notes that "it suddenly occurred to me that I was surrounded by my own life, my own four walls, my own husband and child"; it is with this epiphany that Sophie begins to see herself as an independent adult as opposed to the inheritor of her mother's anxieties (*BEM* 196). Finally owning a place in the world, she recognizes that she is "not a guest or visiting daughter" as she first felt in America but is now "the mother and sometimes, more painfully, the wife" (*BEM* 196). As a result of bilateral migration, Sophie views her place of habitation as home just as much as she views Haiti as a space of cultural origin. The statement above stresses the lingering effects of Sophie's self-mutilation, and more specifically, the pain that accompanies physical intimacy. Also significant is that this realization is confined to her roles of mother and wife, without consideration of her identity as a daughter, woman, or immigrant. With this, the novel links the attainment of selfhood with normative intimate arrangements while recognizing the role that gender and migration play in identity development. The centrality of Joseph to Sophie's reconsideration of identity highlights the importance of an outside perspective. Joseph, someone outside of Sophie's culture, brings her to a space of reflection. Indeed, it is the character of Joseph, whose name is a Biblical allusion, who offers an example of what is means to be "African-American" as opposed to simply "American" (*BEM* 72).

It is clear that physical location plays a central role in the protagonist's healing journey. Although Joseph sets the process in motion, Sophie does not fully come into her own as a woman, wife, and mother until her mother's death forces her to come to terms with her legacy of abuse. As Dana Williams aptly argues, Martine plays an important role in Sophie's healing; Williams points out that it is through the reestablished mother-daughter relationship that Martine teaches Sophie that liberation can be achieved by reconciling the people and place of her past (4). While moving to the United States prompts Sophie to reunite with her mother, it is with two trips to Haiti and through the (re)connection of place and people that the protagonist reconciles what were before disparate identities. At the conclusion of the novel, Sophie enters a space of liberation, not one of physicality, but of interiority; this brings her to view herself as belonging to the land and to the people she has spent so much of her adult life being troubled by.

For Sophie, the juxtaposition of lived experience in Haiti and a vastly different life in the United States engenders a fusion of her Haitian and American identities. In particular, the nation of Haiti grounds Sophie's sense of self and propels her integration of identities at the conclusion of the text. For example, when Uncle Bazie questions Grandmè Ifé about where Sophie comes from, she responds, "Here . . . she's from right here" (*BEM* 116). This short but significant statement connects Sophie as an individual and Haiti as a place in possessive terms and joins Sophie with the land. Grandmè Ifé claims Sophie as a member of "a family with dirt under [their] fingernails" (*BEM* 20). For Sophie, what began as a "short vacation" turns into a transformative event after which she refers to Haiti as "home" and replaces her earlier identification of "home" with her birth nation. It is when Sophie returns to bury her mother that she is identified as a member of the community, someone who is recognized and greeted on the way to her grandmother's house. When Sophie accompanies her mother's corpse on its journey from New York back "home" to Haiti, the emancipatory process is set in motion. That is, Sophie's return to Haiti enables her to move from an individual experience to a collective one.

At the conclusion of the text, Sophie realizes that Haiti is a place where "we are all daughters of this land"; this is evidenced by the fact that Martine wanted to return to Haiti in death (*BEM* 230). Much in the same way that the Caco family is characterized with "dirt under [their] fingernails," this depiction explicitly ties residents to the land (*BEM* 20). Perhaps rooted in the language of slavery and the reality that slaves often did not know their birthplace, these statements connect belonging, nationalism, and nature. It is interesting to consider these lines in light of Martine's rape and pregnancy. Potentially serving as a euphemism of sorts, the connection with women and the land suggests a more mystical view of lineage. In *Breath, Eyes, Memory*, stories that are passed down are often connected with the land. For instance, Sophie notes that for Haitian women "breath, eyes, and memory are one, a place from which you carry your past like the hair on your head" (*BEM* 230, 234). Though one may try to escape the past, it is improbable and is instead an essential part of one's identity. The Caco women are "from" Haiti but often attempt to forget the nation and its legacy of trauma. With Martine's passing at the conclusion of the text, Sophie reconnects with her cultural past and comes to terms with the trauma that has shaped her into a young woman who is now 'libéré,' or free (*BEM* 234). In Haiti, Sophie is able to gain clarity surrounding the link between trauma and control and to reclaim control over her body and her future.

Whereas Haiti functions as a space of reconciliation for Sophie, it is necessary to consider the ways that New York is depicted as a place where "you can lose yourself easily" (*BEM* 103). Tante Atie, Martine's sister and Sophie's aunt, states, "Grand or not grand, I am losing myself here too" (*BEM* 104). This statement suggests that migration alone does not contribute to a loss of one's identity; for Atie, the lack of migration (in that she has never left Haiti) has resulted in a loss of self. To explain, Atie sacrificed herself in service to her ill mother while her sister left home to ease the trauma of her rape. On the whole, Atie feels isolated. Martine left Haiti for New York shortly after Sophie's birth and Atie remained, ever the steadfast daughter and stand-in maternal figure until Sophie was sent to join Martine at the age of twelve. Atie's statements suggest that emotional clarity does not always correlate with physical location. One does not have to migrate to "lose oneself"; this is perhaps most explicit with the use of dissociation in the text. Through the character of Atie, Danticat implies that incremental loss of self and soul can occur without regard to location. While trauma can engender a split identity, the acknowledgment of its impact can also offer the possibility of healing. Supporting the link between place and the negotiation of trauma is Michelle Balaev's assertion that "the trauma novel demonstrates that the reorganized self is relational and emerges relative to a specific place that produces a specific articulation of a transformed identity" (163).

In *Breath, Eyes, Memory*, a more integrated sense of self offers peace for one woman; to be clear, I do not mean to suggest that the development of a transnational identity should be a goal for immigrant-exiles. Much in the same way that Danticat addresses the theoretical tension between lived experience and fictional representation in her afterward to the novel, readers must be careful not to assume that the result for a single protagonist is the ideal situation for those in similar positions. For Sophie Caco, it is her physical return to Haiti and her reunion with her mother in the shared space of trauma that allows her to liberate herself from the inherited trauma of rape and her own sexual abuse. That is, the element of place functions as a means of oppression as well as a catalyst for liberation. As the novel makes evident, speaking her truth is essential to the protagonist's healing process. The narrative concludes just as Sophie begins this next step in her recuperative journey. It is flight—both as dissociation and as migration—that affords a limbo-like space of emotional protection that later allows Sophie to broach the seemingly impenetrable silence. With *Breath, Eyes, Memory*, Danticat makes public the impact of sexual abuse because "secrets remain only if we keep our silence" (*BEM* 121).

FOLKLORE AND FLIGHT IN *KRIK? KRAK!*

In the short story collection entitled *Krik, Krak?*, Danticat continues her exploration of the impact of silence and suffering. The author employs the theme of shapeshifting to reveal the difficulties inherent in migration. The collection of ten short stories features interconnected characters and explores themes including exile, migration, and violence. The author serves as a storyteller and draws on oral tradition to recount tales for a contemporary audience. As suggested, Danticat's work reflects her experience as a Haitian migrant; however, it is misguided to think of *Breath, Eyes, Memory* and *Krik? Krak!* as purely autobiographical. Nevertheless, the author's application of the Haitian custom of storytelling, evident in the text's translation into the terms "honor" and respect," positions her as someone connected with that tradition and more globally with the griot tradition of offering alternative historical accounts. In *Krik? Krak!*, Danticat translates folklore into print and utilizes oral lore to proffer her own reading of Haitian history.

The stories in *Krik? Krak!* explore characters' suffering and highlight women's resilience. Danticat explores themes such as loss and dreams in her other works and connects characters through the common ancestor and revolutionary figure of Défilée.[5] The metaphor of flight, understood as "the action of fleeing or running away," "a way of escape," or "the action or manner of flying or moving through the air as with wings," links personal and political resistance in the text (OED). In *Krik? Krak!* Danticat moves from depictions of dissociation in the short story "Nineteen Thirty-Seven" to migration in "Caroline's Wedding." Through the figure of Défilée, she gives voice to often-silenced experiences. More specifically, *Krik? Krak!* utilizes the medium of folklore to reclaim and reimagine the figure of the soucouyant and depict the blending of cultural traditions. Although many of the characters in the collection reside far from home, their ties with Haiti persist via folklore. The author's use of folklore, then, speaks to enduring cultural traditions and the need to recreate or remember home. On a broader scale, the title, a reference to the call and response format of oral tales, invites the reader to participate in this traditional storytelling ritual.

The figure of the soucouyant, witches who "shed [their] skin by night and suck the blood of [their] victims," is central in "Nineteen Thirty-Seven" (OED). Danticat incorporates references to soucouyants to explore how folklore propagates social mores and socializes women to patriarchal values. In *Krik? Krak!*, folklore serves as a cornerstone of culture that the author adapts into print. Despite the admittedly formulaic nature of folktales, Danticat pens a complex and connected collection of short stories. Through characters such as Défilé Azile, the protagonist's mother, she rewrites traditional beliefs and behaviors to reconfigure the figure of the soucouyant. In adapting oral lore and infusing legend into her work, the author engages with the tradition of Caribbean literature as a body of work that often engages with the tropes of flight and escape.

Danticat's "Nineteen Thirty-Seven"[6] introduces the historical figure of Défilée, "a national heroine whose meanings are suffused with political resistance, anti-imperialism, and patriotic reclamation" (Braziel 60). In this short story, Danticat calls on historical narrative to ground her work within the particular historical frame. The author combines the figure of the soucouyant with the feminist figure of resistance, Dédée Bazile, to explore how the state responds to subversive women. In "Nineteen Thirty-Seven," Danticat conceptualizes the figure of the flying woman and highlights the link between monstrosity and social convention. Though prison guards enforce propriety and act as agents of paranoia, they also attempt to strip imprisoned women such as Défilé, referred to by the protagonist as Manman throughout the text, of her power of flight to prevent her from shedding her skin and killing innocent children. In the story, Manman, an elderly woman, joins the collective accused housed in the prison; the prisoners are "bone-thin women with shorn heads, carrying clumps of their hair with their bare hands, as they sought the few rays of sunshine that they were allowed each day" (Danticat, *Krik? Krak!* 35).[7] Nearly every aspect of the prisoners' lives is censored—their femininity, their conversations, their exposure to daylight. Living in inhumane and dehumanizing conditions, the narrator's mother, Manman, presents with "her skin barely clung to her bones, falling in layers, flaps, on her face and neck" (*KK* 36). This graphic description stands alone. It is implied that Manman is literally starving to death. The text, like the prison guards, questions and accuses by positioning Manman as a threat instead of a victim.

The work links the legend of Défilée and the folkloric figure of the soucouyant to highlight how traditional beliefs can be used as a form of social control. Specifically, Défilé/Manman is accused of being a witch or lougarou when a child in her care passes away. The figure of the lougarou,[8] "derived from the French term loupgarous," is often associated with resistance and transgression (Braziel 61). In "Nineteen Thirty-Seven," the author joins folklore and flight to rewrite the lougarou myth. As the epigraph explains, "We tell the stories so that the young ones will know what came before them." In addition to detailing Manman's path to prison, the narrative traces the protagonist's reclamation of her mother's memory. As a whole, "Nineteen Thirty-Seven" explores the gendering of folklore and highlights the link between oral lore and political control. The character of Défilé and the figure of the soucouyant emerge as victims of scapegoating; gossip and folklore converge when Défilé is accused of being a "*lougarou*, witch, criminal" after a colicky baby she was watching dies (*KK* 39). This accusation results in Manman's face "bleeding from the pounding blows of rocks and sticks and the fists of strangers" after the child is found lifeless (*KK* 39).

In "Nineteen Thirty-Seven," Manman/Défilé is "accused of having wings of flame" (*KK* 35). The use of "wings" in this line positions Manman and her fellow prisoners as suspected soucouyants, who are forced to throw cups of cold water at each other so that "their bodies would not be able to muster up enough heat to grow those wings made of flames, fly away in the middle of the night, slip into the slumber of innocent children and steal their breath" (*KK* 37–8). The women, all accused by community members, are victims of hysteria. The guards, complicit in the mass hysteria, focus on the inmates' skin because soucouyants are believed to shed their skin each night. The guards watch Défilé more closely because they think "the wrinkles resulted from her taking off her skin at night and then putting it back on in a hurry, before sunrise. This was why Manman's sentence had been extended to life" (*KK* 36). In this passage, the author highlights the mutability of folklore and the degree to which superstition influences Haitian culture and women's lives. The entrenchment of traditional beliefs is illustrated by the fact that Défilé's body is cremated on the afternoon of her death to "prevent her spirit from wandering into any young innocent bodies" (*KK* 36).

Through Défilé's untimely death, Danticat turns the soucouyant figure into a contemporary tale of resistance. In writing Défilé as a woman incarcerated by accusation but not destroyed by it, Danticat paints a female character who resists oppression by remaining strong of spirit. By aligning personal and collective violence during Trujillo's reign, the author depicts the height of terror and abuse in early twentieth-century Haiti. It is only after Défilé's death that readers learn that the character's flight across the Massacre River during the Haitian Massacre "gave her those wings of flames" (*KK* 41). While traumatic memories press to the fore for Défilé and for all the women who crossed the river that day, loss engenders the ability for mystical flight and establishes a community for the women who are later incarcerated for being threats to their nation. In "Nineteen Thirty-Seven," Défilé's flight transforms from an act of migration and escape to a psychic practice deployed to transcend the abuse experienced at the hands of prison guards. Although Défilé cannot physically escape confinement, she finds some relief in dissociation. It is when prison guards become increasingly suspicious of Manman's loose skin (for them a sign that she is indeed a soucouyant) that they slate her for execution via fire. In aligning mysticism, folklore, and Haitian history, the author transforms loss into legend and highlights the individual costs of tyranny.

VIOLENCE AND OPPRESSION

"Nineteen Thirty-Seven" moves between the present (Manman's captivity) and the past (the horrors of Rafael Trujillo's regime). As a young woman, Manman flees violence in the Dominican Republic and crosses back over into Haiti; her daughter, Josephine, notes, "On that day so long ago, in the year nineteen hundred and thirty-seven, in the Massacre River, my mother did fly" (*KK* 49). This description employs mysticism to narrate one woman's escape. In crossing the Massacre River, Manman "escaped El Generalissimo's soldiers, leaving her own mother behind. From the Haitian side of the river,[9] she could still see the soldiers chopping up *her* mother's body and throwing it into the river along with many others" (*KK* 40).[10] Overall, the tale speaks to politically motivated flight when Défilé "leaped from Dominican soil into the water, and out again on the Haitian side of the river" (*KK* 49). In narrating the tale of a character who crosses borders out of necessity, Danticat draws attention to an oft-silenced genocide while complicating traditional understandings of migration and the reasons behind geographic "leaps." Somewhat paralleling the present situation (Manman's imprisonment and impending death) is the narration of her own mother's death. Despite the years between, both women fall to dictatorial regimes—Manman to Duvalier and her mother to Trujillo. In joining the women's deaths and placing them at the hands of the nation's dictator, Danticat decries the blatant disrespect for human life and, in particular, the loss of powerful Caribbean women.

What is largely omitted from the text is a discussion of the political tensions between Haiti and the Dominican Republic. While readers are likely aware that the two nations share an island, few may recall that Haiti occupied the Dominican Republic until 1844. More than responding to an isolated incident, Manman's flight comes as a result of long-standing tensions. The two countries, with distinct languages and cultures, historically feuded over borders; tensions escalated with Trujillo's plan to "whiten" his nation's population by exterminating Haitians living in the Dominican Republic. While certainly an attempt to flee a dangerous situation, Manman's journey across the border also opposes the tyranny of Trujillo's regime. Through fiction, Danticat stages her own resistance by telling the story of a genocide that is largely silenced to this day.

Danticat's text questions issues of authority and legitimacy. Although the rebellious figure of Défilé is ultimately subdued by masculine power, her power lives on through folklore. Manman's neighbors are quick to blame her for the child's death. Because a medical explanation for sudden infant death syndrome did not exist at the time, the community condemns Manman and holds the caregiver at fault. This suspicion is reinforced by and replicated via the state's prison complex, and the community is representative of the state's interest in suppression. Gisele Anatol's work on the subversive nature of the soucouyant figure helps to explain the connection between local and national resistance. Anatol finds that the figure "disobeys social mores . . . remain[ing] a suspicious figure in the community [and] occup[ying] a space outside of accepted boundaries" (50). Défilé, then, can be read as an early figure of female agency and "illegitimate power." The character emerges as a woman who contests the violence and oppression around her in subtle ways, most notably by creating a community of sorts with her fellow prisoners.

FOLKLORE AS SUBVERSION

Like "Nineteen Thirty-Seven," the short story "Caroline's Wedding" explores the connection between flight and identity. "Caroline's Wedding" centers flight via one family's migration to New York City. In "Caroline's Wedding," Danticat explores the tension between migration and cultural connection. For characters Caroline and Grace, like Défilé in "Nineteen Thirty-Seven," folklore affords a means of subversion. Although Haitian traditions survive in the form of food and religious customs, the family's migration to the United States comes at a great cost. Most explicitly, Caroline, one of the two daughters and the only one born in America, is born missing a forearm, and her birth defect can be read as symbolic of the severing of the immigrant family from their homeland. While Caroline and Grace's parents attempt to retain elements of Haitian culture through traditions and proverbs, the family lives in a state of exile.

In "Caroline's Wedding," folklore is deployed in an attempt to control destiny. For instance, Ma's bone soup is said to "cure all kinds of ills. She even hoped it would perform the miracle of detaching Caroline from Eric, her Bahamian fiancé" (*KK* 159). For Ma, a woman more Haitian than Haitian American, the desire to dissolve her daughter's relationship stems from the fact that no one in the family has ever married outside the Haitian community. In response, Ma turns to folklore and culinary concoctions to ensure the preservation of Haitian ideals; she hopes that her daughter will retain her Haitian name. The mother's attempts to break up the relationship ultimately prove unsuccessful.

While folklore offers first-generation immigrants Ma and Pa a means of retaining part of their Haitian culture, lore also affords a means of resistance. Indicative of this is the fact that the girls insist on wearing black panties to induce supernatural visitations from their deceased father. This small act of rebellion, of wearing black panties instead of the red ones given to them by their mother to ward off her father's beyond-the-grave visits, evidences a desire for familial and otherworldly connection. The sisters detail, "We had *never* worn the red panties that Ma had bought for us over the years to keep our dead father's spirit away. We had always worn our black panties instead, to tell him that he would be welcome to visit us. Even though we no longer wore black outer clothes, we continued to wear black underpants as a sign of lingering grief" (*KK* 172).[11] Although second-generation immigrants Caroline and Grace are "Americanized," they turn to folklore to connect with their deceased father.

In "Caroline's Wedding," flight surfaces in the form of dreams, the practice that allows us to "travel the years" (*KK* 189). For the daughters, dreams offer escape every night; dreams mystically give voice to the father figure, a man who indeed had "the same scratchy voice he had when he was alive" (*KK* 188). Caroline and Grace rely on folklore when they eschew the wearing of the red panties that are believed to serve as a form of protection from "Papa and all the other dead men who might desire [them]" (*KK* 170). "In Ma's family, the widows often wore blood-red panties so that their dead husbands would not come back and lie down next to them at night. Daughters who looked a lot like the widowed mother might wear red panties too so that if they were mistaken for her, they would be safe," Danticat writes (*KK* 170). Together, these lines offer an allusion to incest; while there was no mention of incestuous propensities while Papa was alive, the passage combines folklore and euphemism to paint the sisters as rebelliously repudiating attempts to keep them "safe." More specifically, Grace and Caroline reject their mother's efforts to keep them "well protected by the red panties" and instead don black underwear in the hope of receiving visits from their father. The sisters oppose traditional beliefs; they either do not think their father would ever harm them or they do not understand the function of the red panties. Further connecting folklore, dreams, and figurative travel, Danticat explains that "Caroline and [Grace] dreamt of him every other night. It was as though he were taking turns visiting [them] in [their] sleep" (*KK* 170). Making the deliberate choice to ensure visits from their father, Caroline and Grace "always wore [their] black panties instead, to tell him that he would be welcome to visit" (*KK* 172).

Folklore is used to exert or strip agency, but it also affords a means of connection. Though Caroline asks, "Is she [their mother] ever going to get tired of telling that story?" the mother's stories bind the family (*KK* 164). Throughout the text, Ma and Papa employ folklore to retain elements of Haitian culture. These attempts are propelled by the fact that their girls are "so American" that they attempt to assimilate by chemically straightening their hair. Caroline and Grace are recipients of these stories much in the way that Danticat positions the reader as consumer of folktales. For the sisters, "These were [their] bedtime stories. Tales that haunted [their] parents and made them laugh at the same time.... They became [their] sole inheritance" (*KK* 180). Through the use of the term "inheritance," Danticat suggests that folklore deserves to be passed on, that it is something to be treasured rather than dismissed or lost.

LOSS

While Pa's death is the most explicit form of loss in "Caroline's Wedding," loss and attempts to remedy loss enter the text in a number of ways, most notably through Grace's passport application and the addition of a prosthetic arm for Caroline. For unspecified reasons, Grace obtains an American passport. Her mother tells her to "'go ahead and get the passport. I can see it when you get it back,' she said. 'A passport is truly what's American. May it serve you well'" (*KK* 158). Ma's directive understands the American passport as a form of social currency, a paper document that conveys all the powers and privileges inherent in its possession. As Ma suggests, the passport will afford mobility. While her father gained entry to the United States through somewhat dubious means by participating in a sham marriage, Grace can now travel anywhere she desires. Instead of citizenship, a driver's license, or owning a home, this small document is what carries power. In contrast to the many who are unable to acquire passports, Grace can now travel freely. Grace easily attains a document that affords politically sanctioned mobility. This document, like Caroline's prosthetic arm, comes at a cost. Grace notes that without the certificate she felt like "unclaimed property" (*KK* 158). Here, Grace equates herself with "unclaimed property" as if the issuance of a passport somehow "claims" her as American and brings her into the fold in ways that citizenship has not; the document, for her, affords a sense of belonging and, more subtly, a degree of ownership. Danticat calls the benefits of migration into question when Grace notes that "we had all paid dearly for this piece of paper, this final assurance that I belonged in the club. It had cost my parent's marriage, my mother's spirit, my sister's arm" (*KK* 214).

Unlike Grace, Caroline attempts to mitigate loss yet is not fully successful in doing so. As mentioned, Caroline was born without her left forearm; "The round end of her stub felt like a stuffed dumpling" (*KK* 159). This condition came as a result of a series of unfortunate events. Caroline details, "My mother was arrested in the sweatshop immigration raid, a prison doctor had given her a shot of a drug to keep her calm overnight. That shot, my mother believed, caused [my] condition" (*KK* 159). Though she has lived with this condition for her entire life, the impending wedding calls Caroline to make herself "whole" because she knows that all eyes will be on her. To mediate discomfort (her own and her guests'), she purchases "a robotic arm with two shoulder straps that controlled the motion of the plastic fingers" (*KK* 198). Illustrating the permanence of loss is the fact that her doctor proclaims that she has phantom limb pain, the "kind of pain that people feel after they've had their arms or legs amputated" (*KK* 198–99). Importantly, Caroline was born with this condition, which suggests that another form of loss is being projected onto the forearm. Perhaps troubling is the fact that the doctor suggested that Caroline purchase a prosthetic to "make it go away" (*KK* 199).

While in "Caroline's Wedding" migration engenders feelings of loss, separation, and insecurity, psychic flight serves as a means of claiming one's inheritance. In Danticat's texts, men place faith in folklore, but it is often women who turn to folklore and mysticism, and are at times persecuted for it. In *Breath, Eyes, Memory* and *Krik? Krak!*, Danticat reclaims folklore to shares these stories with a broader audience. While some may critique this adaptation and popularization of oral lore, it is worth stressing that the author retells rather than rewrites. In the concluding tale in *Krik? Krak!*, Pa questions Grace in a dream: "What kind of legends will your daughters be told? What kinds of charms will you give them to ward off evil?" (*KK* 211). It is through the role of dreams, therefore, that the importance of folklore becomes clear. For Danticat, it is perhaps the act of writing that wards off evil. As a bearer of folklore, Danticat's work propels the transformation of oral lore into print culture.

Danticat connects with the gendered tradition of storytelling in her work. It is through this format that the author confronts painful histories to ground historical remembrance and open up possibilities for the future. In a sense, she serves as a "guardian of folk knowledge" as she furthers the legends that were passed down to her (Bush 764). In *Breath, Eyes, Memory* and *Krik?*

Krak!, Danticat situates readers as recipients of folklore and explores the tension between written and oral mediums. In her work, writing serves as an act of rebellion, as "an act of indolence, something to be done in a corner when you could have been learning to cook" (*KK* 219). While in Haiti, "Writers are tortured and killed if they are men. Called lying whores, then raped and killed, if they are women," Danticat's flight to the United States at the age of twelve informs her writing today (*KK* 221). It is through writing and folklore, then, that the author comes to terms with her own flight; she uses storytelling to quell the "old spirits that live in [her] blood" and to "have something to leave behind" (*KK* 223, 140). *Breath, Eyes, Memory* and *Krik? Krak!*, both concerned with the individual's place in society, point to a larger negotiation of immigrant identity and celebrate the affirming impact of migration. Throughout her work, Danticat centers the struggles of Haitian women and draws on the motif of flight to confront silence and disrupt the cyclical impact of trauma.

CHAPTER TWO

DIVIDED ALLEGIANCES AND ALTERNATIVE HISTORIES
Michelle Cliff's and Margaret Cezair-Thompson's Focus on Psychological Exile

> Exile is strangely compelling to think about but terrible to experience. It is the unhealable rift forced between a human being and a native place, between the self and its true home: its essential sadness can never be surmounted.
>
> —EDWARD SAID

In *Caribbean Women Writers*, Emilia Ippolito contends that "nation favours a language of collectivity and exile is narrated through individual experiences. While nation allows for consensus, exile thrives on dissonance" (38). This chapter explores the individual experiences of exile presented in Michelle Cliff's *Abeng* (1984) and Margaret Cezair-Thompson's *The True History of Paradise* (1999). While the exilic condition can be productive in that "in exile, Caribbean women can ironically politicize their discourse [and] resist assimilation," the texts reveal the consequences of resistance (Chancy 93). Cliff and Cezair-Thompson highlight the effects of personal violence and advance alternative histories that have been lost in contemporary Jamaica. Their novels explore the relationship between exile and migration. In *Abeng* and *The True History of Paradise*, migration is provoked by circumstances that render the homeland unsafe or unbearable; violence and interpersonal conflict operate as precursors to the female characters' emigration.

Cliff and Cezair-Thompson position psychological exile as central to the migratory experience. Put simply, personal and political violence engenders the feelings of exile that spur migration. The characters' divided familial allegiances sets their migration from Jamaica into motion. Each hyperaware of their difference, the protagonists, Clare and Jean, are primed for flight. Whereas the central character in *The True History of Paradise*, Jean Landing, negotiates her sister's death and the political chaos of her country, Clare Savage in *Abeng* reconciles opposing cultural identities. Cliff's novel explores the connection between colonial history and slavery. The author sheds light on the buried history of the Maroons, a group of escaped slaves who have since gained notoriety for their resistance of colonial authority.[1] In *The True History of Paradise*, Cezair-Thompson highlights mounting violence in early 1980s Jamaica, a time characterized by conditions so desperate that the novel concludes with the line, "Panic and history are mine" (346). Clare and Jean's individual journeys parallel their nation's postindependence identity crisis, and the authors establish the connection between the characters' bodies and the figurative body of Jamaica. In *The Difference Place Makes*, Angeletta Gourdine asserts that the term "'Caribbean' denotes a specific geographic locale and connotes paradise, relaxation and adventure" (81). As a number of scholars have argued, the myth of the Caribbean circulates in the popular imagination. Through counterhegemonic narratives, the authors counter the paradise myth.

Abeng and *The True History of Paradise* highlight the emotional and physical consequences of exile by linking past and present. The authors give voice to the "polyvocality of the Jamaican past" and call romanticized portraits of the Jamaican landscape into question (Gillespie 149). This polyvocality is reflected in the ancestral voices that enter Cezair-Thompson's text and the competing influences that pull Clare in opposite directions in Cliff's work. Importantly, the protagonists reclaim their bodies and their histories and migration is but the first step in the protagonists' reconnection with history. While *No Telephone to Heaven*, the prequel to *Abeng*, details the departure and subsequent return of Clare Savage, *The True History of Paradise* narrates a departure in progress. Together the works query the degree to which one can fully "depart" one's homeland.

NOT QUITE/NOT WHITE

Abeng traces the development of Jamaican youth Clare Savage as she navigates life as a mixed-race adolescent. Writing on the intersection of race, class, and identity in *Abeng*, H. Adlai Murdoch notes that for Jamaican residents, "the inescapable fact of their blackness had always marked a tangible and material link with their origins in Africa, and the ethnic, cultural, and linguistic traces and patterns of the continent in the daily lives and intersections of these communities had long played a central role in the articulations and affirmations of Caribbean cultural identity" (66). Murdoch's definition of the term "creole"[2] is useful in understanding the relationship between identity and exile in the text. Murdoch finds that the term "creole" is "linked to displacements of place rather than race, and identifies the descendants of any ethnic group born outside their country of origin" (74). While Clare's mother Kitty is often described as "red,"[3] comes from the country, and has a lineage associated with the Maroons, Clare's lighter-skinned father, Boy, identifies with his slaveholding ancestors. The narrative centers Clare's navigation of binaries such as black/white, English/Maroon, and city/country. Through the character of Clare Savage, a young girl largely unaware of her family history and the history of her nation, the author explores the connection between colonial history, slavery, and the present.

In this semiautobiographical novel, Cliff develops a character who is in the process of self-definition and self-articulation. The author blends historical past and present to highlight a history of subversion that has largely been lost in contemporary Jamaica.[4] A trained historian, Cliff "sees literature as a form that serves the needs of historical recovery" (Adjarian 17). Instead of discussing *Abeng* as a bildungsroman or in the context of gender, as scholars have tended to do over the years, my analysis focuses on Clare's search for her own identity. Clare's racial background and her parents' polarized identities prompt her negotiation of her English and Maroon heritage and bring her to incorporate both identities instead of one. While Clare is not a transnational citizen in the narrowest sense of the term because she does not physically leave Jamaica during the course of the narrative, her migration between city and country and her fusion of disparate cultures functions as a form of transnationalism. Viewing Clare as an individual blending cultures and traditions provides the context for understanding the development of her identity as a process rather than a product. Caught in between parents from very different backgrounds, Clare operates as an internal migrant in a nation on the cusp of independence.

As a light-skinned Jamaican female, Clare is what Homi Bhabha terms "not quite/not white"; Clare, then, is positioned as a familiar, though different, Other (86). This dynamic enables the author to disrupt fixed identity categories. Clare identifies with each of her parents' pasts and each of their racial identities, yet the allegiances operate as polar opposites. Notably, Clare passes as white in the city, but when she is in the country with Zoe, her darker-skinned best friend, her racial privilege establishes difference and is largely a bane. Clare has been taught to bury her blackness to pass for white. Her parents largely silence all discussion of race, racism, and racial politics. When Clare probes for more information regarding her racial background, her father insists that she is white despite the fact that "she knew that her mother was not" (Cliff 36). This contradiction prompts the protagonist to contemplate her racial heritage. Clare is both "pale and deeply colored"; she is caught between the binaries of colonizer/colonized, loyal/rebellious, and city/country (Cliff 36).

In *Abeng*, Clare grapples with her racial identity. Her status as her father's daughter, and thus a Savage (the family last name), allows her to claim racial and linguistic authority, but it comes at the cost of a connection with her maternal roots. Throughout the course of the narrative, she moves "away from the white, imperial, patriarchal authority her father represents and toward an embrace of the black matrilineal legacy of her mother" (Moynagh 117). As Farrah Griffin points out, Clare is the "fair skinned, mixed blood, middle class great-great-granddaughter of white slave owners and black slaves" (531). As such, she represents the complex subjectivity that often accompanies growing up in a colonized country as well as the position of growing up as a mixed-race child in two very different locations.

FEELING DANGEROUS

In her efforts to recover history, Cliff calls on the concept of creolization[5] and presents a "rewriting [of] Caribbean landscape as the site of history" by interspersing flashbacks and historical information throughout the novel (Rody 172). The novel, much like its protagonist, embraces fusion. Although Cliff's evocation of traditions such as a Maroon hunting ritual complicates a reading of the text as a historical novel, it is important to recall that the text is billed as fiction. While the term "creole" was first used to refer to slaves born in the Americas and later to any colonial subject born in the New World regardless of racial ancestry, creolization operates as both a literal mixture and the process of negotiation and assimilation that Clare navigates. For Kamau Brathwaite, creole society is predicated on a process whereby "the society concerned is caught up 'in some kind of colonial arrangement' with a metropolitan European power, on the one hand, and a plantation arrangement on the other" (xxxi). Notably, it is when Clare accidentally kills Old Joe, her grandmother's prize bull, that she recognizes her role in the larger power structure and begins reclaiming her Afro-Caribbean heritage.

As a result of this act, she is formally exiled; away from her parents' home she confronts personal and cultural oppression. Although Clare did not kill Massa Cudjoe, the boar whose name is symbolic of the Maroon leader and who eludes death, her shot signals her move away from the framework of violence associated with her family name and exposes the dangers of imitation. More than "usurp[ing] a traditional masculine role," as M. Keith Booker and Dubravka Juraga claim, Clare's actions bring her closer to reclaiming her ancestral inheritance (120). By taking her grandmother's gun and "feel[ing] dangerous," Clare begins to reconfigure her identity (Cliff 111).

In arming herself with a loaded rifle instead of a machete, Clare adapts Maroon tradition. Significantly, she borrows a rifle, often viewed as a symbol of European violence, and, with Zoe, goes to hunt the boar. In an interesting juxtaposition of symbols, the protagonist takes up arms to kill a boar. Much like the Savage ancestry that Clare distances herself from while in the country, Massa Cudjoe cannot be killed. It is important, then, that the bullet from the rifle strikes not Massa Cudjoe or the cane cutter, but an accidental target, Old Joe. The narrator sheds light on how men searched "for the animal only at certain times of the year and arming themselves with nothing but machetes and spears. It was a man's ritual—the women took part when the pig was brought back to the settlement" (Cliff 112). In borrowing her uncle's rifle, a weapon that, by being loaded, reflects the charged nature of this time in the protagonist's life, the character carves out an identity for herself outside of gender norms. By going against the gendered nature of the hunting ritual and sneaking out early in the morning to perform this imitation of ritual, Clare negotiates tradition. In contrast is Zoe, who as a child of the bush wields a machete with ease. Clare's revision of the ritual's weaponry, the substitution of gun for machete, reflects her increased comfort with blending cultures and traditions. The author utilizes the character of Zoe to introduce Clare to the richness of black identity. Throughout the text, Cliff proffers the possibility of a hybridized, or creolized, identity rather than a sense of self predicated on assimilation.

One of the primary ways that Clare pushes back against dominative culture is through the rejection of gender norms. While her use of the rifle has been read as a masculine act, it calls gender norms into question and points to the character's more fluid understanding of gender roles. As readers learn in *No Telephone to Heaven*, Clare identifies as lesbian. Though she is not yet fully aware of her sexual orientation in *Abeng*, Cliff suggests that Clare is beginning a process of sexual exploration. In *Abeng*, readers witness what can be interpreted as a scene of intimacy between Clare and

Zoe. Importantly, Cliff leaves the question of Clare's sexual orientation unanswered. The passage depicts two girls with "touched hands. Brown and gold beside each other. Damp and warm. Hair curled from the heat and the wet. The warmth of the sunlight on their bodies—salty-damp" (Cliff 120). Writing on the macotte relationship, or same-sex friendships that create structures of socialization, Antonia MacDonald-Smythe calls attention to how the "macotte relationship becomes the testing ground for the affectionate behavior and sexual responsiveness that will become advantageous to the young woman in her future . . . the macotte relationship does not generate a separatism that isolates the young girl from the outside patriarchal world; rather, it allows controlled access to that world" (225). To stress, Clare and Zoe's bond does not threaten masculinist paradigms but instead operates as a site for the erotic that precedes Clare's self-labeling as lesbian. Significantly, the tender moment between Clare and Zoe is interrupted by a cane cutter and the subsequent shooting of Old Joe.

Clare's killing of Old Joe, an act rooted in defiance and independence, occasions the negotiation of her racial, cultural, class, and sexual identities. When Clare aims her uncle's rifle at the cane cutter, a weapon that can be read as a symbol of class and gender disparities, she misses. To explain, the unnamed man stumbles upon the girls bathing and screams, "Coo ya! . . . Two gals nekked pon de river-rock" (Cliff 122). Cliff writes, "He only stared at her—slightly smiling at the sight of a naked and wet girl—trying to be dangerous while protecting her private parts from his sight" (122). After telling the man, "Get away, you hear. This is my grandmother's land," she "began to squeeze the trigger—and at the last second before firing, jerked the gun upward and shot over the man's head. . . . Before either girl could say anything, there was a scream, a bellow, and then a huge thumping of hooves toward them" (Cliff 122). In this scene, Clare uses the rifle, a signifier of violence; when threatened by the man's presence, she deploys the rifle as a counter-threat. The cane cutter's intrusion functions as a symbol for the violence that can accompany homosexual intimacy as well as an interruption in Clare's sexual and racial awakening. The upshot is that Old Joe is shot by "a bullet she meant for no one" (Cliff 123).

Clare's shooting of her grandmother's bull positions her as a "dangerous" young woman in need of behavioral remediation. Her understanding of her African heritage is largely confined to the country until this seminal act places her outside the bounds of terms such as "appropriate," "ladylike," and "desirable." This decisive moment and its unintended consequences, most explicitly Clare's removal from her parents' home and her resettlement with

Mrs. Phillips, a white lady from one of the oldest families in Jamaica, forces her to come to terms with the African side of her identity and begin to reconcile it with the privileged white identity that she has been living in the city. Near the conclusion of the text, Clare joins the multitude of conflicting identities that shape her as a person. She develops a hybrid identity as a result of historical and cultural negotiation as she moves from the city to the country.

The female socialization process in *Abeng* works to solidify privilege. For instance, Kitty tells Clare that she has "to learn once and for all who you are in this world" and stresses that Mrs. Phillips, as a "lady," can teach her things she cannot, thus bringing her closer to her white heritage (Cliff 150). More specifically, Kitty encourages Clare to leave Jamaica. In this discussion, immigration is figured as opportunity, and it is Clare's complexion that will allow her to "someday leave Jamaica behind" (Cliff 150). At the same time, though, the opportunity to leave her homeland is predicated on her acculturation. Clare must "learn the rules" and grasp how to perform the identity of a white woman in order to take advantage of what it offers (Cliff 150). This runs counter to the Maroon history that Clare has explored; for Kitty, being a lady does not mean taking up a gun and going into the hills, but rather "tak[ing] advantage of who you are" (Cliff 150). Even more interesting is the fact that it is the protagonist's maternal grandmother, Miss Mattie, who insists on maintaining traditional gender roles. Following Clare's accidental shooting of Old Joe, Miss Mattie "made a judgment—that Clare was only what she appeared to be; not of Miss Mattie at all, but of Boy's side of the family. The child had no sense of country" (Cliff 145).

Clare's parents do not understand that the act of shooting Old Joe is informed by her exclusion from a boy's hunting trip and her desire to speak back to those who told her "who she was to be in this place" (Cliff 114). In reprimanding their daughter, neither parent is able to "recognize the simplicity of her actions.... A girl of twelve was feeling her way into something. A girl of twelve thought that by taking a gun she acquired some power, some independence" (Cliff 149). Notably, it is Miss Mattie who denied Clare's request to watch the slaughter of a hog; instead, Clare "had taken her place in the kitchen and watched only partly" (Cliff 56). In a somewhat related event, her cousins, Ben and Joshua, exclude her, making her feel "invisible to the boys"; therefore, Clare's desire to find and kill Massa Cudjoe can be read as being rooted in feelings of alienation. Clare's emotional exile is compounded when her parents send her to live with Mrs. Phillips and her sister, Miss Winifred. It is Clare's racial identity that places her "outside" her mother's family; Kitty notes that "there are no opportunities" for Clare in Jamaica (Cliff 150). In this exchange, Cliff positions assimilation as a form of medicine. Kitty sees her daughter's stay with Mrs. Phillips as something that at first may be bitter but will ultimately yield great advantage. According to Kitty, Mrs. Phillips can convey the social norms specific to white womanhood. Clare, exiled to live with a white woman, is constantly reminded of the consequences of her transgression. Sadly, Mrs. Phillips fails to offer her the emotional support that she craves; as a result, Clare turns to self-reliance and nurtures herself.

THE BEST OF BOTH SIDES

In contrast to Boy's unwillingness to discuss his daughter's racial heritage is the reminder that "gradations of shading reach into the top strata of the society" (Cliff 5). Importantly, racial creolization enters the text via Cliff's narration of rape. The unnamed narrator describes the rape of black women by white colonists whose wives often remained in England. The narrator stresses that the abuse of black women would have occurred "with or without the presence of white women" (Cliff 19). Though this voice claims that "all was in the open," the narrative suggests otherwise (Cliff 19). While the term "creole" is now understood as indicating a "black' person or a person of mixed racial heritage," in *Abeng*, racial creolization carries connotations that run deeper than many definitions suggest (Bauer 40). More than simply referring to race, the term "creole" generally refers to people or cultures "derived from the Old World but developed in the New" (Bolland, "Creolisation and Creole" 1). Nigel Bolland explains, "In common Caribbean usage, 'Creole' refers to a local product which is the result of a mixture or blending" ("Creolisation and Creole" 1). What the term does not fully convey is the fact that racial intermixture, as the novel illustrates, was a cruel and brutish process. As a mixed-race adolescent, Clare must confront the legacy of her white, slaveholding grandfather alongside her Maroon ancestry. Throughout the course of the novel, she becomes an agent in the larger historical process that views Caribbean culture as a result of synthesis instead of imposition.

Cliff renders synthesis explicit through the figure of Clare, a young woman whose mother is "both Black and white" but whose people are called "red" (Cliff 54). In contrast to Boy's attempts to downplay his ancestors' indiscretions, Kitty's family is not ashamed of their ancestral background. The Savage family seeks to perpetuate their whiteness, but the Freemans strive to "preserv[e] their redness" in favor of cultural reclamation (Cliff 54). In her community, Clare is seen as her father's child and is deemed "lucky" to have his green eyes. She is depicted as "the best of both sides"; this characterization attests to the duality of her physiognomy as well as her personality (Cliff 61). While Kitty's origins reflect the impact of Jamaica's past on the present, Boy's insistence on Clare's whiteness brings his daughter to interrogate her racial, gender, sexual, and cultural identities. Her privilege sets her apart; she does not "fit in" in the black world or the white world. As a whole, Cliff's work reifies the consequences of racial and cultural exile. Ultimately, Clare's green eyes are a responsibility as well as an inheritance; she is expected to pass them on by marrying "light" and has a "duty to try to turn the green eyes blue" (Cliff 127).

Although Clare's face "gives her away completely," she becomes more accepting of her racial hybridity[6] and begins to think about racial characterizations more critically (Cliff 158). In *Abeng*, hybridity affords the ability to deconstruct labels. Cliff develops a character who, rather than despising her own skin, grows to see her competing allegiances as an opportunity for refined sight. Coming to a greater understanding of the racial discourse surrounding her, Clare begins to prefer her racial heritage to the hateful ways of "narrow-mindedness" (Cliff 158). Marginal characters such as Miss Winifred, Mrs. Phillips's sister, profess that "only sadness comes from mixture," but by the end of the text Clare is able to see the racial landscape around her with more clarity, perhaps because she has been confronted with such bigoted notions (Cliff 164). Most notably, Clare tells Miss Winifred that "there's all kinds of mixture in Jamaica"; this statement points to a more global understanding of creolization as opposed to a focus on racial identity (Cliff 164). With this line, Cliff suggests that Clare is becoming more aware of the oppressive conditions of her society. As this rather symbolic line attests, Clare is developing an increasingly critical perspective.

Though Cliff positions Clare as "inching toward wholeness" in the novel, the protagonist's life is made up of a series of negotiations and contradictions (namely of class, color, and sexual orientation) (Adisa 276). In narrating one woman's exploration of cultural identity, Cliff presents the reclamation of a heritage the protagonist has been taught to despise. Though Clare may be a "fragmented character," as Cliff notes, her cultural reclamation counters social norms. Per Wendy Walters in *At Home in Diaspora*, *Abeng* can be read as an anti-bildungsroman in that Clare's education does not move her toward wholeness but rather encourages a fragmented sense of self (28). Perhaps this "undoing" is central to a reshaping and is thus an essential part of the maturation process. Much like Sophie's use of dissociation in *Breath, Eyes, Memory*, Clare's struggle with disjunction provides the strength needed to one day reclaim her maternal heritage in the face of the immense pressure that her father imposes. In this way, then, Clare's movement toward wholeness is contingent on the rejection of individual and cultural division.

DUALITY

An examination of linguistic creolization affords a view of how the protagonist integrates very different cultural identities. Initially halting Clare's acceptance of the country dialect are the implicit signals she receives from authority figures. Most notably, Clare's teacher, Mr. Powell, is directed by the British-based education board to downplay his accent. The use of "country" language is discouraged in the classroom; the most explicit privileging of English comes in the form of Mr. Powell's instruction manuals, which specify that the poem "Daffodils" is to be "spoken with as little accent as possible" (Cliff 84). Messaging such as this subjugates local dialects to the hegemonic power structure and the curriculum and instruction methods engender historical erasure. Not only do the manuals seek to erase linguistic variation, but their lack of adaptation suggests a fear of change on the part of the governor's office. Mr. Powell receives the same directions year after year. The teacher's acquiescence to the demand to largely strip cultural reference out of his instruction speaks to the realities of the postcolonial state and the precariousness of his position. As the British-based instruction implies, colonial ties persist in nuanced but destructive ways.

Similar to how patois is discouraged in the Jamaican school system, Clare receives influence via Hollywood movies that "[teach] her to drop her patois and to speak 'properly'" (Cliff 99). The protagonist's relationship with language comes to a head when she addresses Zoe and the unnamed cane cutter at the conclusion of the novel. When the cane cutter finds Clare and Zoe at the baths, Clare speaks to him using "buckra language," telling him to "Get away, you hear. This is my grandmother's land" (Cliff 122). By using "the Queen's" English, Clare "reclaim[s] her material history"; she deploys the "white language" to give instructions on her grandmother's land (Rody 151). The command separates; in this instance, Clare accepts and uses "proper English" to her advantage while her actions align her more closely with her Maroon heritage. By speaking in "buckra tongue," Clare creates distance between herself and the cane cutter, and ultimately with Zoe. This linguistic and cultural divide gives her a sense of authority and privilege in the "wild" environment of the parish country.

In *Abeng*, the trope of duality is reflected in the complex and conflicting meanings of the term "abeng" and the name of the protagonist. Simon Gikandi notes that the word "abeng" is the "African word for 'conch shell'"; more subversively, it was used as an instrument of rebellion (237). Similar to the way the term "maroon" originally referred to wild cattle but came to connote human resistance and rebellion, "abeng" has a variety of meanings. An abeng is a conch shell that represents a means of communication, both to call slaves in the fields and to send messages among troops of Maroons who defied the plantation system. In a similar way, Clare's name reflects two very different meanings. As Supriya Nair observes, "Clare indicates light (skin), which stands for civilization, domesticity, soft speech, and knowing one's place" (45). While Boy thought he was naming her in this context, her name has a second meaning that is associated with her mother's memory of her friend Clary, a woman who once nursed Kitty back to health. Kitty's acceptance of the name of Clare for her daughter serves as a subtle form of resistance to her husband's influence and recalls the close relationship that Clare and Zoe share.

In *Abeng*, creolization also functions in a social and environmental context. Similar to eighteenth-century theories of cultural and physical degeneration, people, plants, and objects in the novel are described as undergoing change upon moving to the "torrid region." For instance, at John Knox Memorial Church, the emigrant school teacher plays a harpsichord that has "never adjusted to the climate" (Cliff 6). It is through the harpsichord that the author foregrounds the difficulties of adjustment and acculturation. The instrument is disassembled and reconstructed yet fails to maintain the correct tune. For the church members, the harpsichord serves as a symbol of their climatic and cultural difference from England. The climate in Jamaica is too warm and humid for the instrument, and the voices of the congregation are too loud. To correct this, the schoolteacher suggests that the congregation "tone down their singing" to sing more like the Englishmen the harpsichord is suited for (Cliff 6).

Central to Clare's identity crisis is the fact that the family visits two very different churches. According to Lizabeth Paravisini-Gebert, "The duality of these churches represents Clare's duality of backgrounds," as she is a member of both her father's more "colonial" church and her mother's church, which has roots in African religions (43). Although Clare is never asked to choose between the two religions, Boy and Kitty implicitly occasion confusion by exposing their daughter to cultural elements in a "separate but equal" fashion. From an early age, Clare learns that differences are not to be discussed, but instead suppressed. Rather than educating Clare on the ideological and cultural distinctions between their religions, Clare's parents perpetuate their opposition by bringing the entire family to two places of worship each Sunday (John Knox for Boy and the Tabernacle for Kitty); the churches reflect the "separate needs and desires of the two parents" (Cliff 49).

In addition to growing up the child of parents with divergent religious ideologies, Clare negotiates the differences between city and country and between English and Maroon. In reconciling the disparate parts of herself, Clare crosses, and at times dismantles, the borders that traditionally stand between these binaries. Clare's parallel practice of two very different religions is mirrored in her relationship with Zoe. Notably, it is only in the "wild countryside" that Clare and Zoe's friendship is expressed. Their friendship is contingent on place, which further illustrates the divide between place and class that surfaces throughout the text. Cliff writes, "To Clare's mind a lady was someone who dressed and spoke well. A lady was a town creature" (98). As this characterization suggests, socioeconomic status is a crucial component of the girls' relationship. For Clare, there is no middle ground between their two worlds. In the country she speaks patois and runs about with Zoe, but in the city she must speak "proper" English. As the daughter of one of the women living on her grandmother's land, Zoe is an acceptable playmate in the countryside but, unfortunately, would not be accepted as an appropriate companion for "city Clare." Instead, her relationship with Zoe, a very poor country girl, can only exist in the "wild countryside."

As a result of these conflicts, Clare feels a "split within herself" that can be read as the beginning of a hybrid identity and the development of a new subject position (Cliff 96). This split comes as a result of the opposing ideological constraints that she is exposed to. Clare is caught between her parents, and the polarity makes "resistance very difficult" (Cliff 49). For instance, Clare's mother "came alive only in the bush," but the country is a source of anxiety for Boy (Cliff 49). Perhaps because the very island she lives on "does not know its own history," Clare is largely unaware of her ancestral connections to the countryside (on Kitty's side) as well as her father's family's involvement with slavery (Cliff 96). When Clare begins to come to terms with these contradictions and articulate her own identity, she is perceived as "stepp[ing] out of line . . . in a society in which the lines were unerringly drawn" (Cliff 149–50). By eschewing her identity as a Savage and embracing elements of Maroon culture, she acts defiantly. Throughout the course of the narrative, the character joins transmigrants who "develop and maintain multiple relations" (Mahler 76). Through movement between spaces, Clare comes to a fuller understanding of herself as an inheritor of contradiction; for Clare, moving between the city and the country and from one home to another allows her to step outside traditional boundaries and carve an identity for herself. It is on the "sad little island" of Jamaica that Clare Savage navigates binaries including England/Jamaica, English/patois, and city/country (Cliff 150).

RECLAMATION

In striving to reconcile her family's very different historical pasts, Clare hopes not to have to choose between black or white, but rather embody a hybrid identity. While previously this "mulatto girl" did as she was told and was oblivious to "herself or her past," Cliff's novel awakens the reader to an alternative history that is often untold (71). It is through the figure of Anne Frank that Clare begins to question societal expectations and locate boundaries for herself. Where before she accepted her father's stories without question, Clare begins to see through Boy's logical fallacies. Unlike her largely silent mother, Clare takes steps to claim an independent identity by reclaiming her cultural past. In *Abeng*, the protagonist's cultural inheritance is largely figured through references to Maroons, which operates as a symbol of resistance in the text.[7] Though Clare is initially unaware of the "true" history of the Maroons who opposed slavery and the plantation economy (the people who resisted the very hegemony she descends from), she begins to negotiate these complex identities. Clare's "failure to learn the truth of her family's history" has an impact her identity development (Sharpe 36). By moving from an individual context to a collective one, Cliff uses the protagonist's struggles to speak to cultural loss and erasure. As a mixed-race progeny with connections to Maroon and slaveholding cultures, Clare moves from a place of assimilation to one of integration. The protagonist cannot establish a fundamental relationship with either her English or Maroon history or her status as both black and white, city citizen and country visitor. In *Abeng*, Clare Savage is not forced to choose or assimilate but rather integrates her identities in a liminal space similar to how transnational citizens negotiate identity.

The author references the multiplicity of identity throughout the text. Clare can be both black and white, Freeman and Savage, city and country—and in fact she is. In *Writing in Limbo*, Gikandi reflects on the identity struggle that Clare undergoes. Gikandi claims that "Clare is entrapped in the very modes of knowledge which have entrapped her" (249). With this, Gikandi suggests that as an adolescent girl who has not yet left the island, Clare remains implicated in the colonial mindset and has not yet been able to move beyond the lines of thinking that position her as white, cultured, and feminine based on her father's lineage. This mindset implies that the rejection of her Maroon heritage is desirable and will lead to social mobility and a host of advantages. By developing her own identity, Clare introduces a contestatory form of history. Through claiming her creole identity and embracing revolution, Clare portrays, on an individual level, what is at stake for Jamaicans. While Clare does not have to travel a great distance to occasion this negotiation, the separation between city and country and English and Maroon brings contradictions to the fore. Armed with the knowledge and awareness of the role the Maroons play in shaping Jamaican history and in resisting colonial power,[8] Clare Savage comes to understand creolization not as a repressive force but as an emancipatory one.

A HISTORY OF VIOLENCE

Much like Cliff's *Abeng*, Margaret Cezair-Thompson's *The True History of Paradise* "sees alternative histories as the antidote to paradise discourse and to a full understanding of the challenges Jamaica faces" (Strachan 267). In detailing personal and political violence through the protagonist's perspective, the author blurs the lines between history and fiction and de-romanticizes "paradise." Set in 1981, Cezair-Thompson's work illustrates the effects of internal violence, and in particular, the violence that followed Edward Seaga's election.[9] As Murdoch observes, the family functions as a "microcosmic representation of the social and psychic splitting eventuated in Jamaica by the trauma of slavery, as past brutalities produce a national identity framework in the present whose key components are critically divided against the whole" (80). *The True History of Paradise* follows the protagonist, Jean Landing, as she leaves her country during a state of emergency. Moving back and forth between the present and the seventeenth century, the novel mingles "African, German, Jewish, Scotts, Chinese, English and Irish ancestry together in the head and the body of Jean Landing" (Kenan 54). The protagonist is attuned to the many voices of her ancestors, but she realizes that she is unable to live on the island that they called home. By integrating disparate voices, Cezair-Thompson illustrates "the complexity of the human drama that is

Jamaica's past and the complicated issues of identity in postcolonial Jamaica" (Strachan 265). Rather than decrying the impact of neocolonialism, though, the historical novel presents the events leading up to the protagonist's departure from Jamaica. In *The True History of Paradise*, readers are hit with violence from the first line of the text: "It's Easter, and Jamaica is in a state of emergency" in which "the city has been divided into war zones marked out by graffiti" (Cezair-Thompson 3, 4). Cezair-Thompson foregrounds how political violence, represented by the PNP and JLP parties,[10] and respectively Michael Manley[11] and Edward Seaga,[12] renders the country divided. The novel "settles its focus on the tragic unwinding of a very special decade in Jamaica's history" and calls the term "history" into question while countering the paradise myth (Manley 203).

The True History of Paradise connects the process of decolonization with the political situation in 1962. Cezair-Thompson writes, "Bustamante's party, the JLP,[13] won the general election, and Jamaica was granted independence from Britain. It was to be official on August 6" (45). As Jean's mother Monica remarks, "Everything gone from bad to wus since Independence" (Cezair-Thompson 120). In giving voice to the lingering effects of colonialism and the struggles inherent in separation from the "mother country," Cezair-Thompson suggests that the retelling of Jamaican history is incomplete. The novel relies on the stories of Jean's ancestors to unfold important personal and political events. Throughout, Cezair-Thompson develops a layered, polyvocal approach to national history and deploys the narrator's journey to comment on the state of postcolonial Jamaica. While Clare's flight in *Abeng* comes as a result of divided allegiances, Jean can only be free by leaving her homeland.

In presenting Jamaica's political strife postindependence, Cezair-Thompson paints a country segregated by violence. For instance, Jean observes that Linstead, a smaller city outside Spanish Town, has not been affected by violence. Cezair-Thompson writes, "The violence has not touched them here. No soldiers, roadblock, curfew, graffiti. There is no vigilance or fear in people's faces. In Kingston everyone lives behind iron bars, ever attuned to the sound of intruders and to news of the latest alarming murder. Here the open verandas and unwalled gardens of croton and hibiscus make Kingston seem like some lunatic's idea of reality" (103). While this more global look at the nation puts localized violence in perspective, it is also a reminder of how chaos has become somewhat normalized.[14] As the text continues, the reality of violence becomes more apparent. After a friend in New York shares a news clipping from their newspaper that recounts a shoot-out between the PNP and JLP, Jean realizes that "she had seen the bloody aftermath; that had been upsetting enough. But to see her city under siege in a *foreign* newspaper—the newspaper there, she here—and in a photograph as true as the ones she'd seen of Cambodia and El Salvador, locked her inside her horror" (Cezair-Thompson 294). Jean subsequently concludes that "if this country splits in two, there won't be anywhere to hide" (Cezair-Thompson 294).[15]

PERSONAL VIOLENCE

Inherent to Jamaica's division is the role of racial politics; the Jamaica that Cezair-Thompson depicts is identified as a "Black man country" and scrawlings such as "GO BACK HOME WHITE MAN" directly addresses tourists and "bukras" (Cezair-Thompson 125, 137). The text reveals that racial tensions are so high that "in this country, a poor white man is worse than a stray dog" (Cezair-Thompson 145). For Faye, Jean's closest friend, Jamaica has become unreal and alienating. For instance, Faye remarks that she "never thought Jamaicans could be so cruel. . . . I feel like it's becoming another country" (Cezair-Thompson 220). Personal violence comes to a head when Faye's lover, Pat, is murdered after Jean and another friend, Ines, are attacked. Cezair-Thompson narrates the attack. "He brought the knife down to her face and slashed [Jean], cutting her hands which she held up protectively before her. He slashed her again" (Cezair-Thompson 244). This results in a minor injury for Ines, while Jean is rushed into surgery with "her left hand . . . nearly severed at the wrist" (Cezair-Thompson 244). Following this attack by bandits in search of valuables, Jean becomes more attuned to the reality of flight as offering the potential to escape a situation in which "no woman in this country is safe" (Cezair-Thompson 280).

Violence becomes even more explicit with Pat's murder. Jean is informed that "she's dead. The gunmen came through a window while they were asleep. Beat them [Pat and Faye]. Police said blood was everywhere. All over the house they draggin' them an' beatin' them. . . . They beat her in the face. Dislodged her eye" (Cezair-Thompson 311). Violence that began with the murder of two diplomats becomes intensely personal. With the understanding that "rape had become so prevalent on the island . . . , it was beginning to seem like a war against women; rape of the nation's women, rich and poor, had become a casual and ubiquitous weapon, like stones in the hands of bad boys," it is no surprise that Jean contemplates migration (Cezair-Thompson 245). In a country that has a reputation for being homophobic,[16] it is perhaps not surprising that women in homosexual relationships face violence. Given the fact that a robbery did not take place, one is left to wonder if Pat and Faye were made to suffer for loving one another. Although Cezair-Thompson yokes post-election unrest with the legacy of slavery, this attack shifts from generalized to targeted violence. The attack, as Sam Vásquez finds, "enact[s] yet another level of violence against historically marginalized bodies" (48). The womens' bodies are marked by bigotry; Pat is found shot and tied up while Faye is shot in the back while running away. Cezair-Thompson details the physical results of the attack: "Faye's surgery lasted till late afternoon. The surgeon told them that he has managed to save her eye. Her jaw had also been badly broken and part of her ear torn away . . . she might be left partially paralyzed" (311).

If a personal attack and the murder of a close friend is not enough to push Jean toward migration, her implication in the death of an innocent man convinces her that she is making the right decision. To explain, Jean's car is stopped in a roadblock when she is on the way to the airport. The narrator relates: "[Jean] didn't see the roadblock ahead, or the car that had stopped in front of her. She rammed into the back of it, hitting her brakes too late. It lurched forward on the impact and knocked down the soldier who had been standing in front of it" (Cezair-Thompson 316). When Jean begins laughing at the absurdity of the whole situation, but most particularly at the soldiers standing idly by with no idea of what they are even looking for, a violent string of events is set in motion. After Jean is handcuffed and ushered toward an army truck, an unnamed man shouts, "Hey! Wait! Soldier what are you doing to that girl?" (Cezair-Thompson 317). When the man inquires about the soldier's approach and his treatment of Jean, "The soldier shoved the man with his rifle, pushing him back against Jean's car; then he raised the rifle and shot him in the chest" (Cezair-Thompson 317). The verbal altercation quickly escalates and leaves the man dead and "Jean gaz[ing] at the man in the white shirt, who had done nothing more than come to her aid in a situation that had gotten out of hand. He lay dead with blood seeping from the bullet wound in his chest, his eyes open, his arms flung wide in alarm" (Cezair-Thompson 317–18). Jean is rendered relatively helpless, only gazing, but not reacting to this tragedy. Much like the violence on the island, the blood cannot be contained. Serving as a martyr and witness, the sacrifice dressed in white lays with eyes open, his arms outstretched like Christ. This event is the last in a string of hardships that brings Jean to realize that she must leave a land that is at war with itself; she chooses to protect her own health and her own sanity.

FAMILY DYNAMICS

In an interview with Randall Kenan, Cezair-Thompson characterizes Jean as "poised between her mother and sister, a woman struggling to find herself" (54). Much like Clare in *Abeng*, Jean is "mixed-up progeny"; while Clare is "mixed-up" in terms of her racial heritage, Jean is "mixed-up" as a result of ancestral influences and family dynamics (Cezair-Thompson 9). As in Cliff's novel, the theme of racial prejudice looms large. Early in *The True History of Paradise*, Monica, Jean's mother, notes that "her good looks came from centuries of washing Black people out of the family's blood" (Cezair-Thompson 31). While in *Abeng* the father figure is the voice of racial prejudice, in Cezair-Thompson's work the sentiment comes from Jean's mother. In contrast to Monica's eldest daughter, Lana, Jean comes as a "disappointment, the baby girl was not, in Monica's opinion, beautiful. She was scrawny and dark, darker than anyone in Monica's family, and she had a deformity: a strange flap of skin on the side of her head that looked like a third ear" (Cezair-Thompson 32). Although Jean may not be phenotypically attractive to Monica, she is believed to possess an otherworldly, intuitive "hearing," a caul that the doctor quickly removes (Cezair-Thompson 32). This gift is later referenced when Jean is described as a young woman "peculiarly attuned to the voices of her ancestors" (Strachan 264). Monica remarks, "She 'ave sharpenin' powers. I know dis 'bout Jean, from she was a likkle girl. She 'ave—wha' dem call it—six' sense" (Cezair-Thompson 245).

Similar to the close relationship between Clare and Boy, Jean favors her father, Roy. Cezair-Thompson paints the relationship as follows: "From the first moment he saw her, Jean was the joy of her father's life. His feeling for her surprised him because he had not especially cared about having children" (33). Through the character of Roy, the author depicts an understanding that moves beyond colorism. Unlike Monica, Roy loves Jean despite her complexion; this bond is perhaps best illustrated by a family portrait. It is via the portrait that Jean's identity, or lack thereof, is highlighted. Cezair-Thompson writes, "Jean found the unfinished painting years later, and placed it on her bedroom wall. The only one Roy had finished painting was Lana. Monica was half-finished. Jean was just an outline; so was he" (50). This passage aligns Roy and Jean as outlines while Lana is the one who stands apart. In describing Lana as "finished" and Jean as an "outline," Cezair-Thompson reflects and comments on societal expectations, racial politics, the privilege of lighter-skinned individuals, and the erasure of those who fail to measure up to racial and social ideals. In leaving himself and Jean as outlines, Roy utilizes art to comment on racial politics and its impact on individuals.

While Cliff details the distancing of mother and daughter, in *The True History of Paradise,* Jean loses her father; readers learn that "she had said good night to him as usual; the next day he was gone" (Cezair-Thompson 51). Following her father's sudden death, Jean "became a solitary, independent little girl, never expecting anyone to pay as much attention to her as her father had" (Cezair-Thompson 51). After Roy's death, Monica instructs Jean to "try to be a big girl now and take care of [herself]" (Cezair-Thompson 51). Although this direction can be read as a bit harsh, Monica's behavior is not specific to Jean. After Lana becomes pregnant out of wedlock, Monica casts her eldest daughter out of the house. "For eight years [Jean] did not see her sister. The women of the family spoke about Lana among themselves but never directly to her," the narrator explains (Cezair-Thompson 104). Here, the family, namely Monica, emerges as preoccupied with appearances and afraid to deviate from social norms. Jean's psychological exile and the distance that her mother creates likely contributes to her decision to leave the country.

MIXED-UP

The term "mixed-up" appears several times throughout the novel. When Jean is described as a "mixed-up progeny," Lana remarks, "What a mix-up family we have" to which Jean replies, "Is a mix-up country. But everything have a way a working out" (Cezair-Thompson 9, 254). Perhaps the most explicit way that Jean is "mixed-up" is through the multitude of voices she hears, the influence of her ancestors who speak to her. As Cezair-Thompson clarifies, Jean "is the descendant, not of runaway Africans, but of African slaves. And not only of Africans but of English, Irish, Spanish, Jewish, Germans, and Chinese. Does this motley ancestry make her spirit a less able traveler? Does confusion of the blood cause the spirits to flounder and lose their sense of direction?" (297). Like Clare in *Abeng,* Jean is a young woman with a rich, multicultural heritage. While Clare begins to come to terms with a number of contradictions in Jamaica, Jean must leave her homeland before the "confusion of the blood" destroys her (Cezair-Thompson 297). In *The True History of Paradise,* Cezair-Thompson details the departure of a protagonist who has the financial wherewithal to depart her homeland. Jean has the ability to afford and secure a passport "with her photograph and someone else's name"

(Cezair-Thompson 6). Unlike millions who cannot leave the country via private plane, Jean has a connection, Alan, her white, English lover, who can "get [her] a visa, passport . . . in a matter of days" (Cezair-Thompson 293). For Vásquez, the description of Alan as a "compass" figures him as a "symbol of Western patriarchy [and] represents a certain unimpeded, directed access to cosmopolitanism and freedom from violent Third World conflicts" (54). Moreover, Jean's relationship with Alan somewhat normalizes infidelity and, in light of conditions in Jamaica, raises the question of Jean's agency in selecting a lover who can ensure her escape.

Cezair-Thompson utilizes the figure of Jean Landing to comment on the relationship between colonialism and contemporary unrest in Jamaica. The author writes, "Because of all the tourist brochures' claims about harmonious mixing, a White, Indian, or Chinese face among the Black people is incongruous. *Too much people. Too much story*" (Cezair-Thompson 91). Through Jean's character, Cezair-Thompson reveals the largely suppressed history of Jamaica and connects past and present violence. The novel counters advertisements with a sustained look at discord. Jean's ancestors present an image of prolonged historical violence. In the first "interruption" to the text, the voice of Jean's ancestor Rebecca Landing (1682–1751) surfaces. Rebecca narrates: "*We eventually reached Spanish Town. The destruction was not so great there, though fires had broken out in many places and the inhabitants were running in great alarm through the streets*" (Cezair-Thompson 20). Jean's chapter, the last in the text, concludes with the line "panic and history are mine" (Cezair-Thompson 331). By constructing parallel depictions of panic, the author points to a shift, as opposed to the eradication, of violence. While Rebecca's account speaks to the chaos that residents experienced following an earthquake, likely the 1692 event that devastated Port Royal and killed three thousand people,[17] Jean is troubled by increasing personal violence.

From a textual standpoint, the ancestral accounts, set in italics, contrast the primary text. The voices work with the text to augment readers' understanding of Jamaican history. Notably, Rebecca remarks that "the history of our island is a history of hell" (Cezair-Thompson 25). This line is repeated before Jean encounters the previously discussed roadblock. In the same moment, an unnamed ancestor affirms that "*Jamaica is our country*"; this cry simultaneously claims the nation as "Black man country" and makes Jean's decision to leave the island exponentially more difficult (Cezair-Thompson 125). Yet another account, that of Moses Landing (1838–1865), specifies that the ancestor "*cannot tell you the history of [his] people, but [he] can tell you the history of a soul*"; this declaration plays off the title regarding the need for a true(r) history of Jamaica (Cezair-Thompson 55). Moses's account details the aftermath of Emancipation. He states that *"Jamaica was still a White man's country. Slavery had ended, but there were still men who were owners and men who were slaves"* (Cezair-Thompson 58). Throughout the text, Cezair-Thompson works to expose the lingering effects of colonialism and the continued inequality that plagues the nation. Moses's chapter renders this connection evident. The ancestor reflects, *"Now one hundred years later, another state of emergency; this time Black against Black"* (Cezair-Thompson 60). As the novel progresses and the voices of Jean's ancestors intensify, she "can't help thinking that some inscrutable meanness of their history—her history, Lana's, Paul's, missionaries', conquiestadores', and slaves'—lies in this fallen notion of love, in some error that can be traced back to those first untranslatable hours in the New World" (Cezair-Thompson 241).

The text concludes with a description of a woman who is only referred to as "she panic" (Cezair-Thompson 331). The description reads, *"The woman with a hundred devils in her, or 'panic' as we say here, staggers toward the car. The driver shouts something obscene, swerves around her, and drives on. The soldiers, hearing the commotion, look across the road and see the half-naked woman waving her arms and cursing. They shout and move as a group toward her"* (Cezair-Thompson 331). In beginning and concluding with scenes of panic, the author suggests that while panic has become individual, it is also pandemic. Here, the woman stands in for the larger sense of madness that threatens the country's stability. She, like the image of the country that Cezair-Thompson paints, is exposed. In writing on political turmoil in 1980s Jamaica, the author links contemporary violence with the violence of enslavement and the incertitude of the colonial period. At the conclusion of the novel, Jean leaves Jamaica to escape a legacy of panic and an island characterized by beauty as well as violence.

ESCAPE

Despite the fact that Cezair-Thompson announces Jean's departure upfront, the novel centers on the vacillation of the protagonist and the difficulty she has in leaving her homeland. Following the attack on her friends Pat and Faye, Jean decides that "she would not leave. This was her country. Rage had replaced fear" (Cezair-Thompson 316). Interestingly, an interjection from an unnamed ancestor enters the text, advising, *"Don't forget that you have the key, not them on the outside"*; this is followed by Jean's conclusion that "Jamaica was at war with itself. But there were many people like Jean who wanted no part of this war, who wanted life here" (Cezair-Thompson 316). Eventually, Jean comes to the conclusion that she must leave Jamaica. She explains this to her mother: "I'm not thriving. I'm dying here.... The brutality is killing me. If I stay any longer, I'll have to accept it, and I can't accept it. I find the acceptance brutal" (Cezair-Thompson 326). While on the one hand Jean's migration can be seen as escape, her statement suggests a repudiation of the widespread violence on the island and her departure can be read as a form of resistance. Although readers are left with little indication of Jean's plans once she leaves Jamaica, her intentions to continue a romantic relationship with Alan may allow her to thrive in a way that is not possible in Jamaica. Similar to her ancestor Rebecca Landing, who relates that her "*soul, too, was divided by a sword. That day we left for England the ship whistled so loudly it drowned out my cries,*" Jean's decision to leave her homeland does not come without debate (Cezair-Thompson 26). Like her forebears, Jean has the luxury of leaving violence to the "sufferers."

The link between violence, migration, and desperation is highlighted throughout the text. Cezair-Thompson develops the image of a crowd waiting to depart. "American expatriates and Jamaicans filled the American embassy and stood in waiting crowds outside its gates," the narrator explains (302). For Jean, "Born in British Jamaica just as the colony was drawing its last breath, she had entered a place of waiting. It was not an exceptional place—the waiting rooms of history were full of people like her—but it was a place of wonder" (Cezair-Thompson 303). In constructing this image of those awaiting collective flight, the author evokes a term popularized by Dipesh Chakrabarty in *Provincializing Europe*. In his analysis of nineteenth-century "rude peoples" such as Africans and Indians, Chakrabarty pushes back against a reading of Africans and Indians as populations "*not yet* civilized enough to rule themselves" (8).[18] Chakrabarty concludes that such a reading "consign[s] Indians, Africans, and other 'rude' nations into an imaginary waiting room of history. In doing so, it converted history itself into a version of this waiting room" (8).

While Chakrabarty's understanding of the phrase "rude peoples" critiques a paternalistic view of postcolonial nations and their peoples, Cezair-Thompson's portrait of the waiting room depicts a temporary "waiting room" full of individuals soon to disperse to multiple locations. The real waiting room, though, is Jean's birth into this particular time in history, the period just prior to independence in 1962. By employing the term "waiting room," the author coyly disputes the notion that post-independence Jamaica is incapable of ruling itself. Jean's departure, as someone born into this "place of waiting," suggests that one can only wait so long. As the metaphor implies, early 1980s Jamaica remains in a state of limbo, so much so that citizens like Jean endure another period of waiting to escape. Throughout, migration is depicted as fraught with emotion and anxiety. The process of leaving, of obtaining "approval" to depart, is like a shared purgatory.

Rather than departing solely for personal reasons, Jean's flight is influenced by a warning from her father, the death of her sister Lana, and her failed relationship with Paul. Jean's deceased father urges her to leave. In Roy Landing's (1918–1963) account, he states, "*I came to warn you: terrible things spinning around you, a wheel that isn't stopping. I sat on your bed and watched you sleeping. You opened your eyes. 'Daddy?' 'Leave this place*" (Cezair-Thompson 285). While this account illustrates a supernatural connection or perception, the directive to "leave this place" rather than to leave "home" strips the impending decision of the emotion associated with the referent "home." After viewing the tombstone of her ancestor Susannah Crawford, Jean remarks that "her sister's death saturates everything. It is crucial that she go now. It is terrible now to go. Should she let herself be run out of her own country, her sister unquiet and confused in the grave?" (Cezair-Thompson 16). Much like Edward Said's statement in this chapter's epigraph, the condition of exile, a psychological as much as a physical state, offers relief as well as grief. Jean connects personal and political mourning when she notes that it is fitting to "leave the country in mourning clothes" (Cezair-Thompson 10). Yet, as seen in the above lines, she struggles with the decision to leave home and the guilt associated with that choice. It is possible that Jean's mourning clothes reflect the death of her sister, the demise of her nation, and the loss of hope for life in Jamaica. Ultimately, the protagonist heeds her father's warning. As the text concludes, Jean asserts that "she didn't dream them: Roy, Monica, Paul, Deepa, Moses, Daphne, Lana, Rebecca . . . they are here" (Cezair-Thompson 328). Jean's decision is complicated by voices who urge her to fight for her nation and ones who advise her to run far away. In *The True History of Paradise*, the "voices" direct Jean to "*escape, live, and be silent among the migratory*" and to "*mek dem know we is here*" (Cezair-Thompson 328).

In *Paradise and Plantation*, Ian Strachan asserts that "Jean's inability to consummate her love for her lifelong friend Paul, a son of the soil, and her retreat into the arms of an older Englishman correspond directly with her inability to feel safe and fulfilled in Jamaica and her flight to North America" (266). Central to Jean's decision to leave Jamaica is when she realizes that

Paul would never leave Jamaica; his unwillingness to leave reassures Jean that she is making the right decision. While Clare's sexual maturity marks a greater consciousness, Jean's development offers escape. To explain, it is Jean's new "womanly look" that attracts the attention of Alan, a white, married businessman from New York, and the man she ultimately chooses over Paul, "a true son of the land" (Cezair-Thompson 320). Long-standing familial discord, along with escalating violence on the island, makes "flee[ing] the island for the symbolic North and her white, English lover" an attractive choice (Vásquez 53). In *The True History of Paradise*, Jean's relationship with Alan facilitates her flight from Jamaica. As Rachel Manley argues, Jean's flight "becomes a metaphor for the Caribbean instinct of survival through escape, an instinct that will forever perpetuate the condition of diaspora" (204). Musing on the process of her own migration, Jean relates, "To leave one's country. It is not a complete sentence, a complete anything. Its infinite possibilities leap from loss to promise and back again from promise to loss" (Cezair-Thompson 328). Near the conclusion of the novel, Jean admits that "she knows now why she is taking this journey" (Cezair-Thompson 301). Perhaps this is because "if [refuge] is to be had at all, [it] lies in the destination, not the journey" (Cezair-Thompson 86).

As Cezair-Thompson notes in an interview, "The fact that Jean doesn't speak in her own voice, that she doesn't become a first-person narrator until the very end is very deliberate. She really has to carry and hear all these voices through her first" (Kenan 59). In presenting heartbreak as a form of inheritance, the author ruminates on "the preoccupation with the consequences of exile on the Caribbean voice" (Manley 206). In *The True History of Paradise* and *Abeng*, violence is rendered personal. Through strained relationships, Cliff and Cezair-Thompson detail the flight of protagonists who feel socially exiled, each keenly aware of their own difference; as demonstrated, the protagonists' psychological exile is an essential part of their migratory experience. While Jean "at times felt strangled by the roots on the island," Clare feels the weight of her own suffocation (Cezair-Thompson 277). With *Abeng* and *The True History of Paradise*, Cliff and Cezair-Thompson position historical erasure as a form of systemic violence and center the reclamation of personal and collective histories. Together, the works counteract the vision of paradise as a nexus of tranquility by painting Jamaica as a land that inhabitants are desperate to leave.

CHAPTER THREE

TRAVERSING THE TRIANGULAR ROAD
Retrieving the Past and Reconsidering Cultural Identity in *Praisesong for the Widow* and *Small Island*

> Immigration offers the chance to reinvent one's identity—
> to be reborn, in a sense.
> —SHARRÓN SARTHOU

In Paule Marshall's memoir, *Triangular Road* (2009), the author reflects on her ancestry: "Perhaps living in their birthplace might help me to better understand them" (99). She details that it was travel to Barbados, and later to Africa, that afforded a greater understanding of her parents and her "tripartite self": her Caribbean, African, and American identities. In connecting their parents' birthplace (the West Indies) with a deeper appreciation of personal and cultural heritage, authors Andrea Levy and Paule Marshall suggest that cultural connection is paramount for immigrants and their children. For second-generation immigrants, individuals who can experience the pain of transnationalism[1] through their parents, the homeland is a force and location that looms large yet often remains unknown. As Marshall and Levy's works reveal, the new homeland can occasion a series of negotiations for immigrant families. In Marshall's *Praisesong for the Widow* (1983) and Levy's *Small Island* (2004), the need for cultural connection is met via travel.

As second-generation immigrants born of Caribbean parents, Marshall and Levy explore the relationship between migration and belonging. Through historical fiction, the authors highlight the trauma of the immigrant experience. In their work, transnational narratives and historical fiction meld to position exile as a painful consequence of leaving one's homeland. The protagonists' sense of separation is mirrored by the larger sense of nation-defining that they encounter in new lands. In *Reflections on Exile and Other Essays,* Edward Said finds that "all nationalism in their early stages develop from a condition of estrangement" (176). With *Praisesong for the Widow* and *Small Island,* Marshall and Levy suggest that the condition of estrangement can both propel migration and function as a result of it. This sense of estrangement intensifies feelings of exile for the characters, and their departure from home serves as the genesis for self-recovery. The characters' experiences outside of the United States and Jamaica are expanding for the protagonists. In *Praisesong for the Widow* and *Small Island,* it is only when characters leave home that they are forced to reconsider their personal and cultural identities.

IDENTITY

Praisesong for the Widow and *Small Island* detail the emotional development of characters Avey Johnson and Queenie Bligh. Marshall's work traces Avey's reclamation of cultural identity, and Levy turns to historical fiction to explore the history of West Indians in England. Importantly, the characters are aided along the way. In *Praisesong for the Widow,* Avey is supported by a host of supernatural or mystical forces,[2] most notably her Aunt Cuney and the practice of doubling.[3] Levy's *Small Island* explores how Hortense's landlord, Queenie, assists in her adjustment to life in London. In very different ways, the authors establish the effect that physical location can have on feelings of belonging. Similar to the struggles that Clare Savage in *Abeng* and Jean Landing in *The True History of Paradise* undergo prior to migration, the texts suggest that psychological exile can serve as a precursor to migration. As the novels evince, migration is often a fraught state. The authors, second-generation immigrants born in the United States and England, respectively, detail the hardship of migration via prose. Writing *Praisesong for the Widow* and *Small Island* enabled Marshall and Levy to relive their parents' migratory experience through narrative. While Avey in Marshall's novel gains a transnational perspective by reconnecting with her African roots, Levy's text illustrates the discrimination that colonial subjects faced in England following World War II.

The authors develop characters who defy categorization based on geographic affiliation. The characters in Levy's text migrate to assist the English war effort or to escape dismal economic conditions in the colony. Marshall's novel focuses on how Avey's negotiation of personal and cultural loss comes after a dream calls her to leave her Caribbean cruise in search of cultural reconnection. *Praisesong for the Widow* and *Small Island* meld fiction and personal experience to highlight the destruction that assimilation can cause for immigrants and their children; exclusion sets in on those who do not fit the mold. By detailing the struggles that accompany distance from home, the works support Carole Boyce-Davies's observation that the "construction of home as problematic space calls into question the notion of stable, continuous identities" (65).

Depicting the homeland as a space of disconnection, the novels position home not as a place of comfort but as a force of propulsion that brings the protagonists to a reconsideration of identity. Avey and Hortense are initially painted as symbols of the "displaced . . . tragic representation of the transnational, capitalist, post-modern condition," but their character development illustrates the centrality of flight to the reclamation of heritage and the amendment of historical record (Boyce-Davies 113). Avey and Hortense live in states of limbo for much of the texts. Before they access feelings of belonging, they suffer a period of personal and social disconnection. Loss and reclamation prove central in Marshall's novel. In *Small Island*, Levy centers the difficulties of colony-metropole relations via a focus on racial politics. Through fiction, the authors connect with their cultural heritage and recreate the struggles that their immigrant parents underwent. Collectively, *Praisesong for the Widow* and *Small Island* position cultural connection as an essential component to feelings of belonging for immigrants and their children.

CULTURAL CONNECTION

Praisesong for the Widow centers on how Avey Johnson navigates life as a middle-aged widow. Throughout the course of the text, Avey, an African American woman of Caribbean ancestry living in New York, comes to realize that she has moved away from the deep cultural connection she once had. Marshall deploys the protagonist as a metaphor for the effects of cultural dispossession; Avey grapples with the trauma of geographic and cultural separation and emerges with renewed purpose. Significantly, Abena Busia points out that "in mythic terms, Avey is the traveler who must first find the answers to questions of origin before she can return home" (205). By internalizing the notion of the American Dream and investing in material acquisition, Avey has gained socio-economic mobility at the expense of cultural connection. It is when she takes a Caribbean cruise that she embarks on an odyssey of healing and self-recovery. By employing a "strong, sacrificing, 'no-nonsense' grandmother figure," the author challenges the postmenopausal archetype to highlight the importance of one's roots (Kemp and Liddell 32). Moving away from the trope of the juvenile bildungsroman, Marshall follows a pattern of "departure, initiation, and return" as she fuses Caribbean and African American cultures via the character of Avey Johnson. In presenting a later-in-life journey to reclaim culture, Marshall "demonstrates how we, as readers and writers alike, may locate and reclaim our respective traditions, myths, and rituals to recall that which we have forgotten" (Benjamin 64).

As a child of Barbadian immigrants, Marshall advocates for cultural reconnection. Though the author is American-born, her parents joined the over fifty thousand West Indians who entered the United States by 1980 (Crowder 82). Perhaps inspired by her parents' journeys, the author employs the tale of Avey Johnson to suggest that there is a middle ground between wholesale assimilation and rigid adherence to cultural tradition. Like the protagonist that she constructs, Marshall embraces the fusion of African American and West Indian identities and her writing illustrates an intimacy with both cultures. Much like the author's journey growing up in a Caribbean home in the United States, Avey "comes to understand her own identity through a series of journeys, physical and emotional, literal and symbolic, that help her piece together the elements which contribute to herself as an African American in the late twentieth century" (Rogers 91). Geographic removal is essential to Avey's personal development; her rather comfortable life is challenged once she leaves the mainland. It is the departure from the comfort of home that propels the protagonist's cultural resurrection. In constructing a character who travels away from the planned itinerary of her cruise, the author links emotional hardship and growth. Indirectly, Avey's extension of her travels comes as a result of loss, most notably the death of her husband and her assimilation into white American culture. In staging physical and emotional turmoil as an essential component of the character's cultural reconciliation, Marshall paints cultural reconnection as a process inherently connected with struggle.

As the title of the text implies, the African oral tradition of the praisesong proves central in Avey's transition into widowhood.[4] In revealing the consequences of repressed grief while illustrating the possibility of recovery and rebirth, the novel plays on Sigmund Freud's notion of diasporic melancholia, which Sara Kaplan characterizes as a "failure of mourning that originates in a loss that cannot be fully known or articulated" (513). More than mourning the death of her husband, Avey is called to grieve, and subsequently reclaim, her cultural legacy. In fact, it is the mystical intervention of Avey's aunt, Aunt Cuney, that brings the protagonist to understand her mourning as incomplete. That is, the dream in which Avey sees her Aunt Cuney serves as the precursor to her reconnection with African folklore and ritual. In the pursuit of happiness and wealth, Avey and her husband lost touch with their racial and cultural heritage. As a result, Avey must rediscover "her true name, her true place, obscured for years by her and her husband's pursuit for material security" (Christian 75). In *Praisesong for the Widow*, Avey moves toward a positive double-consciousness, an alteration of African American remembering that focuses on constructing a new identity out of a painful past.

Marshall positions Avey Johnson as transnationally and transculturally dislocated. As suggested, travel propels the emotional crisis that ultimately results in the protagonist's psychological and emotional liberation. While it is Avey's embarkation aboard a Caribbean cruise that affords the possibility for transformation, mysticism, understood throughout as a "belief system based on the assumption of occult forces [such as] mysterious supernatural agencies," proves central to Avey's emergence from emotional and cultural exile (OED). In fact, it is Avey's doubling, or "imagined travel," that affords the emotional healing that allows her to promulgate the complex identity she embraces at the conclusion of the novel. While scholars often discuss Avey's transformation at the conclusion of the novel as being a religious initiation involving purging and cleansing, a connection has yet to be made to the protagonist's use of doubling. The figure of Papa Legba, the loa in Haitian Vodou who stands as the intermediary between the other loa and humanity, serves as Avey's guide, but doubling also plays an essential role in the character's identity development.

DOUBLING

Although travel plays a central role in Marshall's novel, another form of travel, doubling, allows Avey's soul to wander from her body. Early in the text, readers witness Avey figuratively transport when "her mind in a way wasn't even in her body, or for that matter in the room" but was rather "down at the embarkation door near the waterline five decks below" (Marshall 10). This scene complicates Roberta Rubenstein's assertion that it is the dream of Aunt Cuney that provokes Avey to imaginatively visit Tatem, Georgia. The passage illustrates that the act of travel can be read as a parallel force of change. In addition to serving as a way to connect with ancestors, doubling allows Avey to return to moments in the past. Later, the protagonist relives a childhood Easter service. As her mind drifts, she realizes that it was after hearing Patois in Martinique that Aunt Cuney visited her in a dream two days later. It is travel that triggers the opening of "a closed-off corner" of Avey's mind and permits her to unlock repressed memories (Marshall 196). While travel outside the United States primes Avey for this psychological experience, the practice of doubling prepares her for further travel. In this way, an aural memory reignites a cultural one. In *Praisesong for the Widow*, the locations of Grenada and Carriacou and the language of Patois trigger a memory of "the sound of voices in Tatem" (Marshall 196). Dissociation allows Avey to feel as if she is "dwelling in any number of places at once and in a score of different time frames," which suggests a multiplicity that extends beyond temporality (Marshall 232). As Avey travels to Grenada and Carriacou, connecting place and people, she bridges past and present and moves from an individual experience to a collective one.

Avey Johnson can be read as a genealogical double. Avey, whose given name is Avatara, is tasked with carrying on the legacy of her grandmother, also named Avatara. Elizabeth Brown-Guillory's work on emotional fragmentation is especially useful in understanding the importance of Avey's cultural reclamation. In *Middle Passages and the Healing Place of History*, Brown-Guillory notes that "the women are fragmented because of a disconnection to their spiritual source: Africa. They must return to Africa, literally or figuratively, as part of their journey to selfhood" (9). *Praisesong for the Widow* reveals how guides such as Aunt Cuney and Lebert Joseph assist Avey in reclaiming her cultural roots. For instance, Avey joins residents' annual trip from Grenada to Carriacou; during the trip, she symbolically experiences the Middle Passage and in doing so reconnects with a spiritual source. Her newfound sense of estrangement from her culture calls Avey to imaginatively connect with her ancestors via this romanticized return home. As nausea overcomes her, she purges inherited and individual trauma. Avey's brief journey aboard the *Bianca Pride* brings her to a fuller understanding of her identity as an African American woman and a deeper knowledge of her ancestral past.

Avey's personal odyssey begins when she experiences a "mysterious clogged and swollen feeling," a "vaguely bloated" sensation that begins shortly after the start of the cruise (Marshall 52). Throughout the text, Avey begins to reconnect with her body and becomes increasingly aware of the messages she receives. Following the literal and figurative expulsion of cultural detachment when she purges aboard the *Bianca Pride*, she begins to construct an identity that incorporates her cultural heritage. Although overhearing Patois in Martinique and Aunt Cuney's appearance in a dream sets the purgative process in motion, Avey's sickness aboard the *Bianca Pride* recalls the experiences of her ancestors crossing the Middle Passage. By staging Avey's purging aboard the *Bianca Pride*, a ship named to reference "white pride," the author narrates the protagonist's cathartic reliving of her ancestors' suffering.

TRAVEL AND TESTING

In *Praisesong for the Widow*, travel is associated with hardship and growth. Marshall uses Avey's Caribbean cruise to position the protagonist in the liminal space of Carriacou;[5] the medium of travel allows Avey to return to her ancestral land and reconnect with African oral tradition. Aunt Cuney's appearance in Avey's dreams is a force of change that directs her to Carriacou, but her aunt's supernatural appearance takes root in the in-between space of international waters. It is in that protective location that Avey's ancestor enters her consciousness; in this space without cultural signifiers, she is free to explore the impact of her cultural influences. In short, physical removal from the space of Western decadence is an essential component of Avey's cultural reclamation.[6] While travel initially functions as a form of leisure for Avey, the trip occasions physical and emotional discomfort when she becomes ill aboard the cruise ship and a smaller ship, the *Bianca Pride*, that carries her from Grenada to Carriacou (Marshall 52). Avey's time on the island of Carriacou brings her to a place of self-confrontation.

Evidencing the impact of travel on initiating change is a description of Avey "moving like a woman half her age, her shadow on the walls and ceiling hurrying to keep up" (Marshall 10). Interestingly, just the thought of leaving the cruise lightens Avey's burden. Again suggesting a mystical separation of the soul from the body, Marshall specifies that Avey's shadow lags behind her body. Here, her shadow functions as a double of sorts in that it acts independently and struggles to keep up with her newly energized self. It is especially significant that Avey "no longer recogniz[es] herself"; this is the first time in months that she "actually looked at herself" (Marshall 77, 99). Together these statements point to a marked physical and emotional transformation. Whereas Avey once avoided confronting herself in the mirror, now she not only looks at herself but observes vast change, change so drastic that she fails to recognize herself.

George Robertson's understanding of travel as a "quest for the acquisition of knowledge and a desire to return to a utopian space of freedom" allows for a reading of Avey's journey as a complex collusion of transportation and mysticism that results in a more culturally aware protagonist (quoted in Siegel 195). In *Praisesong for the Widow*, Avey is called to join cultures and to incorporate African traditions into her African American identity. As suggested, the practice of doubling proves essential. Somewhat similar to the function of doubling in Danticat's *Breath, Eyes, Memory*, dissociation prepares the protagonist for change. Transportation aboard the cruise ship moves Avey from American to Caribbean culture, but people are essential to her emotional transformation. In addition to the undeniable influence that Aunt Cuney's supernatural appearance has on Avey's decision to disembark the cruise and follow her instincts, the people of Carriacou, who have preserved African oral traditions, assist Avey in reconnecting with her culture.

Avey's travels begin when she embarks on a Caribbean cruise with a group of friends. However, it is after her decision to abandon the cruise and extend her travels in the region that the protagonist's homecoming begins. Avey explicitly addresses the role of transportation on her own evolution when she wonders if the location makes her speak so freely. She notes, "It was the place: the special light that filled it and the silence, as well as the bowed figure across the table who didn't appear to be listening. They were drawing the words from her, forcing them out one by one" (Marshall 170). Here, the mystical effect of the islands, and more particularly the insular space of Carriacou, imparts change. Later, the figure of Lebert Joseph, a guide-like figure similar to Aunt Cuney and a double for the Vodou figure Papa Legba, "saw how far she had come since leaving the ship and the distance she had yet to go" (Marshall 172). When Lebert Joseph enters the text, he replaces Aunt Cuney as Avey's guide. Through this pair of guide figures, Marshall suggests that change is not so much about a particular place or a particular person as it is a process of awakening and rebirth initiated by the intersection of an unfamiliar place and familiar ancestral figures.

Before Avey can find cultural reconnection and a more unified identity, she must undergo a process of testing or challenging. As she begins to experience emotional dissonance aboard the *Bianca Pride*, she feels that "something in her suddenly felt . . . exposed and vulnerable" (Marshall 56). Emotions are turned upside down and her eyes begin playing "frightening tricks" on her, which stresses the fallibility of sight (Marshall 171). While sight is often associated with "knowing," especially through the figure of Lebert Joseph, the man who "had known all her objections before they were even born in her thoughts," Marshall focuses on her character's intuition (Marshall 184). Avey remains in a state of hazy vision until the conclusion of the novel; this state is directly attributable to her cultural disconnection. At the beginning of the text Avey's sight is fallible, but after disembarking the cruise ship, "a change came over her" on a Grenada beach when "she felt the caul over her mind lifting and she began looking around her" (Marshall 154). In this line, the reference to a caul suggests "a person born with a veil of inner fetal membrane, or 'caul,' over his/her face, [who is] gifted with the power of second sight; such a person can see *duppies* (ghosts) and is insightful spiritually in other ways" (McNeil 191). Cauls, in Caribbean literature, are typically associated with sight into the spirit world. The reference to a caul in this line points to an underlying perception that has yet to surface. After the caul is lifted, not unlike W.E.B. Du Bois's concept of the veil, Avey begins looking around her with a "child's curiosity."[7] While previously Avey's eyes deceived her, she looks about her surroundings with a new vision. She begins to see through her own eyes rather than seeing herself through the eyes of others; this change in behavior reflects Du Bois's understanding of double consciousness and marks the start of Avey's metamorphosis.

In addition to Avey's change in vision reflecting a figurative transformation, she notes that everything around her appeared "fleeting and ephemeral. The island more a mirage rather than an actual place. Something conjured up perhaps to satisfy a longing and need" (Marshall 254). It is place (real or imagined) that works alongside Avey's spiritual guides, Aunt Cuney and Lebert Joseph, to lead Avey to a space of cultural reconnection. While the island of Carriacou and its people are largely static instruments that facilitate Avey's awakening, Lebert Joseph and Aunt Cuney act as more dynamic forces. Avey's presence in Grenada, and later in Carriacou, allows her to connect with these instruments of change. The role of socioeconomic status, though, is key. As a result of her wealth, Avey can participate in the kind of heritage tourism that offers up the island of Carriacou as a romanticized image she can locate herself in. It goes without saying that this kind of flight is not available to all. It is only as a result of her wealth that the protagonist is able to access this space of change.

AVEY'S ODYSSEY

In bringing Avey to reconnect with her cultural heritage, Marshall favors a Pan-Caribbean association that stresses the celebration of commonalities. Although Avey was born in the United States, it is her African ancestry that connects her with the residents of Carriacou. Locals accept Avey on the basis of shared connection; this acceptance allows her to experience a sense of belonging that has been absent in her life. In *Praisesong for the Widow*, the author presents one woman's fusion of cultural ties. In moving Avey outside her literal and figurative comfort zones, Marshall highlights travel's role in the protagonist's negotiation of cultural estrangement. Throughout the text, it is insinuated that Aunt Cuney is pursuing Avey, calling her to reconnect with her cultural heritage and come to a greater awakening. Significantly, the woman born with a caul is being "called" and Avey suspects that it is Aunt Cuney "who put her up to abandoning the cruise" (Marshall 83).

Language plays a central role in Avey's journey to Carriacou. She notes that "the vaguely familiar sound of the Patois might have resurrected Tatem and the old woman [Aunt Cuney]" (Marshall 67). This line emphasizes the power of language in that the term "resurrected" suggests an otherworldly connection reflected in the Kongo Cosmogram,[8] a "cross with one line representing the boundary between the living world and that of the dead, and the other representing the path of power from below to above" ("Magic Bowls"). Throughout the narrative, Avey moves from a place of doubting to accepting and even championing mystical connections. After the Big Drum festival,[9] Avey comments that "for the first time since she was a girl, she felt the threads . . . streaming out from the old people around her in Lebert Joseph's yard. From their seared eyes. From their navels and their cast-iron hearts. And their brightness as they entered her spoke of possibilities and becoming" (Marshall 249). In referencing these "threads," Avey speaks to the intrinsic connection that she shares with residents of Carriacou. The passage foregrounds a transmission that goes beyond the physical, and that, interestingly, is reflected in the eyes. For instance, the reference to "seared" eyes suggests that the people of Carriacou have seen too much because they have been able to lift the veil from their eyes. Nevertheless, the connection that Avey feels with the people in Carriacou, rooted in their navels, is the most primal of linkages. In Marshall's novel, the strangers in Carriacou "become one and the same with people in Tatem" and bring Avey to an awakening and evolution (250).

In *Praisesong for the Widow*, Avey's transportation to Grenada and Carriacou paves the way for a reconnection with her cultural heritage. Simone Alexander finds that "this claiming, epitomized in Avatara Johnson ... is symptomatic of an unwavering acceptance and celebration of the spiritual mothers and the homeland, a celebration of cultural unity within the diaspora[10] among diasporic peoples" (27). Indeed, this inheritance comes by way of Aunt Cuney, a woman who "always usta say might be in Tatem but her mind, her mind was long gone with the Ibos"[11] (Marshall 39). Through the characters of Aunt Cuney and Lebert Joseph, Marshall connects ancestral heritage and folklore with a legacy of doubling. Aunt Cuney's dissociation, termed "long gone," speaks to a deeply internalized identification with her African heritage and the link between oral tradition and Afro-Caribbean ancestry. While at the beginning of the text Avey is driven by materialism, by the end of the novel she has "slipped without being conscious of it into a step that was something more than just walking" (Marshall 248). Avey comes to terms with repressed grief and emerges "centered and sustained ... restored to her proper axis," able and willing to "speak of the excursion to others elsewhere" (Marshall 254–55).

Before Avey can reclaim her Caribbean heritage, she must shed her attachment to materialism. While Avey's process toward transformation is guided by Aunt Cuney, and, later, Lebert Joseph, she reaches autonomous subjectivity at the conclusion of the text. With the help of her guides, Avey moves from materialistic individualism to inclusion in a community. The protagonist's transformation is perhaps best illustrated by the fact that she is excited to share her experiences with her grandchildren. The luxury of travel fuels the realization of Avey's latent self; with the character of Avey Johnson, Marshall furthers knowledge of Caribbean culture vis-à-vis the materialist individual turned ambassador. That is, the protagonist reconnects with her past and propagates the legacy handed down to her. Via travel, she moves from a place of cultural disconnection to one of incorporation and acceptance. By uniting mysticism with transportation and transformation, the work positions Avey as an inheritor of the legacy of doubling; the process allows her to transport herself emotionally and cope with the loss her husband, her culture, and her self.

In Marshall's novel, transportation works alongside people and mysticism to engender a space of "something new." This fusion parallels the integration of African, African American, and Caribbean influences in the text. Avey's personal odyssey "culminates not only in her own psychic return to Africa, but in the symbolic return home of all African Americans" (Kemp and

Liddell 37). While place figures prominently, the people who surround Avey are equally important to her efforts to recover her identity and "achieve closure as she learns to acknowledge and come to terms with the contradictions of her cultural heritage" (Mardorossian 135). Although the novel is certainly a tale of connection, "It is even more a conscious and womanist examination of the liberation process" (Kemp and Liddell 38). Marshall's work calls readers to heed the warning and become cognizant of the ways we are all disconnected.

In moving Avey to a space of psychic liberation, the text participates in the literary construction of home. If migration spurs the desire for home, which Boyce-Davies argues, then the importance of travel becomes compounded when Aunt Cuney "evokes a very specific identification and redefinition of the meaning of home" (94). Avey returns to New York at the conclusion of the novel and the text celebrates her new understanding of home. Avey Johnson's journey demonstrates "how we, as readers and writers alike, may locate and reclaim our respective traditions, myths, and rituals to recall that which we have forgotten" (Benjamin 64). Reflecting on her journey to rediscover her "tripartite self," Marshall reminds readers that the "Middle Passage, buried and pathless it may seem in the Atlantic, can never be forgotten, indeed must be remembered by all who are its 'heirs and descendants,' and perhaps in that retelling its pain may be brought to the surface and the nine million recognized" (Diedrich 267). Ultimately, *Praisesong for the Widow* reinscribes the protagonist's return as essential to remembering and rewriting history.

MAKING HOME "SOMEWHERE ELSE"

Whereas Marshall positions the "mother('s)land, the Caribbean . . . as an extension of the Motherland, Africa," Levy decries the ill-treatment of Jamaican citizens in an "other-land," or a "site where each character experiences alienation and Othering" (Alexander 4, Barnwell 451). In *Small Island*, Levy queries the relationship between colonial subjects and the motherland; in the novel, she recreates, on an individual level, the ostracism that West Indians faced in England in the late 1940s.[12] To explain, following World War II, the West Indies was "somewhere else": not Europe, not Africa, not India. In *Making Men*, Belinda Edmondson argues that this "somewhere elseness" has become a central trope of West Indian discourse, with its attendant notion that "the *space* of the West Indies is more metaphorical than it is material"

(20). This is reflected in the title of the text; in *Small Island*, the West Indies function as a metaphorical space for English citizens who express grave misconceptions of Jamaica. Conversely, it is in England, itself located on a "small island," that the limits of transnationalism are stretched. Londoners' lack of understanding of the Caribbean region leaves two West Indian characters feeling unwelcome in their new homeland; as the work reveals, the West Indies are understood as wholly foreign, a place "somewhere else," and therefore largely unknowable. Hortense and Gilbert, as cultural ambassadors of sorts, make the space of "somewhere else" more concrete for the English citizens they interact with. In disabusing misconceptions about the West Indies, the immigrants render the "small island" of Jamaica more material.

As the daughter of Jamaican parents who immigrated following World War II, Levy explores somewhat hazy definitions of the West Indies. Throughout *Small Island*, she examines the sense of exile that alienated West Indian subjects experience in the British metropole. As a prominent black British author, Levy "openly acknowledges the fact that she writes about the experiences of part of the British population that has been silenced" (Fernandez 146). By tracing the journey of Gilbert Joseph on the *MV Empire Windrush*,[13] the vessel that carried the first large group of West Indian immigrants to Britain following World War II, and the same vessel that her father took, Levy presents a contradictory view of the metropole. As the child of West Indian immigrants, she is positioned to address the collective "cold shoulder" that well-intentioned Caribbean subjects receive in England. With *Small Island*, the author "focuses on the consequences of the Empire [and] reiterates the fact that all members of British society are forced to make adjustments and redefine their sense of belonging" following the war (Fernandez 150). In examining how Hortense and Gilbert locate home in Britain, Levy punctuates the exilic experience.

Levy's novel "serves as a necessary reminder that before Caribbean workers came to rebuild the UK in the late 1940s, they had participated in the war effort" (Munoz-Valdivieso 159). In the fourth novel by this self-defined English author, she "explore[s] issues of identity and belonging for contemporary characters who participate in a complex double heritage" (Munoz-Valdivieso 162). With the work, Levy critiques the racist and exclusionary treatment of West Indian subjects. Early on, she explores how the term "immigrant" operates as a racially coded term for non-white individuals. Illustrating this is repartee between two young girls in Jamaica, Hortense Roberts and Celia Langley. Celia proclaims, "When I am older, Hortense, I will be leaving Jamaica and I will be going to live in England"

(Levy 11). Here, Levy sets the tone for the work's focus on migration. As the text suggests, misinformation and ill-treatment often accompany the migratory condition. Seldom do migrants find their new homelands welcoming; seldom do migrants meet the ideal image of citizens in their new nations. The protagonist, Hortense, soon learns that conditions are not always what they seem. To leave Jamaica, Hortense agrees to marry a man she does not love. The wedding takes place within weeks of Hortense and Gilbert's meeting. After a six-month separation, with Gilbert departing for England shortly after the wedding, the young bride is met with disappointment. Instead of a beaming husband greeting her upon arrival, Hortense finds a "shabby" house and a room that is "just this" (Levy 12, 21).

Small Island details life for two Jamaican immigrants in England after World War II. In contrast to Avey's life of excess, Hortense and Gilbert's bare-bones apartment attests to the economic and material conditions in England following the war. Gilbert relates, "Everyone lives like this. There has been a war. Houses bombed. I know plenty people live worse than this" (Levy 21). Through the genre of the historical novel, Levy connects two couples, Hortense and Gilbert and Queenie and Bernard, in the aftermath of war. The novel depicts the relationship between a West Indian couple and their white, English landlords, to explore post-WWII racial politics. The couple's relationship, undoubtedly shaped by economics, is complicated by the fact that Queenie's actions are synonymous with a nation state that exploits the usefulness of Caribbean migrants. Hortense and Gilbert prove economically and personally useful to Queenie throughout the course of the text. By revealing what life was like for immigrants such as her parents, the author portrays a less appealing, less enlightened England. In the process, she presents a more complete picture of the "mother country" and the difficulties of migration.

The text's focus on migration begins when Hortense arrives on the dock. Hortense is mistaken for a woman named Sugar immediately after disembarking from her long journey. An unnamed Englishwoman asks, "Are you Sugar?" to which she replies, "No, I am Hortense." The woman promptly responds, "She's one of you. She's coming to be my nanny and I am a little later than I thought. You must know her" (Levy 15). With this exchange, Levy establishes a sense of alienation through the use of stereotypes. By using reductive phrases such as "one of you" and placing Sugar in a position of service, the author renders feelings of Western superiority intensely personal. Hortense may be "fresh off the boat," but she smiles in the face of such treatment (Levy 31). Closely related to Hortense's difficulty with adjusting to life in London is her self-consciousness regarding her accent. Though her "accent had taken [her] to the top of the class in Miss Stuart's pronunciation competition," she is frequently misunderstood and told to "speak English" (Levy 16). As the text continues, it is mentioned that "they [the West Indians] speak it just like us, only funnier" (Levy 138). In the attempt to ameliorate her own discomfort, and to escape such mockery at her "funny" accent, Hortense is "determined to speak in an English manner" (Levy 449). She resolves to alter her speech by listening to BBC radio programs (Levy 449). Whether pushing herself to change the way she speaks or how she dresses, Hortense feels pressure to present herself much differently. For the protagonist, England is a "very cold country" (Levy 466). Her migration, no doubt influenced by long-standing attitudes of English superiority and the accompanying sense of colonial inferiority, "engenders ambivalence and fuels feelings of alienation, loss, and separation" (Brown-Guillory 3).

Small Island presents marriage as a means of escape and socioeconomic elevation. Women such as Queenie, Hortense's white English landlord, are forced, or rather "elect" to marry men to escape less desirable circumstances. Through these arrangements, Levy comments on the options available to women at the time. For instance, Hortense "steals" Gilbert from her friend Celia and proceeds to wed him "three weeks and five days" from their first meeting (Levy 98). To be clear, Hortense sees Gilbert as her ticket out of Jamaica; she recognizes his ambition to return to England and the significance that he attaches to that return. She then capitalizes on his ambition to secure her escape from Jamaica. The return, for Gilbert, "was a mission, a calling, even a duty" that Hortense elects to join (Levy 98). Although Hortense can be read as a woman with few options, the fact that she uses Gilbert to migrate is significant in that is reflects agency. Hortense and Gilbert's union is a transaction, an agreement that Hortense initiates. Setting the terms, she offers, "I will lend you the money [to travel to London], we will be married and you can send for me to come to England when you have a place for me to live" (Levy 100). Because Hortense is aware that social convention dictates that "a single woman cannot travel on her own . . . but a married woman might go anywhere she pleased," she views this transaction as a means of securing mobility (Levy 100). While on the one hand Hortense inverts power dynamics by lending Gilbert money, her mobility is contingent on their marriage. The couple is not in love but instead is bound by a shared interest in survival amid trying conditions. Far from home, West Indians Hortense and Gilbert serve as a support system for each other; over a period of time, this reliance brings a closeness that neither anticipated.

Like Hortense, Queenie dreams of something more than her present circumstances; coincidentally, Queenie also leaves home. Much like the function of Aunt Cuney in *Praisesong for the Widow*, it is only after Queenie's Aunt Dorothy takes her in that she escapes from rural farm life. The protagonists' aunts effect change. In ways that the mothers cannot, Aunt Cuney and Aunt Dorothy sweep in as surrogate mother figures who, perhaps because of their removed perspective, are better positioned to assess what their nieces need. Like the mystical figure of Aunt Cuney in Marshall's work, Aunt Dorothy utilizes her relative privilege to change Queenie's life. With this physical remove comes a change in name (from Queenie to Victoria) as well as lessons concerning proper speech and gait. Though Queenie attempts to break off her courtship with Bernard, the man she later weds, her aunt's death solidifies their relationship. Interestingly, this is all done without input from Bernard. To explain, Aunt Dorothy's decease places Queenie in a precarious position. When Queenie's mother informs her that she "can come back home now. There's plenty for you to do around the farm," Queenie replies, "I've some good news for you. I'm getting married, Mother, to Bernard Bligh" (Levy 258). In *Praisesong for the Widow* and *Small Island*, therefore, death offers the chance for escape; although Avey's status as a widow frees her, Queenie's impending marriage to Bernard allows her to remain in London, far from life on the farm. Queenie seizes the opportunity to alter her course in life. In this novel, Levy illustrates the sacrifices that women were forced to make.

FACING ILL-TREATMENT

Much like Hortense, Gilbert experiences prejudice upon arriving in England. Levy describes the sentiment among colonial subjects during the early years of World War II and illustrates the strong sense of nationalism that is inculcated in the British colonies. She writes, "There is a war over there. The Mother Country is calling men like my son to be heroes whose families will be proud of them" (Levy 59). Though Gilbert is told by recruiters that he "will mix with white service personnel," he faces rampant discrimination and estrangement from fellow servicemen (Levy 129). Through Gilbert's experiences, the author sheds light on the racial politics at the time. Gilbert relates, "We were allowed to live with white soldiers, while the inferior American negro was not"; with this line, Levy details a socially reinforced hierarchy that is closely associated with nationalist rhetoric (131). The exchanges between

British and American soldiers illustrate how different forms of racism came into contact in England. In brief, Gilbert, a "guest" in an American camp in England, is regarded as a more acceptable other, one who is "lucky... not to be treated [as a] negro" (Levy 129).

The use of the term "allowed" in the above passage connotes a begrudging acceptance; Gilbert's living arrangement only serves to shift prejudice onto the African American servicemen. In Levy's novel, American servicemen stationed in England are deeply prejudiced. While in England at a training camp, the question is asked, "How coloured is he?" and the response is "enough sir"; enough to make him "offensive" to American soldiers and therefore unacceptable company (Levy 150). In a well-stated rebuttal, Gilbert exclaims, "You know what your trouble is, man? Your white skin. You think it makes you better than me. You think it give you the right to lord it over a black man.... You wan' know what your white skin make you, man? It make you white. That is all, man. White. No better, no worse than me—just white" (Levy 525). Levy uses the character of Gilbert to call prejudice into question and highlight the ill-treatment of "foreign" servicemen who assist their "mother country." The author calls attention to how immigrants faced prejudice and exile upon their arrival in England. In detailing the hardship of migration through her characters, the author reifies the struggles of transnational citizenship.

After a short time in England, Gilbert comes to realize the ill-treatment that West Indians face in England. In particular, he notices how his fellow countrymen regard those who have dutifully served their country. After he is asked, "Why would you leave a nice sunny place to come here if you didn't have to?" he launches into a diatribe (Levy 138). Gilbert proclaims, "Let me ask you to imagine this. Living far from you is a beloved relation whom you have never met.... Then on one day you hear Mother calling—she is troubled, she need your help" (Levy 139). Continuing this metaphor, Gilbert relates, "The filthy tramp that eventually greets you is she. Ragged, old and dusty as the long dead. Mother has a blackened eye, bad breath and one lone tooth that waves in her head when she speaks. Can this be the troubled relation you heard so much of?" (Levy 139). For Hortense and Gilbert, the motherland "offers you no comfort after your journey. No smile. No welcome. Yet she looks down at you through lordly eyes and says, 'Who the bloody hell are you?'" (Levy 139). Through extended metaphor, Levy complicates the term "mother country" and brings racial discrimination against Commonwealth citizens to light. As in *Praisesong for the Widow*, migration comes as a result of indirect hardship; to stress, Gilbert travels to England to serve in the war and decides to return to the nation where he served. It is, therefore, the larger sense of strife that brings Gilbert, and later Hortense, to the "mother country."

In evoking the mother figure, Gilbert employs description to paint England as a Mother, but also as a tramp. He uses imperialist discourse to critique how the mother country fails to fulfill its duty to protect colonial citizens. By terming England a "filthy tramp," Gilbert inverts the maternal-paternal power structure to satirize colonial relations. In adopting a chastising tone, he rejects the idealized image of the mother country. In particular, his description details his treatment as a West Indian in England. He subtly makes the case for a consideration of West Indian nationals as "relatives" rather than those to be disparaged; importantly, it is England that is in need in this situation. Through Gilbert, Levy evidences enduring colonial ties and the ironic turn of events that results in citizens from the colony offering aid. Viewing these passages side by side affords a view of the cognitive shift that Gilbert and his fellow servicemen undergo. Although Gilbert initially answered the call for help with the hopes that his contributions would be appreciated, he is soon disappointed. He comes to realize that England falls far short of his expectations just as much as he falls short of theirs.

In addition to exposing the ill-treatment of "outsiders," the novel evidences white Britons' lack of cultural awareness. For instance, Englishmen often assume that Jamaica is located in Africa. In true sardonic fashion, Gilbert's response is, "Give me a map, let me see if Tommy Atkins or Lady Havealot can point to Jamaica.... But give me that map, blindfold me, spin me round three times and I, dizzy and dazed, would still place my finger squarely on the Mother Country" (Levy 142). Here, Levy makes the point that knowledge is not related to socioeconomic status; somewhat humorously, the "superior" Englishmen, represented by the surname "Havealot," are found wanting. Despite obvious economic advantage, the English have difficulty locating the colony, which, importantly, is a supplier of servicemen who aid the "mother country." In this passage and throughout, Levy highlights the lack of dialogue between the two locales; while Jamaicans can clearly pinpoint England on a map, the reverse does not hold true. By titling her novel *Small Island*, the author subtly critiques colonial relations and paints the colony as rather insignificant and unidentifiable to the English. The two English citizens fall prey to racial generalization when they mistakenly associate Jamaica with Africa. While certainly significant on an individual level, on a larger scale this speaks to a cultural blindness and ignorance on the part of those with privilege and power. As a result of migration, Gilbert is able to see England more objectively, and his critique of the mother country supplements Hortense's story. Levy summarizes relations between Jamaica and England with the following line: "Jamaica is a colony. Britain is our Mother Country. We are British but we live in Jamaica" (157).

THE IMPACT OF RACISM

Levy's work calls attention to the prevalence of racist ideology in post-WWII London. For instance, questions such as "how can you think of being a woman alone in a house with coloreds" abound (Levy 116). Though "those people" are fine elsewhere, Queenie is often told that "these darkies bring down a neighborhood" (Levy 117). In *Small Island*, prejudice enters England as a result of war and the racial intermixing that accompanies the influx of servicemen of color. Comments by servicemen, in particular, inform conceptions of migrants from the colonies and illustrate how "white fear and guilt are projected onto black people" (White 181). Given that "until the mid-twentieth century, the black presence in Britain remained well below 20,000 [people]," Levy's novel suggests that English servicemen were influenced by their American comrades' prejudice, which then trickled down into the community (Haynes 140).[14] Despite the passing of the Nationality Act in 1948, which "extended British citizenship to all subjects in the empire," migrants such as Gilbert and Hortense face ill-treatment and suspicion in London (Haynes 141).

Queenie is met with resistance when she offers her home to boarders and works with a community project to resettle migrants. Although Bernard, her husband, was away for years, trolling around Europe following the end of the war, he has no qualms expressing disgust at her acceptance of Gilbert and Hortense as tenants. Exemplifying this is an exchange between Bernard and Queenie. When Queenie asserts that the immigrants do not have anywhere to go, Bernard's response is "they're not our sort.... There are places that will take care of them" (Levy 277). Though Bernard is complicit in the effects of war, he takes no pity on those who are affected. Instead, he regards them as pests to be dealt with by others. Interestingly, Bernard shares this opinion shortly after returning home; this sentiment echoes his neighbors' fear of colonial subjects arriving en masse. Instead of viewing West Indians as capable, independent individuals, Bernard's remarks further an understanding of colonial subjects as always in need, always beholden to the "mother country." On the whole, the West Indian migrants in the novel are seen as "population, not people" (Levy 278). One example of this is when Queenie tells Hortense that she doesn't "mind being seen in the street with you. You'll find I'm not like most. It doesn't worry me to be seen out with darkies" (Levy 231). While on the one hand this statement illustrates Queenie's willingness to flaunt social convention and the white gaze, it also reads as condescending and overtly racist. The inclusion of the word "darkie," in particular, aligns Queenie with the exclusionist rhetoric that her neighbors espouse and challenges her purported liberalism.

Queenie's sexual relationship with a serviceman named Michael illustrates how racial and sexual discourses align. In the first physical description of Michael, Queenie notes that he is "the colour of a conker—not ruddy and new from the shell but after it had dulled in your pocket for a bit" (Levy 297). Overall, Queenie views Michael as an object of curiosity, wondering what the texture of his hair feels like and whether he looks like "tanned leather" all over. She relates that when she is with Michael, "It wasn't me. Mrs. Queenie Bligh, she wasn't even there. This woman was a beauty—he couldn't get enough of her.... This woman was as sexy as any starlet on a silver screen" (Levy 301). Here, Queenie isn't dissociating, as seen in Danticat's *Breath, Eyes, Memory*, but is becoming more comfortable with her sexuality and seeks validation through sexual relations with Michael. To stress, Queenie's sexual relationship with Michael facilitates her transformation into a "starlet"; her access to his black body is consumptive and is reductive in its centering of her experience. As such, Michael runs the risk of being read as the "magical black man" who prompts a white woman's sexual awakening. George Yancy's work on the objectification of black bodies sheds light on this dynamic. Yancy finds that "from the perspective of whiteness, the Black body *is* criminality itself. It *is* the monstrous; it is that which is to be feared and yet desired, sought out in forbidden white sexual adventures and fantasies" (xvi). Queenie's relationship with Michael, then, serves as commentary on the deep-rooted anxieties held by London's racist white patriarchal society that position black bodies as "ugly, dirty, uncivilized" in contrast to the norm of white purity (Yancy 183). For the Londoners in Levy's novel, people such as Michael should be segregated from spaces that afford white comfort. Queenie's fascination with the "strange other," here represented by Michael, evokes England's treatment of colonial servicemen. The empire, like Queenie, seemingly welcomed people of color and subsequently rejected them. Queenie's officious neighbors in particular reflect the tendency to marginalize and erase the black presence in post-WWII London.

Despite the brevity of their relationship, Queenie's association with Michael offers rejuvenation and rebirth (including an actual birth). As the text comes to a close, Levy details the birth of Michael, the mixed-race child of a white English woman and a West Indian serviceman on leave. The newborn, termed an "ample secret," emerges as a "lovely, perfect boy" (Levy 477, 481). Hortense marvels at the emergence of life, but it is also "the ugliest sight [she] had ever beheld" (Levy 479). While Queenie's neighbors may be offended by the birth of a "half-caste" child, Hortense relates that "every tissue in [her] body was tingling with repulsion," not at what the presence of the child implies, but at the act of birth (Levy 480). For Queenie, the child offers a connection to a man she briefly loved. Hortense observes how Queenie's eyes "alighted on this grumpy-faced child and saw it as someone she could love" (Levy 481). Following the birth, Hortense reminds Queenie that she has "a coloured child" and describes the mother as "serene as a Madonna on the messy bed" (Levy 483).

Perhaps problematically, it is Queenie's time with Michael that initiates her sexual awakening. Levy writes, "We kept inside, living like mice. . . . We's eat it [bread and jam] like newly-weds. Feeding it to each other, before licking the sticky cones from each other's mouth and wriggling about to get rid of the crumbs" (495). The long weekend results in a lovechild who is proof of their sexual relationship. When Queenie's pregnancy starts to show, she wraps her midsection "tight as a mummy, round and round," not because she was ashamed, but because she "didn't want prying eyes making it sordid" (Levy 496). With this statement, Levy points to the rather officious nature of English society; because her community is well aware of Arthur's absence, Queenie's burgeoning belly would likely occasion neighborhood gossip. To avoid this, Queenie takes measures to keep her pregnancy a secret; she is a married woman who is expected to remain chaste until her husband returns. The fear of social estrangement prompts Queenie to shield her body from scrutiny. By wrapping her stomach and withdrawing from society, Queenie temporarily enters a state of exile brought on by the growing child within her womb. Queenie's desire to hide her pregnancy from view of those who would comment on her position speaks to the impact of propriety. The culturally ingrained pressure to adhere to the social norms that preclude interracial relations inspires Queenie to deny her more conservative neighbors the knowledge of her impending motherhood.

Levy swiftly moves from a glimpse of Queenie's pregnancy to the narration of her son's birth. In doing so, the author symbolically recreates the way in which the serviceman came into and quickly changed Queenie's life. Their sexual union results in a son who "looked so like Queenie. Her son, no doubt—despite his skin" (Levy 510). With this line, the author calls the logic of prejudice and racism into question. The relation between Queenie and her son is undeniable, and that resemblance trumps racist ideology that would try to deny the affiliation. During a time in which prejudice against blacks in Britain runs high, Queenie's resemblance to her son challenges the link between race and nationalism. Narrating the birth itself, Levy writes, "All at once, Mrs. Bligh's private parts let forth a burp then spat out on to the lap of my best white wedding dress a bloody-soaked lump of her insides" (482). Through vivid detail, the author comments on the aftereffects of birth. Much like the loss of life that the war has occasioned, the afterbirth marks Hortense. This staining of her wedding dress invites a deeper reading of the scene and is suggestive of the expelled colony in relation to the mother country; the afterbirth is not unlike the discarded colony of Jamaica. Much like the West Indians who arrive on English soil, the afterbirth brashly announces its presence.

FEELING "OTHERED"

As Kattian Barnwell finds in "Motherlands and Other Lands," the motherland may be "variously defined as place of birth, land or home of the mother, the site, of the self. . . . Conversely, the other-land refers to the site where each character experiences alienation and Othering, the place of exile" (451). In *Small Island*, Levy employs Queenie's pregnancy to comment on the nature of isolation and challenge inflexible boundaries. Queenie expresses, "We live on an island, for God's sake, everywhere is blinking overseas" (Levy 288). Through historical fiction, the author takes Hortense and Gilbert from the moment they are told, "We don't want you. There's no job for you here," to the day that a white woman (Queenie) begs for the couple to take her baby (Levy 313). While for Hortense and Gilbert the motherland initially proved to be a site of alienation and ill-treatment, as evidenced by Gilbert's ironic portrait of the motherland as a "filthy tramp," it is, interestingly, a citizen of the "motherland" who turns the couple into parents. Although the pair was initially excluded on the basis of their race, their race is what prompts their adoption of Queenie's mixed-race child.

In this post-war society in which "Britain required a new backbone," Hortense and Gilbert gain a sense of inclusion through their adoption of Queenie's child (Levy 365). By having Queenie and Bernard experience their own forms of dissonance, Levy makes the case for a leveling of sorts following the war. For instance, Bernard expresses that "England had shrunk. It was smaller than the place I'd left. . . . I had to stare out at the sea just to catch a breath. And behind every face I saw were trapped the rememberings of war" (Levy 424). Though the war succeeded in making "death a reasonable thing" for Bernard, by the end of the text we see him advocating for Queenie to keep Michael (Levy 429). Alternately terming the infant Michael "an imposter child" and a "dear little thing," Bernard conveys the contradictory feelings that come with the situation that he returns to—his wife pregnant with a black soldier's child (Levy 508–09). Bernard proclaims that "the war was fought so people might live amongst their own"; perhaps ironically, the work concludes with Hortense and Gilbert's adoption of Michael so that he can do just that (Levy 469).

As the text concludes, Queenie asks Hortense to "take [Michael] and bring him up as if he was your son. Would you, would you, please?" (Levy 519). Most pressing for Queenie is the fact that she does not "know how to comb his hair" (Levy 520). This comment speaks to significant cultural differences and her reluctance to adapt; it is simply more convenient for Queenie to arrange her son's adoption. The fact that she is placing a burden on Hortense and Gilbert never crosses her mind; her racial and socioeconomic privilege blinds her from the economic and emotional realities of her request. Although Bernard proposes keeping Michael and telling him that he was adopted, Queenie refuses to budge, asking, "And what will we tell him when he asks? That we left him too long in the sun one day and he went black?" (Levy 520). Queenie fears that "one day he'll do something naughty and you'll look at him and think, the little black bastard, because you'll be angry. And he'll see it in your eyes" (Levy 521). In these lines, the author points to prejudicial sentiment that shirks acknowledgment of interracial relations. Undercutting Bernard's suggestion to raise Michael is his wish to tell him that he was adopted. Similarly, Queenie's attempt at humor fails and instead presents a reductive understanding of race.

Queenie decides that it is best for Michael to be "with people who'll understand. . . . His own kind" (Levy 522). Ironically, the woman who treated Hortense with suspicion ends up begging, "That's what I'm on my knees for—my darling little baby's life" (Levy 522). Hortense reflects, "I never dreamed England would be like this. Come, in what crazed reverie would a white Englishwoman be kneeling before me yearning for me to take her black child?" (Levy 523). In becoming an instant family, the West Indian couple offers the cultural homeland to Michael that Queenie is unable to. Though at first they are told to "go back to the jungle," Hortense and Gilbert make a home for themselves in England (Levy 317). Ultimately, the couple's adoption of Michael at the conclusion of the text highlights the prevailing attitudes toward race at the time. Queenie is wholly unprepared to raise her child. Her desire to have a black couple raise her child suggests an internalized understanding of race that determines that a West Indian couple is better prepared to raise a mixed-race child. In bringing characters together in interesting and unexpected ways, Levy makes "the history of Caribbean people [in England] more visible and show[s] that their story is an important part of British history" (Munoz-Valdivieso 163).

Through the vehicle of fiction, Marshall and Levy counter the dominant historical narrative. Together, the authors show that migration is closely associated with trauma and propose that historical trauma cannot and should not be forgotten and "indeed must be remembered by all of us who are its 'heirs and descendants'" (Diedrich 267). Ian Strachan observes in *Paradise and Plantation* that "Caribbeans must wrest control of their lives from the hands of neocolonial forces and reenter time. By doing so they will reenter history" (236). While increasing attention has been paid to Caribbean literature, and Caribbean culture more broadly, little attention has been paid to the treatment of immigrants and those who have left the Caribbean region. In turning to the genre of historical fiction, a form that has traditionally been coopted to promote nationalistic identity, the authors trace the development of characters who thrive after they leave home.

As their works reveal, "Home cannot be defined simply in opposition to a place or land of exile. Home is experienced by the post-colonial individual as both Motherland and Other-land" (Barnwell 451–52). In fictionalizing the struggles associated with life away from home, the authors explore how migrant characters find belonging in new places. As children of immigrants, the authors present works that cross geographic boundaries and center transnational exchange. They call for a more fluid understanding of kinship and cultural belonging. Though Avey and Hortense are humbled in the course of the narratives, the texts attest to the connection between ancestry and the individual journey. Collectively, Marshall and Levy's works highlight the sense of reconciliation that can accompany flight; while hardship initially propels the migratory experience, the characters' lives are transformed once they arrive in unfamiliar lands.

CHAPTER FOUR

REDEFINING BEAUTY
Elizabeth Nunez's and Pauline Melville's Exploration of Illness, Migration, and Transformation

> As she spoke I could feel the richness of whatever was beginning to take place inside her. . . . But most of all, she felt deeply alive, as if something were opening up inside her.
> —PAULINE MELVILLE, "Lucifer's Shank"

Pauline Melville's *The Migration of Ghosts* and Elizabeth Nunez's *Anna In-Between* and *Boundaries* feature female characters who are transformed by illness. In Melville's short stories "Lucifer's Shank" and "The Sparkling Bitch" from *The Migration of Ghosts* (1998) and Nunez's *Anna In-Between* (2009) and *Boundaries* (2011), physical suffering offers the protagonists a reconsideration of identity and increased comfort with their bodies. Nunez's work explores how breast cancer alienates the matriarch, Beatrice. In her novels, the protagonist's battle with breast cancer unites her family in temporary migration while she pursues effective medical treatment abroad. Melville's "Lucifer's Shank" follows breast cancer patient Ellie during her journey, and "The Sparkling Bitch" deploys Susan's battle with anorexia nervosa[1] as a vehicle for neocolonial critique. Collectively, the texts attest to the life-altering impact of disease. The protagonists' illnesses, rooted in their dis-ease with their bodies, their relationships, and their privilege, highlight the emotional side effects that can accompany physical maladies.

In the works under study, physical illness is paired with travel. For instance, in "The Sparkling Bitch," Susan's eating disorder manifests after a trip to Nigeria. Melville's "Lucifer's Shank" and Nunez's *Anna In-Between* follow breast cancer patients Ellie's and Beatrice's journeys to secure quality medical care. While flight offers a way to negotiate sexual abuse in novels such as *Breath, Eyes, Memory*, the women in these works turn not to dissociation for relief, but instead engage in travel during health crises. The severity of the protagonists' physical conditions demands an immediate response. Through flight, the women return home, in a literal as well as metaphorical sense; although Ellie loses her battle with cancer, Beatrice's prognosis is optimistic. Melville's and Nunez's texts highlight how disease functions as a force of inertia that propels temporary migration and intensely introspective experiences. Together, the texts afford a closer look at the relationship between disease, migration, and familial reconnection.

Melville's and Nunez's prose details the intersection of illness, migration, and transformation. In the works, and most particularly in Nunez's novels, exile[2] operates as an initial reaction to a loved one's illness and functions as a cover for a much deeper emotion—fear. Although the protagonists are vastly transformed by health crises, their relationships undergo similar trials. Disease complicates their relationships by introducing the threat of death; in the majority of cases, personal bonds emerge strengthened. In the texts, good health, or lack thereof, affects feelings of citizenship and belonging. Melville's works focus on the relationship between migration and physical decline. Nunez's texts detail how travel brings Beatrice to reconsider her status as a citizen, wife, and mother. In works by Melville and Nunez, the ill suffer through a period of socially sanctioned ostracism before their loved ones come to terms with the consequences of the protagonists' illnesses. Perhaps more important than the physical transformation that accompanies disease is the emotional growth that the journey offers. The texts shed light on the impact of severe illness, read temporary migration as central to the characters' physical and emotional journeys, and position disease as a catalyst for transformation.

MIXTURE, MYSTICISM, AND TRANSFORMATION

Pauline Melville's *The Migration of Ghosts* explores issues including migration and exile as she infuses the collection of short stories with her own brand of mysticism. The Guyanese-born author's short stories employ magical realism[3] to call the operations of multinational corporations into question. In "The Sparkling Bitch," the author delivers a critique of neocolonial conditions through Susan's transformation from a seemingly healthy woman into an ill recluse. Susan's health crisis, used as a symbol for large-scale abuses and neocolonial practices such as her husband's attempted cover-up of an oil spill in Nigeria, suggests that such actions cannot remain under wraps.

Melville constructs the character of Susan as a vehicle for social critique, most notably of the environmental disaster that her husband has no qualms in covering up. Yet disease offers Susan a means of resistance. Her journey from her place of relative exile in the countryside to the London banquet hall at the conclusion of the text allows her to strike a blow against her husband's professional reputation. By turning her rail-thin body into an object of curiosity to be scrutinized by a room full of influential people, Susan pushes back against the greed, corruption, and abuse that her husband and Hay Oil represent. She is the haunting presence, not Charles's exploitative actions or the ensuing environmental devastation, that brings embarrassment. That is, Susan's possession turns her into a haunting reminder of the oil spill and weaponizes shame to render her a ghost-like figure who challenges her estranged husband's façade.

Born of a British mother and a Guyanese father, Melville describes herself as the "whitey in the woodpile" (Robinson-Walcott 101). As a champion of mixtures, her work emphasizes the "shape-shifter, the trickster, the indeterminacy of gender, race, sexuality and nationality" (DeLoughrey 67). In incorporating a variety of influences and voices in her writing, such as the use of Haitian Vodou in "Erzulie" and the humorous voice of a well-traveled parrot in "The Parrot and Descartes," Melville embraces polyvocality and boundary crossing. While feminism "has long conceived of the body as a prison for women," "Lucifer's Shank" and "The Sparkling Bitch," among her other works, depict women breaking free (Savory 55). Although the women are unable to fully break free of their bodily prisons, their emotional outlook distinguishes between physical and emotional captivity. Though breast cancer ultimately claims Ellie's life, she embraces the more youthful appearance that her mastectomy brings. Perhaps even more explicitly, Susan's physical degeneration publicly embarrasses her husband. Overtly aware of the shock and disgust that her physical transformation will occasion, Susan turns her "six stone"[4] body into a walking accusation of her husband's personal and professional negligence (Melville 132). Expecting to greet his lovely wife, who he has not seen in over six months, in a green silk gown, Charles, the ultimate "sparkling bitch" with his manicured nails and a Rolex watch, goes pale and "betray[s] his wife by refusing to stand and show her where he was" (Melville 133). Whereas Susan suffers the exile of what readers can only assume is a loveless marriage, Charles's neglect and embarrassment of his wife solidifies his portrait as a greedy, self-obsessed man.

As Susan Bordo writes in *Unbearable Weight*, "The *physical* body can be an instrument and medium of power" (143). The relation between the body and agency plays out in Melville's "Lucifer's Shank," a short story that draws on allusions from Dante's *Inferno*. Most explicitly, the protagonist, Ellie, reads about "following the pilgrim's journey through the circles of Hell"; Ellie's literary journey precedes her own (Melville 63). In one scene, the pilgrim-like figure, Ellie, looks "like a different person, blind and not knowing where to go" as her best friend, the unnamed narrator, takes her arm and serves as her guide (Melville 67). In this line, Ellie's blindness suggests the beginnings of a transformation; by "blinding" Ellie, Melville alludes to a larger cultural blindness and positions Ellie as relatively powerless. Although the narrator does not know where she is leading Ellie, the protagonist's blindness engenders a reliance that amplifies the friendship between the two women. While the unnamed friend is initially overwhelmed when Ellie shares that she has been diagnosed with breast cancer and avoids Ellie's calls because of her own discomfort, she soon realizes that her actions are selfish and hurtful. Much like the restored familial connections that are central in Nunez's work, disease prompts the revitalization of a long-standing friendship. The women were close prior to Ellie's illness, but the friend becomes a near-permanent fixture at Ellie's side following her diagnosis.

In "Lucifer's Shank," magnification and disappearance are directly related to sight. Interestingly, Ellie's lack of sight attributes a fallible "second sight" to the narrator. For instance, the narrator notes that she had a premonition that "something terrible was going to happen" (Melville 67). The premonition is later revealed to have been misplaced; rather than serving as a "warning about the holocaust," as the narrator thought, the premonition is suggestive of the protagonist's personal holocaust, her battle with cancer (Melville 67). By connecting one woman's illness with a cornerstone of history, the author suggests that although transformation can certainly be global, it can also be personal. While the Holocaust the narrator refers to resulted in mass casualties, this short story follows one woman's illness and subsequent death.

THE BEAUTIFUL EMPRESS

Through the character of Ellie, Melville calls definitions of beauty into question. Although cancer ravages her body, Ellie's physique is transformed into something majestic. With the voice of the unnamed narrator, Melville paints the transformed Ellie as a sight of beauty, a "strikingly beautiful empress" lying in her hospital bed (83). Ellie's beauty at the conclusion of the story does not come without physical reminders of her fight for life. As Ellie battles cancer, her body is transformed in the fight against the disease. The narrator remarks, "This was another self come true, the self that could have been. She lay there with a magnificence that I had never seen or understood before" (Melville 83). Through her friend's admiring gaze, Ellie appears as a counter to normative conceptions of beauty; her emotional transformation far eclipses her physical one and it is only when Ellie is most true to herself that she appears "strikingly beautiful."

The most noticeable physical change comes when Ellie undergoes her mastectomy. For Ellie, the operation threatens to strip her femininity and render her deformed. Ironically, the surgery reverses time in that it transforms Ellie into a Peter Pan-like figure with the "strange androgynous look of youth" (Melville 70). The progression of Ellie's breast, and later bone cancer, highlights surgery's capability to mark the body. Notwithstanding the obvious physical reminders of Ellie's cancer, the disease is at times largely invisible; the narrator notes that despite the recurrence of cancer, "There was no sign of anything wrong" (Melville 76–77). The disease retracts and reemerges into view when Melville shifts the focus in this text. It is telling that Ellie's mastectomy does not immediately occasion discussions of reconstruction, but rather the championing of her new look. If the body is a medium of culture, as Bordo claims, then it can be argued that Melville presents an alternative model of femininity through the character of Ellie. In developing an image of survival as opposed to vanity, the author links disease and transformation when Ellie's surgery leaves a visible marker of her battle with cancer.

Like the unnamed boy in "The Sparkling Bitch," Ellie's body is shaped by external factors; aside from her obvious shrinking as a result of weight loss, perhaps the most salient reminder of cancer is Ellie's mastectomy scar. Despite the emotional and physical scars that cancer brings, Ellie tries to embrace change; she states that she quite likes the scar because it serves as a physical reminder of her disease (Melville 70). In fact, the most explicit marker of Ellie's personal growth is her changing opinion of her mastectomy scar. While at first the character sought to minimize or hide the scar and "retract herself from view," as the story progresses "she walked the length of a shopping centre and triumphantly bought a scarlet cotton dress with a low neck and tiny black pattern" (Melville 72, 77–78). Here, the protagonist moves from a sense of vulnerability related to the potential observance of the scar and a desire to take on an alternate persona to a healthier acceptance of the changes that disease brings. This becomes clear when Ellie dons a low-cut dress that showcases the most explicit physical reminder of her battle with cancer. Through Ellie, Melville highlights the change that life-threatening illnesses can enact on the psyche and the body; in essence, the author models a way of coming to terms with the forces that disrupt our lives.

At the conclusion of the text, Melville incorporates indigenous beliefs surrounding death when she explains that "according to some groups of South American Indians, it is the manner of death, the way that you die, that determines your after-life.... The real self is revealed only in death" (83). As a result of cancer, Ellie's true self is revealed. According to Elaine Savory, "In Melville's stories the body is essentially a misleading disguise and there is often an ironic relation between the façade of a personality and its actual nature" (50). If the body is a disguise, as Savory claims, then as Ellie's body begins to fail, the disguise strips away, revealing her true nature. Throughout the course of the narrative, Ellie emerges with "a magnificence that [she has] never seen or understood before" (Melville 83). For the narrator, and for the reader, the protagonist offers a new way of thinking about beauty and the transformation that death can bring. The narrator begins to view Ellie, and death, in a new way. In understanding flight not as escape but as a process that affords growth, it is clear that disease is the catalyst that brings Ellie to a place of peace. To stress, cancer serves as the impetus for Ellie's spiritual awakening through literature. In reading and discussing works such as Dante's Alighieri's *Inferno* and Salman Rushdie's *Is Nothing Sacred?*, she ponders the destructive power of popular religion and reexamines her political views. As a result of this exploration, the character "felt deeply alive, as if something was opening up inside her" (Melville 65). Ellie's movement toward acceptance serves as a reminder that living with disease, and especially an incurable one, is indeed a process of navigation.

Specifically addressing the bodily changes that can take place during terminal illness, Melville proclaims that "life is the mask that drops off and death protrudes from underneath as the reality" (83). In "Lucifer's Shank," she offers a warning and cultural critique against passively moving through life. If the body can become an avenue of escape, as Savory claims, then Melville's story can be read as a force that brings readers to confront their own mortality. Indeed, the text suggests that "the bod[y] is a misleading disguise and there is often an ironic relation between the façade of a personality and its actual nature" (Savory 50). In "Lucifer's Shank," it is cancer, perhaps ironically, that strips Ellie of the ability to hide. Despite the potential for disfigurement, Ellie's beauty emerges and is magnified when she is observed immobile and incoherent on her deathbed. Ellie's disappearance is incremental, but nonetheless a warning against being one in the "silent crowd drained of life" (Melville 66). The work attests to the masks that we wear everyday and the equalizing, and penetrating, power of cancer.

THE SHRINKING VIOLET

Like Melville's "Lucifer's Shank," "The Sparkling Bitch" details one woman's transformative journey. Similar to how cancer brings emotional growth and physical change in "Lucifer's Shank," "The Sparkling Bitch" employs a disease, anorexia nervosa, to deform the body of Susan Hay, the wife of oil executive Charles Hay. The story begins in Nigeria, a country that, according to Charles, has "too much heat and too much oppressive emptiness" (Melville 119). The work develops a parallel between poverty, corruption, and Susan's metamorphosis. While Ellie's battle with cancer was invisible for a period of time, Susan's physical decline is quickly noticeable. In "The Sparkling Bitch," Melville presents the protagonist's eating disorder as a debilitating condition that drives her into exile. The author fuses disorder and mysticism to connect the shrinking female form and the corrupt postcolonial state.

It is a chance encounter in Nigeria that brings change for Susan. When Charles is on a trip to tidy up "business" in a nation that his company left "stinking of oil spillages," Susan has a brief, wordless exchange with an unnamed boy and is never the same (Melville 119). Susan's battle with anorexia nervosa can be traced to the moment when she observes a "boy of about thirteen . . . , clearly the victim of starvation: his thin black limbs were crossed and sharply folded like those of a spider playing dead" (Melville 120). In this scene, Melville explores issues of power and privilege when she positions Susan as a colonizing figure through her gaze. Charles, the personification of exploitative behavior, is omitted from the scene, perhaps because his quest for fame and fortune has blinded him from seeing the results of his actions, symbolized here by the figure of the emaciated boy. Instead, the author paints Charles's partner in materialism, a rich, white woman, as gazing at an impoverished African boy. The scene uses the figure of the Nigerian boy to showcase the costs of neocolonialism via a starving child who "plays dead" at a rural gas station. The boy's long-legged and angular form evokes Anansi, the West African trickster figure who takes the shape of a spider. Moreover, the title of the short story collection, *The Migration of Ghosts*, suggests that the boy's ghost-like essence moves from Nigeria to London through the character of Susan to morph into a new haunting presence in England. The shapeshifting element here evokes questions of female disembodiment, and Susan's submission to the force gives new meaning to the term "possession."

While in "Lucifer's Shank" disappearance is figured in terms of Ellie's desire to mask her scar and retract from view, in "The Sparkling Bitch" disappearance is introduced when Susan fails to recognize the figure as human but notices the "angularity of the black body outlined against the pale concrete forecourt and the faded red gasoline pump made her freeze with shock when she realised. Despite skeletal thinness, the boy's figure resonated with a sort of violent power" (Melville 120). It is evident that it is the boy's malformed appearance that captures Susan's attention; as a victim of neocolonial practices, he stands in for those who cannot speak. He never utters a word, yet an exchange occurs. When Susan acknowledges the boy's monstrosity, she begins to uncover her husband's monstrous dealings in Nigeria. Melville infuses the political context in the background by depicting the Nigerian boy through Susan's view. The author furthers an image of an exoticized, captivating "other" to complicate the colonizing gaze. In collapsing the construction of the boy with Susan's observation through the voice of an unnamed, omniscient narrator, readers are left with the white, colonialist perspective. The image of the boy remains shrouded in mystery, approachable only through the lens of mysticism.

Like the wasteland that Hay Oil has left in its wake, the image of the boy and the faded gasoline pump contrast with the immense corporate wealth represented by the figure of Susan Hay. Though the boy is not inherently violent, he appears to possess, or rather is possessed by, a "violent power" that will later reign over Susan. The unnamed boy does not deploy political influence, but his physique radiates a strong, silent power. Melville highlights the "unseen within the visible"; the author calls readers to look beyond physical description, to ponder the other forces at work in Susan's physical transformation (Francois 39). The boy is clearly emaciated from malnutrition; in a similar but very different way, Susan's body shrinks when she denies herself sustenance. Through magical realism, Melville suggests that Susan's bodily changes and eating disorder stem not from a dissatisfaction with her body, but from a "spell" that, ironically, transforms a white, wealthy body to reflect the "skeletal thinness" of a boy she met in Nigeria (Melville 120).

As the story continues, the author develops the suggestion that Susan is influenced by a supernatural force. Melville writes, "A strange and powerful god gradually emerged to stalk the clearings.... He began to rule her with a rod of iron until there was no distinguishing between her and himself. She welcomed this implacable god of starvation, who opposed all fertility, excess and fecundity" (130). With this passage, the author references the "efficacy of obeah"[5] and lends credence to the mystical while leaving much open to interpretation (Melville 101). By specifying the force of change as ruling with a "rod of iron," but not directly naming the influence, she weaves an often invisible level of knowledge within the visible. In providing these signifying characteristics, the author implies that Ogun, the god or loa of iron in the Yoruba religion, is the force that renders Susan a "living accusation" (Melville 132). "An iron will had her in thrall. She moved one leg after the other as if she were fitted with false limbs," Melville details (132). Through an unnamed force that is implied to be Ogun, Susan learns that the answer to "everything" is simply not to eat. As a result of her dedication, she is transformed into a "blazing witness" and a physical representation of the neglect and exploitation that corporations such as Hay Oil exact on less advantaged peoples (Melville 133).

It is during the brief encounter with the Nigerian boy that Susan feels the violent power that transforms her into the "murderous ghost" who horrifies guests at the London gala (Melville 132). In this moment of contact, neither party speaks but an exchange takes place. "The brief contact enabled her to break free," the narrator notes (Melville 121). While on the one hand the notion of breaking free can be read as referring to the intense, wordless interaction, it also forecasts the sense of purpose and freedom Susan feels in surrendering to "the god she honoured" (Melville 133). Melville's trickster-like writing style brings readers to ponder what exactly is exchanged in this moment. If indeed the boy is possessed by the same power that takes hold of Susan, then perhaps this moment is what incites her transformation. By placing Susan in the position of benevolent colonizer, a woman who "squatted down and pulled a US fifty-dollar note from her purse," Melville suggests that money cannot right corruption or economic disparity (120). What the boy needs is clearly food, yet Susan offers him money—money that, even more ironically, is not legal tender and would require conversion to yield sustenance.

While it is likely guilt that influences Susan to offer money to the boy, it is "an irrational empathy [that] kept her there" (Melville 120). Through the voice of the narrator, the author questions whose behavior is "irrational." Susan is initially aligned with Hay Oil and Western influence as seen in her default reaction, but her subsequent response exemplifies the beginnings of a divergent journey and the power the boy holds over her. Notably, Melville writes that Susan "needed some response from the figure at her side in order to be released from the spell. . . . It was not gratitude that she needed exactly. She was not sure what it was. Perhaps just an acknowledgment of her existence" (121). With this line, the author suggests that Susan's captivation comes as a result of her own feeling of disappearance. Perhaps because she feels insignificant to Charles, Susan has never fully developed (emotionally or physically) and instead remains in a liminal state.

The acknowledgment of existence that Susan craves comes via the character of the unnamed boy. In a key scene, the boy's eyes are magnetic because they are equally disgusting and compelling. The author writes, "His eyelids had been bitten by insects but the eyes beneath were huge and dark and compelling" (Melville 121). Here, the boy represents the costs of colonialism and the neglect that often characterizes the postcolonial state. After twenty-two years of marriage, Susan's "appearance was still slender and girlish," but from an emotional standpoint, "her abilities, for some reason, [were] never developed" (Melville 125–26). By constructing Susan and the boy in this manner, as physically compelling in very different ways, Melville invites comparison. The author paints two characters in stages of halted development to highlight their parallel exploitation. To be clear, Susan and the boy are in subordinate positions of power relative to Charles and Hay Oil Incorporated. While the levels of exploitation certainly vary, with Susan's neglect serving as a reference to Hay Oil's investment in extractive practices, it is clear that the corporation privileges profit over the health of the landscape and the people who live there.

LIVING ACCUSATION

The most explicit illustration of Susan's transformation comes in the final scene when she joins Charles at an important social event. Again referencing themes of disappearance and invisibility, Susan is not noticed upon entering the hall, but her physical deterioration soon attracts the attention of the guests who are shocked by her changed appearance. A mystical force has shaped her figure. Susan's illness/possession (depending on one's interpretation) has turned her into a rail-thin figure. By honoring the god Ogun in refusing food and becoming a "blazing witness," Susan signifies the effects of colonialism, big business, and extreme poverty (Melville 133). Eating disorders "reflect and call our attention to some of the central ills of our culture"; in "The Sparkling Bitch," Melville deploys disease to highlight corporate corruption and the economic disparity between more and less developed nations (Bordo 139–40). This is evident in Susan and Charles's relationship. Despite her husband's attempts to lock his rebellious wife away in a cottage, Susan's rebuttal, a play on shrinking space and form, magnifies his discomfort while taking power back through perhaps the only means possible. By accepting Ogun's command, Susan uses her charged body to call attention to her husband's actions.

The final scene of the story transforms Susan into a witness of the costs of colonialism. In the concluding lines, Melville writes, "When Susan rose shakily to her feet, uncontrollable diarrhoea had stained her dress and dripped from the chair. White with fury, Charles Hay took her by the arm and led her slowly from the hall" (134). It is interesting that Charles turns ghostly white rather than darkening to a shade of red; Charles seeks to disappear, like Susan, rather than call attention to himself. Unlike the narrator in "Lucifer's Shank," Charles is not a supportive figure, but, like Susan's neighbors, pretends that he does not see her. J. Brooks Bouson's work on shame helps to explain Charles's reaction. In *Embodied Shame*, Bouson emphasizes how "shame, and its related feeling states—chagrin, embarrassment, mortification, lowered self-esteem, disgrace, and humiliation—can lead to withdrawal or avoidant behaviors, which reflect the desire of shamed individuals to conceal or hide themselves in an attempt to protect against feelings of exposure" (6). In "The Sparkling Bitch," Susan, who according to Charles, is "clearly dying," causes him to "burn with rage" when her foul breath and emaciated appearance engender great embarrassment (Melville 133).

Bouson also writes on the connection between shame and bodily fluids. She notes that feelings of shame, loathing, and disgust are "associated with body substances and waste products—such as tears, saliva, feces, urine, vomit, and mucus [because] the abject is defiling and disgusting [and because] it cannot be totally expelled or rejected" (Bouson 4). This is especially true in the case of Susan's diarrhoea, a symptom of her eating disorder that mirrors the oil spill that her husband attempts to cover up. Like Susan's diarrhoea, the oil spill cannot be fully expelled from record. Her accident turns her into a living accusation that renders personal the damage that Hay Oil causes. In this scene, Susan's diarrhoea marks a place of wealth and a symbol of Western materialism with a stain. This incident serves as a physical reminder of a common condition that residents of Nigeria suffer and even die from. Ellie in "Lucifer's Shank" dies a beautiful empress, but Susan shrinks from view, morphed into a "murderous ghost" because anorexia has transformed her into a horrific, accusatory sight. While Ellie's body is physically and emotionally scarred from her battle with cancer, Susan's corporeality serves as a "living accusation" of the costs of neocolonialism and the ghostliness that can accompany the pursuit of wealth. Her ravaged frame stands in contrast to the opulence and waste surrounding her, engendering in observers the same guilt that she initially felt while gazing at the Nigerian boy. Ultimately, the author's short stories evidence the transformation that disease offers; while Ellie takes flight in death, Susan's journey to Nigeria sets off a chain of events that exact her metamorphosis. In *The Migration of Ghosts*, the author uses the protagonists to highlight a range of social ills.

RELATIONSHIPS

In an interview with Barbara Lewis, Elizabeth Nunez notes that she is "very interested in this tension between our private desires and our public responsibilities" (204). The tension between public and private matters is centered in *Anna In-Between* and *Boundaries*; in the novels, Nunez examines how late-stage breast cancer alters one woman's appearance and her outlook on life. Through a focus on the family's reactions to Beatrice's diagnosis, the author highlights the strengthened relationships that can arise from caretaking arrangements. Similar to how Ellie's best friend remains by her side, Beatrice's daughter and husband feel that it is their duty to render care. While Anna, Beatrice's daughter, serves as the primary caregiver, largely because her gender ostensibly makes her better equipped to handle this "women's disease," she must repress feelings of revulsion in favor of outward-facing strength. As an Afro-Caribbean woman living in the United States, Nunez often speaks about "life as an exercise in denial and 'voluntary exclusion'"; this sense of exclusion surfaces through Beatrice's avoidance of medical care and her attempts to shield her family from her illness (Lewis 202).

Much like the figure of Anna Sinclair in *Anna In-Between* and *Boundaries*, Nunez migrated to the United States as a young age after "arriv[ing] here from Trinidad, for the first time, in 1963, on a student visa" (Nunez, "How I Came" 373). Her migration at the age of nineteen serves as fodder for writing that explores the intersection between disease and migration. In Nunez's *Anna In-Between* and *Boundaries*, Anna is stuck "in the middle between her mother and father" (*Anna In-Between* 110).[6] As an immigrant, she is positioned as neither "fully at home on the island of their birth, neither fully at home in America" (*AIB* 314). Through a focus on the physical form, Nunez paints Anna as phenotypically and ideologically exiled. Her physiognomy as a light-skinned woman establishes difference from those closest to her and her insistence on the quality of her mother's medical treatment eventually brings the two closer. While Beatrice self-isolates as a result of her illness, avoiding treatment for the lump in her breast for over two years, Anna's geographic distance spurs emotional disconnection. As a "visible immigrant," Anna is trapped in a state of limbo. By returning home to care for her mother, she comes to a fuller understanding of herself as a young woman. Whether freeing oneself in the service of others, or coming to terms with oneself as a woman, breast cancer in Nunez's works serves as a force of change for patient and caregiver alike.

Breast cancer affords physical and emotional rebirth for the protagonist, Beatrice. Though early in the novel Beatrice is depicted with "dull" skin and "lackluster" eyes, *Anna In-Between* concludes with an image of Anna's parents as "two bodies . . . glued together as one. . . . The man, her father, is holding the woman, her mother, close to his chest, folded in his arms. He presses her head into the well of his shoulder. Light bounces off her mother's bare scalp, the skin stretched taut across hard bone. Her head glitters; it shines. Her father draws her mother closer to his heart" (*AIB* 20, 312). This scene of Anna's parents dancing to Nat King Cole features a revitalized marriage. It is disease that strengthens the bond between the couple. By juxtaposing harsh elements (bare scalp, hard bone) with tenderness (glued together, folded in his arms), Nunez illustrates the duality of disease and the complexity of human relationships in response to personal crises.

In *Anna In-Between* and *Boundaries*, the admission of disease is deferred; it is revealed that Beatrice had "felt it for two years" (*AIB* 110). In terming the tumor "it," the author parallels the physical distance between mother and daughter, a distance so vast that it is termed a "safe distance," in that "in their household, they do not expose their bodies, not to each other. Husbands and wives may have to bare their naked bodies to each other, but not mothers and daughters" (*AIB* 41). For Beatrice's mother, distance is "safe"; propriety and fear give way to the necessity of medical treatment. Perhaps strange to some, intimate relationships in the text bring husbands and wives to "have to" bear their naked bodies, as if intimacy or stripping down is prohibited. As the text continues, Nunez provides readers a glimpse of the tumor, the "lump pushing out beneath the skin on her mother's left breast [with a] thin trail of partially dried blood beneath it" (*AIB* 42). Despite the fact that Beatrice waited to show Anna the tumor, she is depicted as "calm" as she lifts her arm to reveal "another large lump, her lymph nodes swollen, pushing against her skin" (*AIB* 43). In this graphic description, the tumor visually expands toward the viewer as the reader encounters Beatrice's tumor through Anna's gaze.

Though it is perplexing why Beatrice would delay medical treatment, one reason why she hesitates to reveal her condition to her husband and daughter is that "in her parent's social circles, any weakness is a character flaw. . . . Sickness and death are the ultimate evidence of weakness and failure" (*AIB* 67). For Beatrice, "Self-control is the holy grail of the upper middle class. To lose control over one's self is to be humiliated" (*AIB* 67). In *Unbearable Weight*, Bordo discusses culture's grip on the body. In particular, Bordo finds that our bodies learn, through routine, "which gestures are forbidden and which required, how violable or inviolable are the boundaries of our bodies, how much space around the body may be claimed, and so on" (16). This observation sheds light on Beatrice's reaction to the insidious lump in her breast. Those in her social circles often equate illness with weakness; she dares not speak of the lump because "to talk of cancer is to stir memories of shame and defeat. To talk of cancer is to conjure pictures of rotting flesh, women reduced to stinking carcasses, raw meat leaking onto ulcerous sores" (*AIB* 228). Beatrice's friends are afraid to talk about cancer because cancer has no regard for class or good breeding. "Cancer does not care if the blouse you are wearing was bought in New York, if the label was a designer's," Anna explains (*AIB* 228–29). As this declaration suggests, cancer evokes aversion because of the fear it inspires; for those with financial means, cancer is one of the few situations they cannot buy themselves out of. While wealth certainly affords access to medical treatment, it is incapable of preventing the conversion of healthy cells into malignant ones.

Beatrice's commitment to socially sanctioned propriety extends to her relationship with her husband, John. Perhaps reflecting the notion that to share the news of her discovery (the lump) would mean that it is real and could even kill her, Beatrice waits over two years to tell her husband. As John relates to Anna, "Your mother and I respect each other's privacy. That is the way we have always lived our lives. . . . I knew she would tell me when she was ready" (*AIB* 53). With this line, Nunez implies that Anna's father was cognizant of Beatrice's illness; perhaps he felt the lump yet elected to remain laconic on the matter. By favoring respect over responsibility, Mr. Sinclair inherently participates in the silence around his wife's disease. In remaining silent, Beatrice and John participate in the "cultural practices that objectify and sexualize us"; treatment is delayed and illness denied in favor of control and cover (Bordo 28).

MEDICAL TREATMENT

In *Anna In-Between*, the "insidious" cancer triggers memories of Beatrice's mother's battle with the disease. Anna explains that Beatrice's mother "died at fifty-six of breast cancer. In those colonial days on the island there was no chemotherapy, not for those without money, not for locals without connections. The tumor on her grandmother's breast just grew larger until it broke through her skin. It was bloody and ugly" (*AIB* 114, 44). Beatrice, like her mother, faces obstacles to effective medical treatment, but her socioeconomic status allows her to seek care abroad. She has seen the emotional and physical damage that breast cancer can cause; her mother's death from the disease helps to explain the avoidance tactics that Beatrice employs. Much like the cancer invading her body, Beatrice's mother's tumor looms as a vilified demon, the personification of petulance that cannot be stemmed. As a result of her mother's cancer, a tumor, a demon that ate away her mother's flesh, Beatrice "fears that the seed for the same disease may be lying dormant in her breasts, biding its time" (*AIB* 68). Here, the seed metaphor enables Beatrice to blame genetics or a higher power for placing an embryonic form of disease within her. Her logic reads cancer as something of a "boogey man" waiting to attack. By contrast, Anna predicts that "the lump on her mother's breast will not be benign. One in five women will be diagnosed each year. For a woman whose mother had breast cancer, the odds increase" (*AIB* 66). However harsh, Anna represents a more a realistic view of the realities that breast cancer patients face.

Anna In-Between and *Boundaries* reveal the polarization that intensive medical treatment can bring. Debate over Beatrice's medical care divides the family; Anna advocates for treatment in the United States while Beatrice "won't go anywhere else" (*AIB* 60). Anna is advised, "Don't oppose her. She has made up her mind. She will be treated here, in our country, in our homeland. She is proud of our doctors" (*AIB* 62). In this passage, medical treatment is aligned with nationalism when Beatrice vehemently resists outside care. Despite the realities of conditions so bleak that "they use newspapers instead of sheets," Beatrice insists on obtaining treatment at 'home'" (*AIB* 60). While Drs. Pak and Ramdoolal examine Beatrice, she is bluntly told that "if you want to die, Mrs. Sinclair . . . stay here" (*AIB* 115). It is significant that Beatrice hesitates to expose her body to further examination. Beatrice and John remain silent and shelter her body from the gaze of medical professionals, but the lump can no longer be ignored. When the lump pushes out from underneath her skin, reminiscent of how her mother's tumor "broke through," and conditions become truly desperate, Beatrice breaks her silence and discloses her condition to her husband. The news soon reaches her daughter, who insists that her mother seek medical treatment in the United States. This insistence from her daughter, who lives abroad, along with a medical professional's advice, influences Beatrice to obtain treatment outside her nation. Perhaps ironically, only those from "outside" can effectively treat her; it is her decision to obtain medical care abroad that saves her life.

Beatrice's medical care is depicted as relatively "hands off." For instance, Beatrice allows Dr. Lee Pak to "press his thumb against the vein in her wrist or to check her pulse at her neck, but he is never allowed to examine her under her clothes, or, God forbid, without her clothes" (*AIB* 73). In yet another instance, "Dr. Ramdoolal takes barely a minute to examine Mrs. Sinclair. He asks her to unbutton her blouse. He sees the tumor, the size of a lemon, pushing out of her bra. He grimaces. He does not need her to take off her bra, he says. He has seen all he needs to see. He asks if there is also a lump under her arm. Beatrice nods" (*AIB* 109). Together, these lines illustrate the entrenchment of norms that privilege propriety and avoidance, and the mores governing visual access to Beatrice's body have significant consequences. In this scene, Beatrice remains fully clothed; the most vital part of her (with regard to her illness) remains covered. The tumor, described as a lemon, visually protrudes, undeniably announcing its presence. Perhaps even more troubling is the fact that Dr. Ramdoolal elects not to perform a manual examination. Instead, he relies on a brief visual inspection and patient testimony to reach conclusions about his patient's health.

Anna is positioned as a witness in this scene, and her reaction is reflective of the sociocultural dynamics that govern the island, its inhabitants, and their attitudes toward medical treatment. At this moment, Anna "wants to hug her mother, put her arms around her shoulders and comfort her. But they do not hug in her house. Stiff upper lip. Self-control. Discipline over the emotions. These are the values they believe in. Yet the trembling has increased on her mother's lips" (*AIB* 106). Beatrice's reaction illustrates Bordo's understanding of the body as a locus of control. In this moment, Anna wants to hug her mother but pulls back and Beatrice largely suppresses her emotions. To stress, this is the first time that Beatrice has betrayed the iron-clad sense of control that she has internalized. Her trembling lips point to fear yet suggest a willingness to comply. In seeking treatment, Beatrice takes the first step in exerting control over her disease; this control, significantly, comes by releasing hold of her emotions and the need for privacy.

Although the novel offers a glimpse inside the doctor's office, the text does not include a view of more intensive treatment. In the only reference to medical treatment in *Anna In-Between*, Nunez writes, "It is almost teatime when her parents return. Her mother's face is drained, her skin gray, her eyes dull. She feels weak, say says. She wants to rest.... *The procedure*, he said, as if the methodically timed invasion of her mother's body with poisonous drugs is no more than the steps to be taken to solve a management problem" (157). As with previous discussions of disease, direct confrontation is avoided in favor of genteelism. Instead of terming treatment as what it is, likely chemotherapy, Anna's father turns to euphemisms to quell his own discomfort and grief. It is safer to refer to cancer treatments as "procedures." Similarly, a subsequent description of Beatrice's health depicts the tumor in a state of limbo. The narrator explains, "The tumor can lie there insidious, waiting, but it is hidden; it is out of sight. For now, they will have breakfast. ... For now all is normal" (*AIB* 196). Here, a sense of relief emerges in that the tumor is "out of sight"; much like the previous description, the tumor is anthropomorphized and painted as lying in wait.

Similar to the protagonist in Melville's "Lucifer's Shank," Beatrice is described as "skin and bones" near the conclusion of the text (*AIB* 221). *Anna In-Between* largely shields readers from the physical effects of Beatrice's medical treatment. Instead, Nunez paints side effects in a positive light as Beatrice's chin "is smooth. Silk smooth.... 'The chemo has destroyed the follicles!' Her mother is still laughing when her husband returns" (*AIB* 275). As the text concludes, the author depicts Beatrice with her head "wrapped in a blue silk scarf that matches the blue flowers on her dress.... She has recovered a bit from her chemo session and her complexion is bright. Her face is not drawn; her eyes are not dull" (Nunez *AIB* 301). In contrast to the opening scenes that are rife with deferral, Beatrice lightheartedly relates, "I'll have one breast. Is that so? One breast? I'll be deformed.' She swings her body toward her husband. 'Deformed, John'" (Nunez *AIB* 308). Interestingly, the scene that most illustrates Beatrice's changing attitudes toward her appearance is when she cuts her hair. While Beatrice is afraid of looking "old" and "terrible," she takes agency in cutting her hair with orange-handled scissors (*AIB* 230). Within a few pages, Beatrice's attitude shifts when she declares that she "want[s] to be a funky white-haired lady now. I don't want to go to the hairdresser. I want you [Anna] to do it" (*AIB* 232). Anna notes that "in the absence of hair, the structure of her mother's face is more pronounced and Anna is struck again by how beautiful she is, how stunning she must have been when she was young" (*AIB* 250). For Beatrice, breast cancer brings increased comfort with her body and a reconsideration of her identity. As Nunez's works illustrate, the body is indeed "an instrument and medium of power" (Bordo 143).

PRIVACY AND PROPRIETY

Nunez's *Boundaries*, the sequel to *Anna In-Between*, picks up where *Anna In-Between* leaves off. In *Boundaries*, Nunez writes, "Everything has changed now that John Sinclair has breached the code of privacy they share. Her secret is out. She will need a mastectomy. It is the only way to save her life" (17). The narrator relates that "this is the natural duty of a daughter whose mother is ill" but John Sinclair, rather than his daughter, tends to Beatrice (*Boundaries* 15). In a dramatic shift, it is not a man who "remains outside, waiting for the results. A man's man leaves matters of a woman's bodily functions to the business of women. But it is her father who does this woman's business; it is Anna who stands outside in the waiting room" (*Boundaries* 157). It is John's involvement in Beatrice's treatment that propels drastic, life-saving surgery. Yet, as the text details, the diagnosis was not willingly shared, but was knowledge that he "breached." John is initially painted as relatively "hands off" and detached from such intimacies but later functions as his wife's caregiver. In short, he risks social retribution to care for his wife, to change her bandages when a female "ought" to be doing that. In constructing a male character who breaches the bounds of propriety to take an active role in his wife's recovery, the author presents an alternative model for caregiving. This reversal of duties, with John attending to Beatrice and Anna taking a more distanced approach, challenges their community's norms regarding women's medical treatment.

Although *Anna In-Between* largely avoids depictions of the physical body and delimits description of Beatrice's cancer, the disease is rendered explicit in *Boundaries*. Readers may expect to see an image of a depraved, diminishing woman, but Beatrice appears "in remarkably good health" (*Boundaries* 83). The seventy-two year old woman is described as able to pass for someone much younger. The author writes, "Her head, bald from weeks of chemo, is covered with a soft navy-blue fleece hat. In the absence of hair, her deepset eyes and prominent cheekbones are more pronounced. Around her neck she has loosely tied a silk Hermès scarf" (*Boundaries* 83–84). With this description, readers are sheltered from a full view of the effects of cancer; the inclusion of the Hermès scarf highlights Beatrice's socioeconomic status and the medical treatment that it affords. Though readers likely realize the devastation that cancer can bring, the character's medical treatment shifts the focus to traits such as Beatrice's fabulous bone structure. Here, medical care offers a means of reflection and appraisal; with the absence of hair, Beatrice's features become more pronounced.

As this scene suggests, it is through clothing that Beatrice attempts to downplay the effects of cancer. Perhaps because Beatrice dresses in such vibrant colors, "Anna is reminded of her [mother's] illness" (*Boundaries* 150). "Not a hint of pallor mars her brown skin," but Beatrice's overcompensation ultimately betrays her (*Boundaries* 150). To Anna, everything about her mother's outfit is awkward. As the narrator observes, Beatrice is "wearing a festive fuchsia-pink cotton dress, the fabric too light and too bright for the fall weather" (*Boundaries* 150). Clothing covers and offers momentary escape as the dress "drapes over her body and hides the bandaged wound on her chest" (*Boundaries* 150). Just three days after her surgery, the choice of clothing is nearly successful in bringing Anna to forget what her mother has endured. Though "the color warms her mother's face so convincingly," Anna sees through the façade (*Boundaries* 150). If clothes are the "semiotics of being, the codes by which they position themselves to be understood in the world," as Savory asserts, then Beatrice's choice of dress can be read as a repudiation of illness and the refusal to identify as ill (54). Though Beatrice's clothing was hardly mentioned before her surgery, the brands that she wears and her choice of apparel are centered following her operation. After the surgery, Beatrice attempts to manipulate the codes/clothes to shift attention away from her illness. In the hopes that high-end items such as a Hermès scarf or a bright dress will somehow remind those around her of her socioeconomic status, and thus downplay the importance of the moment, Beatrice attempts to emphasize her privilege as opposed to her medical condition.

Similar to Beatrice's use of clothing as a distraction tactic, prayer offers her a momentary escape. Beatrice's doctor proclaims, "My patients who pray recover faster. Prayer gives them hope, a positive attitude that helps them heal. The ones who don't pray often sink into despair" (*Boundaries* 81). While on the one hand, "Her prayers had not stopped the relentless march of the malignant cells multiplying under her arm and in her breast," near the conclusion of the text the doctor again offers commentary when he tells Anna that her "mother knows better than I do how to heal herself" (*Boundaries* 107, 208). With this line, the author stages a practitioner of Western medicine giving credence to prayer. In doing so, Nunez, through Paul, one of Beatrice's doctors, recognizes the power of faith and outlook in the recovery process. After the success of Beatrice's medical treatment, Paul notes that he has never had a patient "recover so quickly after major surgery" and acknowledges that "the mind is a powerful instrument" (*Boundaries* 245–46).

While at the conclusion of "Lucifer's Shank" Ellie disintegrates into a former version of herself, Beatrice's physiognomy "sags, but it does not crease" (*Boundaries* 156). Beatrice's body is termed "exquisite" regardless of the fact that she "has not denied herself her passion for mangoes or coconut ice cream" (*Boundaries* 157). Despite Beatrice's age, "There are no wrinkles on her back. The skin is smooth, fluid, butterscotch-brown flowing from fleshy shoulders down to a certain defined, if thick, waistline, flaring out to voluptuous hips" (*Boundaries* 156). With perhaps a hyperattention to her "voluptuous hips" and a heightened sense of propriety, Beatrice "had strict rules regarding the extent to which a doctor was allowed to examine her" (*Boundaries* 227). Specifically, her "breasts and the triangle between her thighs were private, off-limits to [doctor] Neil Lee Pak" (*Boundaries* 227). It is only when "the size of her tumor finally terrified her" that Beatrice breaks the culture of silence to seek medical treatment (*Boundaries* 227). Even then, there are rules that govern her medical care. Through descriptions of the cordoned-off female body and Beatrice's reluctance to bare her body, even for medical professionals, the author comments on the compartmentalization of the female form. As Nunez's works attest, physicians as well as the public at large are sometimes comfortable with viewing only what needs to be seen. In respecting the wishes of more modest patients such as Beatrice, the physicians reinforce social mores and favor moral codes over more thorough medical exams. Beatrice's tumor must become oppressively large and intrusive before it is treated; this delay in treatment reflects a larger sociocultural tendency to conveniently ignore our own mortality.

Whereas *Anna In-Between* details Beatrice's active avoidance of medical care, *Boundaries* expands on this elision. For instance, it is noted that "Beatrice Sinclair did not tell her husband that tumors were growing in her breast and under her arm, and even when they bled on her husband's vest that she wore to bed, she kept her silence—though by then she knew he knew" (*Boundaries* 93). John, too, is tight-lipped; he "would wait until she gave him permission before admitting what he knew" (*Boundaries* 93–94). Because Beatrice "belongs to the old school . . . sucking it up is their badge of courage," John elects not to confront or question Beatrice but rather wait until she is ready to share her concerns with him (*Boundaries* 112). In this way, he is rendered complicit in the progression of her disease. More specifically, it is this "learned restraint that allowed [Beatrice] to endure a tumor blooming in her breast" (*Boundaries* 146). Though his restraint is reinforced by the group of women who are afraid to even speak of cancer, it is informed by the fact that Beatrice's mother died from the disease. Nunez writes, "Beatrice Sinclair could not bear to be in the same room with her mother when she was dying of breast cancer. The stench of rotting meat put on her mother's leaking tumor revolted her. For it was the prevailing wisdom then among the women on the island that since cancer eats flesh, it will be satisfied by any flesh, even cow's flesh" (*Boundaries* 147). In contrast to Anna's hesitation to enter the room when her mother wants to show her the tumor for the first time, Beatrice's repugnance is visceral. Likely ineffective, the old wives' tale of putting meat on the site speaks to the hungry, ravenous nature of the disease, a disease so relentless that it pursues human flesh.

PROGNOSIS

Beatrice's breast cancer is surrounded by a sense of shame. This is most notably expressed through Anna. Anna's reaction to her mother's illness is to "[stand] there, minutes passing by as she tried to build a wall around herself, a barrier that would shield her from longing, or perhaps rejection, and would not leave her exposed, vulnerable. It is shame now that seals her lips, shame for the relief she felt" (*Boundaries* 160). Anna avoids confronting what she already knows. She left the island for formal education in the United States, but cultural experience proves ineffective in combating entrenched mores. In recalling this moment, Anna feels shame. Much in the same way that she attempts to freeze time, following her mother's surgery, Anna is "glad for the domestic chatter, glad to put a bandage on the sore that had begun to bleed moments ago" (*Boundaries* 154).

Likely as a result of her travel to the United States, Beatrice's surgery is termed a "success." The first image of Beatrice following her operation is one in which she is "surrounded by all that white, her mother's brown face shines as if bathed in a sort of celestial light. She is bald, there is not a trace of makeup on her face, her skin is slack, the muscles still loose after hours of sedation, but to Anna her mother seems more beautiful than she can remember" (*Boundaries* 99). Much like Ellie's physical transformation at the conclusion of "Lucifer's Shank," Beatrice is framed in a feminine, heavenly light with the contrast of the harsh white hospital linens breathing life into her face. Though she may be bald, she has become more beautiful. For

Beatrice, surgery provides relief and this catharsis is evident on a physical level. Beatrice claims deformity to be her "most personal fear" and worries that the physical reminder of her surgery, her scar, will be repulsive, but John proclaims, "From now on, Beatrice, you and I will have our showers together" (*Boundaries* 100).

The duty to care for Beatrice following surgery lies with Anna; she is advised to change her mother's dressing twice per day. Anna is informed that "there is an intricate web of blood vessels lying beneath the breast. He has sutured them, but fluid and blood sometimes collect beneath the stitches. He has put a drain at the end of the incision. It looks like a straw for drinking soda, and it will drain the excess fluid and blood onto the dressing. So she must change the dressing to prevent infection" (*Boundaries* 144). While the novels detail the "hands off" relationship between mother and daughter, their bond becomes intensely personal following Beatrice's mastectomy. As in Melville's works, disease, and caretaking in particular, strengthens bonds. Much like Ellie and her best friend, Beatrice and Anna were close in a distanced, respectfully intimate way; before her mother's mastectomy, Anna would never have gazed at her mother's breasts, much less touched them. Beatrice's surgery forces Anna to become more comfortable with another form of intimacy, one that is more at ease with the human form. Within a short period of time, their relationship moves from one in which Beatrice shielded her daughter and husband from her disease to a place where her daughter must now "remove the drain the surgeon has inserted at the end of the sutures to release the blood and fluids that have collected there. Her mother must expose her body to her. She must touch her naked skin" (*Boundaries* 154–55). Indeed, it is physical connection, the laying on of hands, that determines Beatrice's recovery. Those hands are not just anyone's, but her daughter's. While on the one hand Anna "is not repelled by blood, or by a leaking wound," she winces at the vision of her mother's bandage, a covering that cannot fully erase the sutures that close "the skin left gaping apart after Dr. Bishop removed her mother's left breast" (*Boundaries* 147,127).

Much like the final view of Ellie after her operation, Beatrice is depicted as "regal." Beatrice's medical treatment leaves her with "no hair on her head, the follicles deadened by the toxins," and ushers in a baldness that becomes "essential to the symmetry of the curves, lines, and planes of her body" (*Boundaries* 157). This image is so arresting that it leaves Anna breathless. While cancer ultimately takes Ellie's life, Beatrice's mastectomy completely eradicates the "insidious" cancer. As Beatrice's physician states, "She has had her miracle. The tumors are gone. She does not think of a future beyond this" (*Boundaries* 200–201). In Nunez's work, cancer can be understood as a facilitator of transformation. While on the one hand disease leaves Beatrice with years in front of her, it has also reshaped her relationships and her understanding of herself. Though she comes to be seen as "regal," she now has no sense of where to go from here. Beatrice is extremely lucky; she will now "live a normal life" (*Boundaries* 245).

Following her medical treatment, Beatrice declares that she wants to go home. "This time she means back to her island, to her own people, her own doctors in her own country," Nunez specifies (*Boundaries* 207). In *Boundaries*, Nunez presents medical treatment as a matter of convenience and ties temporary migration to effective medical care. By placing Paul as Beatrice's primary doctor, Nunez uses someone "familiar" or from "back home" in treatment abroad. To stress, Beatrice's medical treatment, while secured by migration, is eased by Paul's presence. On the whole, *Boundaries* can be read as cautiously optimistic. Melville's "The Sparkling Bitch" and "Lucifer's Shank" illustrate the destruction of physical bodies and Nunez's *Anna In-Between* and *Boundaries* offer a second chance to a woman who ignored the signals her body sent her and deferred medical treatment for two years. While over half a million women worldwide die from breast cancer each year, Beatrice Sinclair is spared.

CHAPTER FIVE

CONSUMING THE CARIBBEAN
Sexuality, Social Norms, and Belonging in *Here Comes the Sun* and *Land of Love and Drowning*

> In its happy tourist avatar, the Caribbean has long figured as the utopian respite from the mechanized, work-driven, capitalistic routines of the overindustrialized world.
>
> —SUPRIYA NAIR

As Angeletta Gourdine asserts in *The Difference Place Makes*, the term "Caribbean" "denotes a specific geographic locale and connotes paradise, relaxation and adventure. Herein the myth of the Caribbean ... is born" (81). Also writing on the constructed image of the Caribbean, Amar Wahab finds that the "trope of paradise is an enduring one that continues to stabilize the Caribbean as a site of consumer fantasy" (29).[1] This chapter investigates how Nicole Dennis-Benn's *Here Comes the Sun* (2016) and Tiphanie Yanique's *Land of Love and Drowning* (2014) undercut the paradise myth through critical representations of tourism, sex tourism, and land development in Jamaica and the Virgin Islands.[2] The works explore the interplay of structural inequalities, foreground the emotional and economic impact of exploitative practices, and question who benefits from the commoditization of land and women's bodies.

The novels point to female sexuality as susceptible to scrutiny while the sex-tourism and land-development industries are largely unregulated. In doing so, the works call attention to the relationship between power, economics, and the surveillance of sexuality. In *Consuming the Caribbean*, Mimi Sheller notes that the Caribbean region has a "deep history of relations of consumption, luxury, and privilege for some" (37). My argument extends Sheller's understanding of the tropical holiday as a "safe new means of consuming the Caribbean environment" by reading the service economies in the novels as a set of consumptive industries that are reliant on consumer fantasies (37).[3] In *Land of Love and Drowning* and *Here Comes the Sun*, development works not to ameliorate poverty, but to serve the interests of the economic elite. While the authors take tourists and developers to task for their destructive conduct, they are careful not to depict residents as victims of Euro-American power. To be clear, the Caribbean "is never a passive landscape only acted upon nor are its residents simply inert victims," as Supriya Nair observes (8).

The hypersexualized image of the Caribbean that the authors engage with relies on an understanding of Caribbean sexuality as excessive, pathological, and unruly. Like the paradise myth that Gourdine identifies, the conception of the Caribbean as an exotic, resource-filled region is grossly inaccurate and has fueled a culture of exploitation. The novels center the space of the beach and the movement to reclaim that space to highlight the consequences of trespass on land and women's bodies. The works illustrate the costs of crossing individual and cultural boundaries, the norms that "make us upstanding citizens" (Amato 223). The women in Yanique and Dennis-Benn's novels resist attempts to control the spaces they inhabit through their own social, political, and aesthetic means. In the texts, environmental devastation parallels the trauma associated with sexual transgression. Eeona, the protagonist of Yanique's novel, copes with the loss of her father, a man who arranged her marriage to end their incestuous relationship, in the space of the newly transferred Virgin Islands. Margot in Dennis-Benn's text is sold into sex work at a young age and later becomes a madam for a hotel developer who razes her town of River Bank. In *Land of Love and Drowning* and *Here Comes the Sun*, the authors use the protagonists' moves away from home, their respective quests for affirmation, to position home as a site of individual and collective trauma.

REGULATING FEMALE SEXUALITY

Yanique's novel, her first full-length fiction work, is set on the islands of St. Thomas, St. Croix, and Anegada. Anegada is especially significant because it is the childhood home of the protagonist's mother and the place that the Spanish named "the drowned land, because it has a history of drowning ships" (Yanique 51). In *Land of Love and Drowning*, Yanique develops a parallel between the regulation of female sexuality and the ownership of land by setting the narrative on the eve of the transfer of the islands from Danish to American rule in 1917. Surveillance over the protagonist's burgeoning sexuality primarily comes via her mother, Antoinette. As discussed in the previous chapters, sexuality frequently operates as a force of regulation that prompts women to cover "that which should not be exposed" (Johnson and Moran 9). One example of Antoinette's attempts to constrain her daughter's sexuality is when she instructs the teenage Eeona to pull her dress down. Antoinette asks Eeona to adjust her dress "so it cover the knees at least.... That is freedom" (Yanique 13). With this exchange, Yanique frames sexuality as a liability by highlighting the fact that women are responsible for controlling visual access to their bodies. Antoinette's instruction is representative of how girls such as Eeona are taught to be embarrassed of their bodies and to be afraid of unwanted attention. For Antoinette, the suppression of female sexual expression affords protection and thus freedom. During the course of the narrative, Eeona learns that her body is not fully hers but is instead subject to "the gaze of others but also to touch and to violence" (Butler, *Undoing Gender* 21).

Eeona's body, though, is not the only one that is subject to observation. In *Land of Love and Drowning*, women are often placed on display for the enjoyment of men, and readers are positioned as witnesses to the enjoyment that men such as Owen Arthur obtain from gazing on women's bodies. The novel opens with a scene of Eeona's father admiring the body of an unnamed girl. The girl is being used in a demonstration of electricity, a parlor trick-like display in which her hair shoots off in all directions with the touch of a vial to her nose. Through the use of a young woman's charged body, Yanique cements the patriarch's status as a "certain kind of man" who admires young girls' bodies (5). Representative of this is when Owen Arthur admits that "the first half of him desired that he had created this little girl. She was a pretty yellow thing. The lower half of him desired the girl. How young could she be?" (Yanique 4–5). Here, Yanique paints Owen Arthur's sexual proclivities as recognizably dangerous. In adopting the voice of a sexual predator, the author simultaneously exotifies and commodifies the girl as a "pretty yellow thing." In this scene, Yanique repeats, but also distinguishes between, two forms of desire; the first use of the term is rooted in reproduction and patriarchal ownership, while the repetition of the term shifts the focus to an inherently sexual meaning. This passage speaks to the liabilities that female sensuality creates, but it also characterizes the father as a potential danger to the unnamed girl. Specifically, the inclusion of the words "little girl" and "desire" acknowledge the girl's youth, and hence the illegality of a sexual relationship with her. The second use of the term "desire" connects male genitalia, vaguely referred to through the phrase "lower half," with the thought of intercourse with the unnamed girl. Interestingly, sex is central in both references; by terming Eeona's father a "certain kind of man," Yanique lays the groundwork for the trauma that follows (5).

Notwithstanding the fact that Owen Arthur's pursuit of censured sexual activity affects his entire family, it is his eldest daughter, Eeona, who bears the brunt of her father's actions. Owen Arthur's obsession with his daughter brings him to collect the "pieces of her hair from the brush and burns them himself, so that no one can steal them and put a curse on her" (Yanique 6). Eeona, a young woman "so beautiful that many call her pure" and her father's firstborn and "only child, thus far, who has survived to life," is groomed for this intimate attachment (Yanique 6). In *The Beauty Myth*, Naomi Wolf comments on the psychological element of female sexuality. Wolf writes, "What little girls learn is not the desire for the other, but the desire to be desired" (126). Wolf's conclusions on desire mirrors Judith Herman and Lisa Hirschman's assertion that "the fairy tale most commonly repeated in Western culture warns girls to expect nothing but abuse from women, and teaches them to look to men for salvation" (1). These claims are important because Eeona's need for salvation renders her susceptible to her father's approach. Owen Arthur's longing to be the sole recipient of his daughter's affection inspires a reciprocal response. Eeona's romantic feelings for her father, admittedly outside the bounds of social norms, are a result of the grooming process.[4] In beginning a sexual relationship with his daughter and treating her more like a mistress than his child, Owen Arthur preys on Eeona's need for validation. Eeona yearns to be claimed, to be desired. In Yanique's novel, attention is conflated with and substituted for affection. Because Eeona's emotional needs are largely unmet, she confuses her father's sexual advances for attention.

Throughout, Yanique centers the importance of purity/virginity. Eeona's parents' obsession with their daughter's sexuality reflects their concern over sexual purity. One example of this is Antoinette's decision that "if Eeona did not pitch away her virginity, for she was a girl too aware of her beauty, they would marry her off early" (Yanique 17). Arguably, Eeona's physical attractiveness is a liability for her. If a "woman's body is an ornamented surface [and] women must make herself 'object and prey' for the man," then Eeona, who is keenly aware of her beauty, can be viewed as a subject positioning herself as an object (Weitz 31, 34). Significantly, the use of the phrase "pitch away" simultaneously positions the daughter as an active agent and interprets her virginity as an asset. Also intriguing is the use of "they"; the inclusion of the pronoun reinforces Antoinette's role in the socialization process. Regardless of the fact that Antoinette plays a rather superficial role in parental decision making, the use of "they," as opposed to "he," stresses her role in reproducing and reinforcing social norms.

In *Land of Love and Drowning*, Yanique stages the incestuous relationship of Owen Arthur Bradshaw and his daughter Eeona against the backdrop of island beaches and within the context of shifting political allegiances. By characterizing the beach as neither land nor sea, public nor private, the text collapses boundaries and questions the line between acceptable and unacceptable sexual expression. The author uses the beach and the politicized reclamation of that space as a means of discussing sexual citizenship and the surveillance of female sexuality. Sexual citizenship, as Diane Richardson lays out, reflects "normative assumptions about sexuality" (211). By situating Owen Arthur's trespass on his daughter's body within the geographic space of the Virgin Islands, Yanique draws the parallel between body sovereignty and land rights as she illustrates the aftermath that results from the rupture of what Carole Pateman terms the "sexual contract."[5] In short, Owen Arthur is unsuccessful in mediating the sexual impulses that drive him to lust for Eeona. These unresolved libidinal impulses cannot be suppressed, which results in a violation of the sexual contract.

In *The Social Construction of Sexuality*, Steven Seidman finds that "sexual behavior that is defined as natural may be celebrated [but that] unnatural desires are condemned and may be harshly punished" (xi). Following Seidman's observation, Owen Arthur's death can be read as closely related to his sexual perversion.[6] Understood thus, it becomes clearer that perhaps the pivotal event of the novel, the patriarch's death, can be read as a suicide. With Owen Arthur's untimely passing, the threat of continued transgression is removed. To explain, the father's death comes the day after he directs Eeona to marry her suitor, Louis, and "go away with him" (Yanique 57). It is not sufficient for Eeona to marry or be "claimed" (legally or sexually) by another man. It is possible that Owen Arthur recognizes that his perverse desire for his daughter requires distance in order to be diverted. Although his death can be interpreted as him having been "called to the island, as though by a siren," an alternative reading infers that he was pushed to the reef by his siren-like daughter and his refusal to let her go (Yanique 59). His inability to pursue a legitimate union with his daughter, "who knew she could sink ships," could be what drove Owen Arthur to crash his ship into a reef near the "drowned land" of Anegada (Yanique 60). That is, he likely dies because he is unable to conform to social norms. While Owen Arthur drowns "for love of [Eeona]," the women he leaves behind must cope with the consequences of his sexual transgressions (Yanique 177).

BLURRED LINES

The author explores the impact of sexual and political power by joining patriarchal and political overreach. Yanique broaches the silence surrounding incest[7] through the vehicle of historical fiction. Although the father figure's demise does not come as a surprise, the consequences of his relationship with Eeona do not become clear until much later in the text. Ketu Katrak's work on female sexuality proves useful in understanding how Eeona is affected by her father's advances. Katrak writes, "In cultures where any talk about female sexuality is repressed and silenced, we need to look more carefully for the relations between 'sexual desire' and 'political power'" (14). In *Land of Love and Drowning*, Owen Arthur emerges as a deeply insecure man who is unable to "bear the thought of his women going on" (Yanique 5). This sense of possession is rendered explicit with the use of the terms "his" and "own" throughout the novel. Also notable is an exchange between father and daughter after an intimate swim. Eeona proclaims, "I love you, Papa" to which he replies, "I love you, my own" (Yanique 42). This is followed by the image of the pair with "wind blowing into [their] sea-wet faces that were pressed cheek to cheek" (Yanique 43). If sexual politics concern the codes that govern moral and sexual behavior, as Saskia Wieringa and Horacio Sívori point out, then the Bradshaw family stands as an example of what happens when social norms collapse (14).

The blurred lines of the relationship between father and daughter bring Eeona to see herself as a young woman who "belonged only to [her] father" (Yanique 42). This sense of belonging transcends death. Several years after her father's passing, Eeona remembers, "I had not wanted to think at all about Owen Arthur having another woman and that woman not being me" (Yanique 65). The lack of proper "claiming," whether from her father or from suitor Louis Moreau, leaves Eeona feeling orphaned; Eeona laments that there is "nothing for which she could say, 'I belong to you'" (Yanique 68). Although there is ambiguity surrounding Owen Arthur and Eeona's sexual relationship, readers learn that he "came to Eeona's room. This was something he had not done since she had left the nursery. This was not a thing that fathers did" (Yanique 57). Moreover, Eeona wonders if her father would "really own her now? With Mama just on the other side of the house? Would he not wait until they could sail away together?" (Yanique 57). In deploying an unnamed narrator to introduce the potential of sexual abuse through terms such as "this" and "thing," linguistic choices similar to the use of "there" to refer to Eeona's genitalia, the author makes it clear that Owen Arthur knowingly defied social convention in his relationship with Eeona. This passage rapidly moves to Eeona's perspective and in the process avoids overidentification with the patriarch. The author's inclusion of "own," likely a thinly veiled reference to sexual intercourse, reiterates the trope of sexual advance and reinforces the extent to which Eeona has been groomed for a romantic relationship with her father. Instead of offering judgment, Yanique highlights Eeona's subservient position by placing her father as the one who would determine when the relationship would be consummated. It is not Eeona who can determine when she will be "owned"; it is "he" who will make that decision. Eeona imagines losing her virginity to her father at the same time that they "sail away."

Apart from the narration of Owen Arthur visiting Eeona's room are several intimate depictions of the two. Eeona relates, "We swam in the sea, nude as the Lord made us. The ship a large shield from prying eyes. I would imagine that it was only we alone in this family" (Yanique 42). With this, Eeona imaginatively erases her mother and sister and views herself as the sole recipient of her father's attention. It is significant that religion is invoked to somewhat normalize the image of father and daughter swimming naked. This reference to a religious figure downplays the biological relationship between the pair, collapses kinship, and stresses divination. The passage shifts when Eeona asks her father if he had ever performed oral sex on her mother. When he responds that he had not, Eeona thinks, "Good, his mouth is mine"; Eeona's sense of satisfaction, a claiming of her own, is dashed when she learns that it was Rebekah, her father's mistress, who introduced Owen Arthur to the practice (Yanique 178).

Throughout, the novel offers a space to consider the repercussions of "unnatural love." Owen Arthur is largely unsuccessful at navigating socially constructed boundaries. This becomes evident when he admits that his bond with Eeona runs counter to social norms. He reflects, "We have always known that this is not the way of a good father or of a good daughter" (Yanique 58). Altogether, Yanique avoids a scathing critique of the patriarch and leaves it up to the reader to evaluate his reasoning. Yanique's use of "good" in opposition to the unarticulated "bad" or "deviant" distributes blame without regard to age, gender, or power dynamics. Consequently, the novel reflects the rhetoric of victim blaming. Perhaps unable to face his perversions, Owen Arthur asks the object of his uninhibited desire to shoulder part of the moral burden. Laurie Vickroy's work on sexual abuse sheds light on the impact of victim blaming. Vickroy explains that "perpetrators promote forgetting and defend themselves through secrecy, silence, denial, rationalizing, and undermining the victim's accusation. In short, they try to define reality counter to victims' experience" (19). Indeed, Owen Arthur endeavors to rationalize his relationship with Eeona; rather than accept this logic, Eeona delivers a wholesale rejection of her father. Her rebuke, offered after she is summarily rejected by him, can be read as an attempt at redirecting shame.[8] Melissa Harris-Perry has cogently argued that "because shame is connected to collective rules and shared expectations, it is a basic tool by which societies create moral order.... Shame makes us view our very selves as malignant" (107, 109). Eeona's response to her father and his death, then, can be viewed as intimately connected to the maintenance of moral order. Instead of admitting that their actions cannot continue, as Owen Arthur points out, Eeona declares, 'Then I wish you would die, Papa. I wish you would just die" (Yanique 58). The outcome of her directive is a "telegram [that] came the following evening: '*Homecoming* wrecked on Anegada reef. Two survivors. Captain not among them'" (Yanique 58).

CLAIMING

In stark contrast to Owen Arthur's sense of shame is his wife's self-assuredness. Antoinette is painted as "wild" and is often admonished for her behavior. For instance, Owen Arthur chastises Antoinette when he tells her that her "influence is causing [Eeona] to have [her] same wildness. She is becoming bold, going beyond herself" (Yanique 15). Given this, it is possible that Owen Arthur began abusing his daughter to "tame" her, to prevent the very self-assurance that Antoinette is known for. The text specifies that Antoinette's condition was a "nervousness brought on by the pregnancies and miscarriages. A woman's wildness" (Yanique 16). The protagonist reflects: "Mama had wild and wandering tendencies.... If a woman was not self-possessed, she was in danger of the wildness" (Yanique 24). In contrast to her mother's "wildness," Eeona craves to be "owned," to transfer responsibility for her wellbeing to someone else. The protagonist remarks on her need for escape following rejection/loss when she admits that "hadn't she, in a wild way, wanted to be stolen?" (Yanique 195). Eeona views herself, and in particular her body, as property that another can easily stake a claim on. In *Land of Love and Drowning*, "wildness" is mediated by external sources, be it developers or patriarchal influence. In evoking questions of ownership and possession, the author highlights the precarious nature of female agency.

Unable to effectively negotiate the events of her adolescence, Eeona seeks to "go where no one would know her history, her losses, and her transgressions" (Yanique 137). In response to her lack of "claiming," she purchases land on the island of St. John and opens an inn; "She owned the inn. . . . She had made her own inheritance. Just so" (Yanique 263). On St. John, Eeona jests about being invisible and wishes that she could "be like a witch flying in the night" (Yanique 252). Speculation about the protagonist mounts when Franky, Eeona's brother-in-law, wonders if she is "one of those women who preferred women" (Yanique 254). Collectively, reactions to the absence of a husband and an inability to successfully procreate reflect the pressure placed on women and the damage that social mores can have on those who cannot or will not conform to norms.[9] Near the conclusion of the text, rumors abound. Eeona is said to have been seen "with her hair flying wings, seen on the road, wandering as though lost" (Yanique 330). Yet another depiction paints her "wandering the roads at night like a ghost. . . . Just last night she *was* a cat with long silver fur in mats and curls" (Yanique 333). More than illustrating what is often identified as a Caribbean hyperactive imagination, Eeona's demeanor points to the tendency to pathologize women who defy social norms. Importantly, such logistical leaps reify the link between hysteria and women. In *Land of Love and Drowning*, Yanique explores the consequences of what society deems "unnatural." An example of this is when Anette, Eeona's sister, wonders if Eeona "had finally gone crazy. No children. No husband. And all that nastiness Mr. Lyte had talked about" (Yanique 333). In this line, Anette's sentiment perpetuates a view of incest as something that the survivor should be ashamed of; in referring to the exchange as "nastiness," Anette, furthers a view of her sister as tainted. This response highlights what happens when there is no outlet to successfully negotiate the effects of abuse.

In the conclusion of the narrative, Eeona finds peace on the island of Anegada, a land that "called Eeona" (Yanique 339). As Lyonel Norman, Antoinette's fiancé (prior to her relationship with Owen Arthur) observes, "People always coming back here trying to find who they belong to" (Yanique 340). Eeona brings closure to her past when she visits the wreckage of her father's ship and "flew, like a witch, above *The Homecoming*" (Yanique 343).

This cathartic event, in which the ship functions as a symbol of collective trauma, draws Eeona from a dissociative-like state. "Eeona awoke. And she was not herself. Not herself at all. She knew where she was. She knew how she had gotten there. She knew she had not made it to touch *The Homecoming*," the narrator recounts (Yanique 344). Significantly, she didn't need to touch the desk to cope with what happened on that ship. "Eeona had never wanted, really, to be anything but her father's daughter" but was unable to cope with the loss of her father or the resulting disintegration of her family structure (Yanique 344). As a whole, the novel deals with secrets and their effects. This is evident when Yanique reveals the double meaning of the protagonist's name. Mr. Lyte, the inn's gardener, explains: "He Own Her. That's the elder daughter. He Own Her because the father hold the girl first.... He ask too much of the girl. He Own. Her turn out witchy" (Yanique 308). In connecting ownership, sexual transgression, and loss, Yanique illustrates the vast effects of personal trauma.[10]

NO TRESPASSING

Paralleling Yanique's discussion of women's bodies and psychological health is the author's treatment of the Caribbean environment. The author expands her investigation into the consequences of patriarchal power with a critical view of beach privatization. In *Land of Love and Drowning*, resistance to beach privatization comes in the form of the BOMB, or the Beach Occupation Movement and Bacchanal.[11] An unnamed narrator relates, "We were marching on the sand and doing wade-ins and soak-ins and—for those who could—swim-ins. Running to the beaches in the middle of the night, past the guards and the dogs" (Yanique 312). Specifically, protesters pretend to be Afro-American tourists by donning hats, cover-ups, sunglasses, and sandals. Once on the beach, the protesters reveal themselves, turn on a radio, scream, "We is the Virgin Islands," rip off their costumes, and run into the water (Yanique 313). This humorously subversive act of announcing themselves and taking back the beach often yielded calls to the police and demonstrators in jail. At the same time, Yanique's inclusion of guards and dogs strips the passage of levity and develops a contentious political atmosphere. Motivated by the contrast between the locals, who are faced with "NO TRESPASSING" signs, and tourists, who are invited onto beaches without passes or permission, protesters combine activism and pleasure by bringing "coolers of rum and Coke" to the beach—hence the term "bacchanal." It is important to note that the events Yanique details are not fiction. "By 1970, only two of the more than fifty beaches on the island of St. Thomas were open to the 'public.' Even though the Open Shorelines Act of 1971 [allowed] public use of the coastal zone . . . , access to that zone to this day is not legally mandated" (Johnston).

In fictionalizing the beach-access movement in the Virgin Islands, Yanique calls the efficacy of public trust doctrine into question. Despite legislation that holds that "certain natural and cultural resources are preserved for public use, and that the government owns and is required to protect and maintain these resources," residents in *Land of Love and Drowning* are often blocked from accessing the island's beaches (Felix 421). According to public trust doctrine, the land above the "mean high-tide land, or dry sand, is often privately owned. . . . As a result of this 'trust,' the public has a right to use the lands and waters [to the land seaward of the line]" (Felix 424). Currently, the US Virgin Islands "upholds the principles of the public trust doctrine through the Open Shorelines Act," which is the same act referenced in the novel (Felix 422). While the act is in place and is enforceable, hotels and property owners often find indirect ways of limiting access. The residents in Yanique's novel, through their protest, fight uncontrolled development and assert that they should have equal access to the shoreline. In 1971, the protest resulted in the creation of an Open Beaches Committee and the Open Shorelines Act. Although the Open Shorelines Act "cemented a right of public use of the coastal zone . . . access to that zone . . . is still not effectively enforced [largely because] . . . there is no specific language [mandating] a right to access these shorelines" (Felix 430, 434).

The BOMB movement, as depicted in Yanique's text, was short-lived. Within one month, the protest was over. The Free Beach Act, officially termed the Virgin Islands Open Shorelines Act, was passed shortly thereafter. When the legislation went into effect, the "last mean hotel and the last stingy family had to take down their PRIVATE signs and remove their chains. [Locals] lay on the beach and felt [their] self-worth rise with the tide" (Yanique 324). This passage is particularly significant because it ties present-day economic disparity to the island's history of imperialism and servitude through the inclusion of the word "chains." While the author artfully connects historic events, the critique of tourism is perhaps more interesting. When discussing life after the BOMB movement, the narrator concludes that the "authenticity, which was really poverty, was pulling in the tourists once again" (Yanique 315). In the end, Yanique's novel calls readers to question whether the destruction of a lighthouse to build a Marriott hotel that will "shine brighter than anything" is worth the cost of a historic landmark (329).

SELLING SEX

As in the Virgin Islands, tourism and sex tourism are multibillion-dollar industries in Jamaica. Ibrahim Ajagunna and Ann Crick observe that sex tourism functions as a separate economic sector and is now a "common practice in many Caribbean Islands" (182). The easy assertion may be that tourism is responsible for the rise in sex tourism. Although the growth of mass-market tourism can fuel sex tourism, it is important not to conflate the industries. The narrative reveals that the sex-tourism industry in Jamaica relies on exoticism and a hypersexualized view of women's bodies. Belinda Edmondson, among others, has linked the public image of Caribbean women with various forms of nationalism. For the working-class characters in Dennis-Benn's text, Jamaica "is no paradise" (44). While islands may be associated with tropical fecundity, for residents such as Margot, Jamaica is not a utopia. As an employee at an all-inclusive resort that relies on the four Ss (sea, sun, sand, and sex), or the key elements that construct the Caribbean picturesque, the protagonist, Margot, is one of many in "a country where they [the help] are as important as washed-up seaweed" (Dennis-Benn 9). This conception of identity recalls European ideas regarding the treatment of colonial lands as places as brimming with limitless resources. As Graham Huggan and Helen Tiffin point out, "Settlers set about rendering them [the colonies] productive and profitable through imported methods rather than by accommodating them to local circumstances" (8). Also addressing how the Caribbean region has been exploited, Kamala Kempadoo explains that "territories that once served as sex havens for colonial elite are today frequented by sex tourists, and several of the island economies now depend upon the region's racialized [and] sexualized image" (1). In *Here Comes the Sun*, Dennis-Benn details how tourists' conceptions of Caribbean women translate into profit for the protagonist, Margot, and her boss, Alphonso Wellington.

In her debut novel, Dennis-Benn exposes the hypocritical surveillance of female sexuality. In the work, heterosexual sex (including prostitution) is permissible while the stigma against homosexual intimacy functions as a site of social control and an important element of state power. Sex work offers economic and psychic escape for the protagonist, but comes at a cost. Although Margot gains social and economic mobility as a result of her involvement with sex work, that lifestyle is possible because she exploits others, most notably by recruiting and training young women to be sex workers and by tricking her girlfriend into abandoning her land to make way for a resort. In *Here Comes the Sun*, Dennis-Benn contrasts the normalization of exploitative practices such as prostitution with the demonization of same-sex intimacy to comment on the ramifications of heteronormativity in Jamaica.[12] By developing an atmosphere that combines pious devotion, exclusion, and the commodification of women, the author calls attention to the relationship between power, economics, and the surveillance of sexuality. Dennis-Benn inverts the colonial gaze and centers the environmental implications of hotel development. The novel calls readers to meditate on the racial, sexual, and economic complexities of Jamaica's service economies. Dennis-Benn utilizes Margot's move to a beachfront villa and the subsequent eviction of River Bank's residents to position the town as a site of personal and environmental loss.

The author deploys the protagonist as a touchstone for the emotional implications of sex tourism and land development. As Dennis-Benn reveals, Margot's "real job" is to provide sexual services to vacationers; she later trains and supervises a group of women who service hotel guests. Each night, "She goes to the employee restroom to freshen up . . . and powder her face before sauntering to the client's room. . . . She doesn't see it as demeaning. She sees it as merely satisfying the curiosity of foreigners; foreigners who pay her good money to be their personal tour guide on the island of her body" (Dennis-Benn 10). Here, the "tour metaphor" affords a reexamination of the long-standing commodification of Caribbean women's bodies and renders questionable the intentions of unnamed foreigners. Notably, the use of the term "curiosity" reinforces gender, racial, and class division and implies that a process of self-relationing is occurring. In the narrative, tourists' curiosity is often fed by racist ideology and stereotypical images of Caribbean women. It is implied that the clients are curious about black and brown women's bodies, curious about what "exotic women" are like as lovers. They pay to satisfy this curiosity. At the resort that Dennis-Benn constructs, a space that was redecorated to remove the "vibrant colors, palm trees, and artwork by Jamaican artists," sex tourism is socially normalized (Dennis-Benn 47). The author writes, "Each man has a girl or two—local brown girls . . . [who] sit around the men like decorative flowers, pretending to listen to the conversation as the men absently stroke their bony thighs" (Dennis-Benn 137–38). In this way, then, the women function as props, ornamented bodies that are positioned just so. By staging these interactions within an environment that reimagines Europe and diminishes the Afro-Caribbean environment, the author calls attention to the impact of appropriation and erasure in Jamaica.

It is evident that Palm Star Resort privileges the economic and political interests of the West. The hotel operates as a place of refuge and exploration for vacationers, but for the protagonist, the resort's gate sharply divides the highly cultivated property from her "shabby neighborhood" in the town of River Bank, a former fishing village that lost its industry to construction and drought (Dennis-Benn 9). Within Margot's community, a place that becomes a site for mapping power, sex work is stigmatized and is viewed as morally corrupt. Although Margot fears judgment from her community and largely succeeds in keeping her source of supplemental income under wraps, sex work affords her a "deep calm, a refuge in which she hides" (Dennis-Benn 59). Amidst a homophobic environment, Margot, a lesbian who is not yet out to her family, is intimate with male clients to support her sister's education. The protagonist's involvement with sex work offers financial gain as well as self-empowerment, and the racial-sexual economy serves as an area for self-definition. In River Bank, Margot navigates multiple subject positions. According to Lynda Johnston and Gill Valentine, "'home' is one site where our identities are performed and come under surveillance and where we struggle to reconcile conflicting and contradictory performances of the self" (111). In River Bank, Margot must evade judging glances, but within the confines of the resort, she enjoys the fact that men become "unquestioning and generous as children, even protective" when around her; her body yields power and she deploys her body's erotic potential (Dennis-Benn 43). For Margot, her clients offer an acceptance that is missing elsewhere. The clients' protectiveness works to combat feelings of childhood betrayal, the most notable of which was when her mother sold her into sex work. It is also possible that performing heterosexuality affords a brief respite from the pressures of being gay in Jamaica. It is by engaging in heterosexual relations that Margot can imagine herself as a woman whose sexual preferences do not need to be "fixed."

In the single depiction of Margot's sexual relations with clients, she draws on her relationship with Verdene, her lover, to navigate a sexual encounter with a client named Horace. While with Horace, the protagonist pictures Verdene's "feminine lips parting, hungry for more than Margot's body" (Dennis-Benn 60). If the body is a "key site in the exercise of gender and racial domination and resistance," as Sheller finds, then Margot's imagined encounter with Verdene pushes back against the state regulation of homosexual activity and operates as an invisible but significant form of resistance (224–25). Margot is drawn to Verdene because she understands her true nature; Verdene sees "not her figure or the nakedness she so willingly offers to strangers, but something else—something fragile, raw, defenseless" (Dennis-Benn 16). In transposing Horace's and Verdene's eyes, Margot imaginatively remains true to Verdene while intimate with Horace. The phrase "hungry for more than Margot's body," in particular, reinforces the idea that Margot craves an emotional connection. Dennis-Benn emphasizes the protagonist's embodied negotiation of power when Margot sets the terms for the sexual-economic transaction. Although Horace justifies his infidelity to his wife by convincing himself that he is "saving" Margot, the protagonist rejects this promise (Dennis-Benn 61). With this, Dennis-Benn develops a character who pushes back against such "generosity" and reinforces boundaries for herself. Margot takes steps to retain power; she declines offers to be "saved" because that response is what "keeps them coming back" (Dennis-Benn 61).

THE BOSS LADY IN CHARGE

Along with servicing tourists, Margot has a long-standing relationship with Alphonso, her supervisor and the white Jamaican owner of Palm Star Resort. Margot's involvement in sex work shifts when Alphonso approaches her with a business proposition. In this pivotal scene, Alphonso says, "The two of us can profit from this. You give me fifty percent of your profit and I make you into a wealthy woman.... We'll sell sex. Lots of it.... You will recruit and train girls you see fit for the business. You'll be the boss lady in charge" (Dennis-Benn 141). In this line, Alphonso positions himself as a partner in selling sex (via the use of "we"); yet the inclusion of "you give me" and "I make you" renders the nature of the arrangement explicit. The use of "make you," in particular, reconstitutes Alphonso's understanding of the relationship. To be clear, the issue is not Margot's pursuit of economic gain, but Alphonso's focus on acquisition and his manipulation of the unequal power dynamic that shapes tourism and sex tourism in Jamaica. The moniker "boss lady," in particular, points to the power differential between the two in that Alphonso likely bestows the nickname to encourage Margot's cooperation. Over the course of the narrative, Dennis-Benn suggests that the exertion of influence is a nuanced process; as revealed, Margot is involved in relations of domination as well as subordination. Throughout the text, Margot functions as a sexual agent who shapes and is shaped by the sexual-economic industry. While Alphonso certainly exploits Margot for his own gain, the protagonist also commands by engineering relationships of dependence.

As the "boss lady in charge," to use Alphonso's term, Margot deploys psychological tactics to spur demand; she exerts power by controlling the availability of the "island girls." Specifically, the protagonist renders clients "helpless" when she "tells them that a particular girl they requested isn't available. No one has ever made them feel so dependent" (Dennis-Benn 149). Margot plays on the clients' racialized sexual fantasies and exerts influence by manipulating power dynamics via the law of supply and demand. In terming the women that Margot supervises as "girls" and the clients as "dependent," Dennis-Benn emphasizes the protagonist's role in arranging paid sexual encounters. Both parties, interestingly, are reliant on Margot to satisfy their sexual or financial needs. The clients who visit "Margot's girls" "exit the hotel with long, conquering strides, whistling softly through the lobby. Days later they might return for another round, another hour with an island girl" (Dennis-Benn 149). The terms "conquering strides," "round," and "island girl" are striking. The young women, between the ages of sixteen and twenty-five, are not in a position of power relative to Margot and especially not to their clients; this is made explicit with the use of the word "conquering." In referring to an intimate encounter as a "round," which evokes alcohol and sports imagery, the author emphasizes clients' casual attitudes toward sex and sex work. This approach, rendered potentially problematic by the fact that underage women are involved, is made evident by euphemisms such as "banana" for oral sex and "sundae" for a kinky sex act (Dennis-Benn 10).

In *Here Comes the Sun*, Margot operates as both a pawn and an influencer. The protagonist functions as a madam for the women she trains. She "feeds them, dresses them, teaches them how to carry themselves among moneyed men" but in the next breath reminds them that they are worthless and disposable (Dennis-Benn 145). As Judith Butler states in *Gender Trouble*, "Sexuality is always situated within matrices of power"; this relationship certainly rings true in the text (123). Though Margot is largely in control of the young women, she is ultimately under Alphonso's thumb. Alphonso pursues financial opportunity with dispossession as the primary consequence of his actions. He is focused on acquisition and utility; his intervention in River Bank relies on taking advantage of the resources at his disposal. In short, Dennis-Benn places Alphonso at the center of this microcosm of the sex-tourism industry. Under his plan, Margot becomes known as the "biggest pimp on di North Coast," the individual who will manage the "hotel dey destroying River Bank to build" (Dennis-Benn 321). Through the character of a "boss lady" who was sold into sex work at the age of fourteen, Dennis-Benn highlights the traumatic and cyclical impact of sex tourism on vulnerable populations. In focusing on Margot's influence on the young women under her supervision, the novel largely omits reflection from the protagonist. Instead, the most notable marker of how sex tourism shapes Margot is the disintegration of her romantic relationship with Verdene.

A LOSS OF REFUGE

Dennis-Benn's narrative supports Seidman's observation regarding unnatural sexual desires. In the novel, female sexuality is policed through a combination of "rules, norms, laws, and structures of inequality" (Sheller 277). In particular, the author develops the character of Verdene Moore to explore the vilification of homosexuality and position same-sex love as something to be condemned. Readers are introduced to Verdene by way of Thandi, Margot's younger sister. Thandi grew up hearing that Verdene "lures little girls to her house with guineps so she can feel them up. . . . Verdene Moore is the Antichrist . . . the witch who practices obscene things too ungodly to even think about" (Dennis-Benn 28). Here and throughout, Verdene is depicted as a predator to be feared; indeed, it is her homosexuality that emboldens her neighbors to imagine predatory encounters. Community members reinforce heteronormativity when they indirectly address Verdene's sexuality by deeming her a threat to "little girls." A number of individuals suspect that Verdene is a lesbian and invent rumors to drive her into exile. In equating Verdene with the Antichrist, residents absolve themselves of any responsibility to be civil to her and evoke religion to vilify homosexuality; her neighbors understand same-sex intimacy as "obscene" and "ungodly" and collectively police same-sex intimate relations. In the environment that Dennis-Benn develops, non-procreative sexual intimacy is sanctioned while the sexual servicing of tourists is conveniently ignored. Women who are read as homosexual face exclusion and violence from their community while sex work, though stigmatized, continues in the confines of the resort. The contradictory restriction of sexuality, as Michel Foucault concludes, supports the state's investment in procreation and is central to the exercise of state power. In *The History of Sexuality*, Foucault finds that bio-power, or the state's regulatory management of its population, operates as "factors of segregation and social hierarchization" that reinforce relations of domination (141).

The social norms surrounding sexuality abrade feelings of belonging for the protagonist and her girlfriend. The author describes the emotional consequences of exile by developing characters who are marginalized by their community. For Margot, her community's adherence to moral order brings her to imagine her own paradise. Margot dreams of leaving Jamaica. Specifically, she longs to "get as far as possible . . . maybe America, England, or someplace where she can reinvent herself. Become someone new and uninhibited; a place where she can indulge the desires she has resisted for so long" (Dennis-Benn 14). As a result of rampant homophobia, Margot cannot label her bond with Verdene; she cannot "see herself this way" (Dennis-Benn 65). Instead, Margot terms her attraction to women as "this." Margot cannot be openly intimate with Verdene in Jamaica and views migration as a means of regeneration and self-identification in a more accepting environment. By repeating the term "uninhibited," used previously when describing Margot's behavior with clients, Dennis-Benn recalls how tourists can be "uninhibited" when away from home and stages a fantasy respite for the protagonist. In this imagined reverse migration, the author links location with feelings of belonging and counters the nation's picturesque image with an alternative paradise. This conception, perhaps problematically, projects the romanticization of ideal places on an unfamiliar environment and shifts the image of paradise from Jamaica to England and the United States.

Because Margot struggles to be sexually intimate with Verdene while in River Bank, she dreams of moving to a more accepting environment. "Her mind races ahead to the possibility of leaving River Bank for a nice beachfront villa in the quiet, gated community of Lagoons—a place far from River Bank where Margot could give freely of herself, comforted by the cool indifference of wealthy expats from Europe and America. It would be like living in another country," Dennis-Benn writes (75–76). This passage introduces the possibility of remaining in Jamaica; herein, the phrase "cool indifference of wealthy expats" stands in for terms such as "progressive" and "liberal." With this, the author positions the expats' antipathy to homosexuality as an antidote to local homophobia. Similar to the fenced-in nature of Palm Star Resort, a space that functions as an invented site/sight of discovery for tourists, the remote place that the protagonist imagines would allow the couple to live "without the neck strain from looking over their shoulders" (Dennis-Benn 76). In other words, Dennis-Benn calls attention to the alienation inherent in all-inclusive resorts by replicating the environment in a residential setting. Through the protagonist, who craves the presence of "indifferent" expats, the author highlights the impact of regulating sexuality. Although the character dreams of life with Verdene in a beachfront villa away from prying eyes, that way of life is replaced with "an office with good air-conditioning, a chair that adjusts to her back as though it is made for her, a mahogany desk with her name on it, a better view of the beach, the ability to slip out of her shoes and wiggle her toes, and a door she can keep locked" (Dennis-Benn 286). While Margot's office affords refuge from direct involvement with sex work, it cannot fully eradicate the reminders of River Bank.

Michelle Balaev's work on the relationship between individual trauma and cultural forces sheds light on how trauma operates in the text. Balaev finds that "the trick of trauma in fiction is that the individual protagonist functions to express a unique personal traumatic experience, yet, the protagonist also functions to represent and convey an event that was experienced by a group of people" (155). Following Balaev's claim, Margot's resulting numbness can be read as both her experience and as representative of one of the many ways that survivors can respond to trauma. Margot remains haunted by the "memory of what her mother had done to her" (Dennis-Benn 15). As previously mentioned, Dolores sold fourteen-year-old Margot's virginity to an unnamed cruise passenger for six hundred dollars to "fix her." Sheller's work on sexual citizenship in the Caribbean considers the relationship between sexual surveillance and the state. Sheller observes that the "desire to constrain women's eroticism thus concerns both eradicating nonreproductive queer sexualities *and* constraining the over-reproduction of heterosexualities of the working class" (240). Likewise, Richardson argues that "hegemonic forms of heterosexuality underpin constructions of citizenship" (212). Dolores's quest to eradicate her daughter's homosexuality, then, can be read as rooted in her adherence to the social norms that condemn same-sex love and her understanding of sexual citizenship in Jamaica as reliant on heterosexuality.[13] Dolores attempts to exorcise the "devil" in Margot by rendering heterosexuality compulsory. She rationalizes the sale of her daughter's virginity as being the "only way dat [she] could save [Margot] from [her] ways" (Dennis-Benn 261). Similar to Margot's description of her attraction to women as "this," the use of "ways" deploys euphemism to emphasize Dolores's evasion of her daughter's sexuality. For Margot, the trauma of sexual exploitation leaves her emotionally "sick." In *Here Comes the Sun*, Dennis-Benn uses Margot's experience with sexual exploitation and exclusion to examine the upshot of regulating female sexuality.

If the trauma novel "explores the effects of suffering on the individual and community in terms of the character's relation to place," as Balaev claims, then the collective loss of land for River Bank residents places Margot's individual trauma in a larger cultural context that reads trauma as connected to the tension between capitalism and relationships (160). Like Dolores, the developers value income over people. The town of River Bank, as a result of hotel development, is transformed from a place of individual suffering into one of collective loss and upheaval. If the landscape is a "referent for the individual's sense of self or identity," then the waterfront area, the contact zone between residents and tourists and the location where Dolores sold Margot into prostitution, can be read as a metaphor for Margot's struggle with same-sex intimacy (Balaev 161). That is, the waterfront can be interpreted as a site where the struggle for money as well as sexuality is constantly negotiated but never resolved. The annexation and subsequent demolition of River Bank homesites, occasioned by the hotel development project that Margot is involved with, is symbolic of the protagonist's shift to an indirect involvement with sex work. In situating the sale of Margot's virginity in River Bank, Dennis-Benn connects the town with individual suffering. It is perhaps because of this linkage that Margot is more willing to see the town demolished and repurposed. With the character of Margot, Dennis-Benn situates sexual exploitation and environmental devastation as parallel forces of destruction. The author positions land development as a potentially traumatic process, one that, for Margot, comes with mobility, but results in displacement for the collective. In essence, Margot and Verdene's exile precedes the mass eviction of their neighbors. By relocating the protagonist, the author can more fully explore the collective suffering that comes when River Bank is transformed into a space for touristic consumption.

THE EXPANSION OF MASS TOURISM

In situating the reader as both a literary tourist and a potential critic of the implications of the tourism industry, the novel harkens back to Jamaica Kincaid's *A Small Place*. Like Kincaid's text, a work that presents a "sustained assault on Europeans' and North Americans' privileged place within the global postcolonial economy," *Here Comes the Sun* sheds light on Jamaica's economic divide and the exploitative practices of the country's economic elite (Huggan and Tiffin 76). At the heart of Dennis-Benn's novel is a critical discussion of tourism that recalls the anticolonial movement in Caribbean literature. Like Kincaid, Dennis-Benn suggests that the "battle is not against development or tourism as intrinsically harmful processes and activities, but rather against the often flagrant human and environmental abuses that continue to be practiced in their cause" (Huggan and Tiffin 79). While tourism is "one of the most important economic sectors for many countries in the Caribbean," studies indicate that tourism has vast social and psychological consequences for residents (Thomas-Hope and Jardine-Comrie 94, 97). Although the hotel industry "requires an endless supply of 'pristine' beaches, 'untouched' coves, and 'emerald' pools, many islands struggle with the water and sewage demands of the hotel industry, and sewage is returned to the same sea in which guests swim" (Sheller 68). The growth of tourism also has implications for natural resources and local economies in that most of the income generated by guests never reaches residents. Although a number of scholars recognize that tourism can be positive for communities if their needs are considered, this is not the case for the residents of River Bank.

Scholars including Edouard Glissant have recognized the language of landscape as a transformative force in the Caribbean. If control of the Jamaican landscape can be read as a language of its own, then the loss of beach access that occurs when resorts such as Palm Star are built stresses how the asymmetrical power relations at play drastically alter the function of the existing landscape. In *Colonial Inventions*, Wahab reads landscape as history and a "way of European self-relationing, between the West and its other" (13). Although his work focuses on how Afro-Trinidadians inhabit the landscape of Trinidad, the concept of self-relationing is woven throughout Dennis-Benn's text. Wahab's study relies on the assumption that "colonial discourse is not given but constructed, is dynamic rather than static and concerns the constant interplay between sites of anxiety and sites of seeming repetition" (16). *Here Comes the Sun* focuses on how hotel development threatens the community of River Bank and denaturalizes the landscape while renaturalizing the island as a space of paradise. The work reimagines the colonial encounter by replacing colonists with developers who partner with lawyers to evacuate residents. River Bank, then, is turned into a site of anxiety, a place where racial and economic tensions play out while the trauma generated by a range of exploitative practices is replicated. Importantly, the hotels that line the coastline, largely indistinguishable from one another, become spaces for tourists to understand their position relative to the "other" and for residents to understand their place.

Dennis-Benn problematizes the impact of mass tourism and the use of development as social control. We would be remiss to forget that "at the center of Jamaica's ethnic and political complexity is race . . . the social and economic division between mostly white 'haves' and mostly black 'have-nots' runs deep"; this is reflected in the fictional resort at the center of the novel (Torregrosa). The resort property stands in for a host of projects dotting Jamaica's coastline. Hotels like Palm Star Resort attempt to bring "order" to the landscape by visually and geographically appropriating the land of non-European peoples and shaping the identity of the surrounding environment. In the novel, tourists "dress like they're going on safari, especially the men, with their clogs, khaki apparel, and binocular-looking cameras" (Dennis-Benn 17). It is not evident who/what tourists are photographing with their telephoto lenses; they eat "fried fish . . . , their backs, shoulders, and faces red from sunburn, their tour buses parked out front" (Dennis-Benn 106). Overall, the author depicts tourists who do not fit in; their pale skin cannot withstand the harsh rays of the Caribbean sun. They come to document (through photos) and to be chauffeured from stop to stop along a tightly controlled itinerary. They misunderstand the culture in that their dress is more at home on an African safari than in the Caribbean. It is clear that readers are not meant to identify with the tourists but, like imagined locals, to laugh at the tourists' dress, behavior, and lack of belonging. In passages such as this, Dennis-Benn destabilizes the imperial gaze to position tourists as objects for readers' amusement. If tourism "can be understood as a form of embodied encounter between foreign travelers and local people that involves corporeal relations of unequal power," as Sheller finds, then Dennis-Benn's use of the counter-gaze is particularly significant (210). The author inscribes tourists with potentially laughable qualities to question the hierarchy of relations that situates the tourist as viewer and resident as object of that gaze. In calling on touristic relations of looking, Dennis-Benn foregrounds the island's occupants and pushes back against a picturesque view of Jamaica.

The text reveals how Jamaican women are sexualized and othered in relation to white, foreign tourists and counters that image with an exacting view of tourists and tourism. At hotels such as Palm Star Resort, Jamaican chefs are fired and foreign ones are hired because "tourists want to eat their own food on the island. They don't come to eat Jamaican food wid all dat spice" (Dennis-Benn 111). Palm Star Resort, a manufactured space that emphasizes cultural and economic differences, is built on a former plantation property. If landscape can be read as history, as Wahab calls for, then it is revealing that Dennis-Benn stages the repurposing of a site of oppression with the construction of a site that perpetuates exploitation. The resort affords vacationers time to "lie flat on their backs and bellies in the bright sun while maids dash in and out of rooms with mops and linens" (Dennis-Benn 285). To stress, the state of relaxation that tourists enjoy is dependent on the exploitation and near invisibility of lower-level workers. Palm Star Resort, while fictional, is an example of how all-inclusives delimit cultural exchange and are instead "built around security [wherein] the guests arrive and they are on property for most of their stay" (A. Hall 62). By situating the narrative at a resort and depicting touristic encounters from the perspective of locals, the author levels a critique against neocolonialism and external (often white) influence in the Caribbean. Here and throughout, the author pushes back against the trope of the "lazy native" by centering the labor of working-class Jamaicans.

LAND DEVELOPMENT

In addition to zeroing in on the cultural impact of tourism, Dennis-Benn showcases the environmental implications of hotel development and uses the destruction of the natural environment as a signal for cultural loss. A number of scholars have highlighted the connection between the Western discourse of nature and the history of empire, and landscape can be read as an instrument of power and a "cultural image that structures or symbolizes surroundings" (Daniels and Cosgrove 1). If land is understood as a site of dignity, as Frantz Fanon claims, then the question becomes whose dignity is being upheld in River Bank. Palm Star Resort exists because the Wellington family, originally from Canada, arrived in Jamaica after Alphonso's father "fell in love with the country, and stayed" (Dennis-Benn 108). By crafting a hotelier who is a second-generation immigrant, the author calls attention to the economic division on the island and the privilege of a family who had the means to relocate out of attraction to a foreign land. The Wellington family's involvement with development attempts to control the landscape and forcefully removes residents from their land. It can be argued that Dennis-Benn narrates this separation to highlight the connection between colonialism's history of "forced migration, suffering, and human violence" and development practices that fail to center residents (Handley and DeLoughrey 4). The forced migration of residents becomes clear when they are met with "no trespassing" signs. Dennis-Benn sets the scene: "The construction workers with their tools aren't on site today. There is a sign that reads NO TRESPASSING on the beach. . . . The hotels are building along the coastlines. Slowly but surely they are coming, like a dark sea" (120). In this passage, residents are painted as "trespassers" who are denied access to the coast. In depicting the sprawl of resorts as an invading "dark sea," which can be read as a play on the loss of coastline access and the denaturalization of the landscape, the author emphasizes class and racial division between those who have access to the beach and those who do not.

The repercussions for residents extends beyond the loss of beach access. The narrator reflects, "Little Bay, which used to be two towns over from River Bank, was the first to go. Just five years ago the people of Little Bay left in droves, forced out of their homes and into the streets" (Dennis-Benn 120). With little regard for the families that live there, the developers, who used to "wait for landslides and other natural disasters to do their dirty work," turn to force to clear entire towns (Dennis-Benn 120). By repeating the term "dirty work," also used when discussing Margot's occupation, Dennis-Benn questions who is really engaging in unsavory practices. In repeating the term, the author sheds light on the emotional and cultural costs of development. In the above passage, locals are represented collectively, perhaps to illustrate how residents and developers function as differentially empowered groups. Residents resist through physical force by "blocking roads with planks and tires and burning them" and steal construction materials "to rebuild homes in other places" (Dennis-Benn 120). In short, Dennis-Benn includes examples of resistance to restore the dignity of displaced characters and to recall the historic struggle for land and resources in the Caribbean.

The town of River Bank functions as a socially constructed space where competing practices play out. Developers bemoan the difficulties of extracting people from their homes and seek a government contract to enforce their commands. The construction equipment wastes away in the sun, battered by the elements; the natural environment rejects those who attempt to unlawfully exercise power. Despite residents' assault on the construction tools, the bulldozers appear overnight; "They stand in place like resting mammoths, their blades like curved tusks. It's as though they landed from the sky or were washed ashore. One by one they begin to knock down trees in the cove and along the river. They also take a chunk of the hill, cutting down the trees that cradle the limestone, which they chip away" (Dennis-Benn 289). In this passage, the bulldozers function as alien figures that systematically erode the landscape. The bulldozers, like the tourists, do not belong. Perhaps an ironic representation of the hordes of tourists who invade the island's beaches, the bulldozers remove the natural defenses of protected spaces. They destroy the environment, lacking drivers, almost as if in a science fiction novel. In short, the bulldozers represent the way that those in charge (here the developers, and most notably, Alphonso Wellington), relieve themselves of responsibility. The bulldozers give those in power a way "out" by partially alleviating their discomfort. Like Alphonso, who mediates his relationship with sex workers by installing Margot as their supervisor, the developers are not directly operating the bulldozers. Instead, they can point to foreign workers as the catalyst of destruction. In both cases, it is rich white men who act exploitatively and damagingly. Men such as Alphonso, who effectively annexes the town of River Bank, fail to take responsibility for the effects of their actions. Their deeds reference the region's colonial history and reimagine resistance to such behavior.

In the novel, the primary consequences of hotel development are environmental destruction and the displacement of residents. The narrator reveals that "the men fold the earth. . . . Bits and pieces of rock scatter as trees are uprooted. When they collapse, the earth shakes. . . . The clouds gather together, and the sun stands still and watches her world crumble" (Dennis-Benn 289–90). In contrast to the previously examined passage, the link between man and environmental destruction is clearly delineated. The men operating the machinery act as omnipotent figures who lay waste to the landscape. It is worth noting that Dennis-Benn specifies that it is men, rather than machines, who "fold the earth." When the destruction of their homes becomes imminent, "People begin to snatch their things from their shacks, forced into the unknown. . . . Those shacks are marked to be destroyed" (Dennis-Benn 290). What is intriguing, though, is the force that stops the bulldozers. The construction workers notice a woman's wild hand gestures, perhaps directing them to stop, and read her as an obeah woman at the exact moment that the earth begins to tremble. As a result, "The men clutched their helmets and searched for safety. They ran for cover, diving behind bushes and under sheets of zinc. . . . Later it was reported that what they had experienced was an earthquake. They decided to halt the construction until a later date" (Dennis-Benn 290). Here, the author stages the woman's presumed association with obeah as the momentary counter to the razing of the landscape. The bulldozers, left in place, serve as a warning with their "engines baring their teeth like a threat" (Dennis-Benn 290). The developers deploy machinery as a symbol of displacement; the "teeth" of the machines are visible for all to see. Much like the yellow tape all over town, the static bulldozers serve as a warning that "in a matter of weeks, River Bank will be no more" (Dennis-Benn 290).

In *Land of Love and Drowning* and *Here Comes the Sun*, Yanique and Dennis-Benn foreground extractive practices to challenge imperialist modes of dominance and shift representations of the Caribbean away from stereotypical depictions of paradise. In both works, ownership of land and bodies is problematic and is frequently tied to social norms. For the women in these works, traditional gender roles are imposed, transgressive sexual expression is punished via exclusion or violence, and purity can be "plucked like a blossoming hibiscus before its time" (Dennis-Benn 96). The International Monetary Fund recognizes that "it is common for only 20 percent of revenue to be returned to the local economy" in all-inclusive Caribbean hotels; the works, therefore, can be read as a counter to the economic and environmental realities of mass tourism ("Caribbean Cruises Leave"). With their novels, Yanique and Dennis-Benn call the ethics of development into question.

In painting residents as participants in as well as recipients of exploitative practices, the authors disrupt the colonizer/colonized binary to complicate understandings of intersecting systems of oppression. Margot, who stands at the top of the hill, hires employees to populate her property because she cannot stand living alone. Like Owen Arthur, her sexual needs cannot be satisfied; she "lives from one orgasm to the next," missing Verdene but unwilling to reconnect (Dennis-Benn 334). *Here Comes the Sun* concludes with these lines: "Everything glitters in the new sunlight, just like Margot had always thought it would. Except for her lone, grainy figure on the water's surface, dark in the face of the sun" (Dennis-Benn 345). Margot, as a "pimp" as well as a lesbian, transgresses social norms and defies the heteropatriarchy, the combination of heterosexism and patriarchy that privileges the heterosexual and masculine. Less successful in flaunting social mores is Owen Arthur, a man who is ruled by paraphilic desire and whose actions have profound implications.

In the works, citizenship is associated with normative understandings of sexuality, and transgressing entrenched notions results in exile, loss, and violence for the protagonists and their families. The protagonists, whose parental figures both attempt to dictate their sexual choices, ultimately pursue seclusion to escape continued reprobation. The works detail the consequences of transgressing sexual norms and situate the environment as a symbol for challenges to the protagonists' physical and emotional wellbeing. The authors situate bodies as well as landscapes as sites of politicized struggle. Interestingly, it is at home where the characters come under surveillance; the characters' moves away from home, then, can be read as a rejection of the judgment and exclusion they face from their neighbors. In highlighting the impact of sexual surveillance and the consumptive nature of Caribbean service economies, the authors counter the tourist avatar image that Nair references. Collectively, Yanique and Dennis-Benn's novels position Jamaica and the Virgin Islands as places of false refuge for tourists and spaces of exploitation for residents.

EPILOGUE

In *Homemaking*, Fiona Barnes and Catherine Wiley assert that "women write in order to negotiate the tensions between definitions of home as a material space and home as an ideal place" (xix). As the works discussed illustrate, the writing and rewriting of home is often a journey in itself, a way of making sense of personal and inherited histories. For the characters, home is steeped with contradiction and can be a site of great tension. In many of the texts, home operates as a place of oppression as well as subversion. The realities of the characters' lives counter a view of home as a place of freedom and security, and it is the act of flight that underscores the connection between trauma, migration, and social norms. The characters' embodied and ideological transgressions in response to social convention render them exiles in or outside their homelands. As a result, the characters embrace change and pursue adaptive solutions to preserve selfhood in the face of violence, illness, and exclusion. These forces propel the characters' migration, but trauma and shame do not define the narratives; rather, the protagonists' navigation of trauma, oftentimes through dissociation and flight, foregrounds the emotional work that underlies and often precedes emigration. The authors position the characters' homelands as spaces of individual and collective trauma and situate migration as the force that facilitates the protagonists' homecoming. The works showcase women responding to challenges to safety with moves toward autonomy and self-determination.

In an interview with Judith Raiskin, Michelle Cliff remarks that "everybody comes from someplace else, and that's the feeling of the Caribbean" (63). Through fiction, contemporary Caribbean women authors such as Andrea Levy and Edwidge Danticat complicate notions of paradise and what it means to leave one's homeland; in essence, they work to redefine the popular imaginary of the Caribbean and inform conceptions of migration and exile. Indeed, emerging writers including Nicole Dennis-Benn and Tiphanie Yanique engage with and build on the work of authors such as

Michelle Cliff and Paule Marshall; together, these prose works advance the continuum of Caribbean women's writing and center Caribbean women's shared experiences. If "we know people by their stories," as Danticat asserts in *Krik? Krak!*, then it can be argued that literature operates as an archive (185). The quest for recognition, driven by the search for belonging, sheds light on the complex identity politics that Caribbean women navigate. In speaking of cultural loss, violence, neocolonialism, disease, and abuse, the authors reject silence and instead advance understanding of how societal ills, systemic racism, and other forms of structural oppression continue to impact Caribbean women's physical and emotional wellbeing.

NOTES

INTRODUCTION

1. In *Sister Citizen*, Melissa Harris-Perry notes that "the first book-length treatment of shame as a clinical concern did not appear until 1971, and the emotion remained neglected until the late 1980s.... Psychologists commonly refer to shame as a belief in the malignant self: the idea that your entire person is infected by something inherently bad and potentially contagious.... When we feel ashamed, we tend to drop our heads, avert our eyes, and fold into ourselves.... Shame makes us want to be smaller, timid, and more closed" (103).

2. Kezia Page observes that late twentieth and early twenty-first Caribbean literature is "predominantly female-authored, celebrating diaspora, open, [and is] direct and iconoclastic on subjects traditionally seen as taboo" (15).

3. For more on Caribbean women's exile, see Myriam Chancy's *Searching for Safe Spaces* and Ketu Katrak's *Politics of the Female Body*.

4. For Hill, also the term transnational includes "people whose family members live in two or more countries. The major transnational Caribbean populations outside the region are in the North American northeastern cities (from Quebec to Washington, D.C.), Florida, Great Britain, the Netherlands, and France" (7).

5. In the works under study, the body frequently operates as a social phenomenon and characters are "taught the subtle, and not so subtle, sex and gender norms required to make us upstanding citizens and eager, compliant consumers" (Amato 223).

6. Scholars including Aida Alayarian note that emotional trauma must meet the following criteria: "1) it is unexpected; 2) shocking; 3) the person was unprepared; 4) helplessness—nothing the person could do to prevent it" (74). While the term "trauma" appeared in medical literature in the mid-1600s, the field of trauma studies did not gain traction until the early 1990s when interest in Holocaust testimony peaked. The field of trauma studies began with a focus on the psychological impact of war on soldiers who served in armed conflicts including the Vietnam War and the Gulf War.

7. In *Trauma, Torture and Dissociation*, Aida Alayarian understands dissociation as a defense mechanism whereby "physical conflicts and threats to self-preservation are regulated in the mind" (157).

8. Migration for Caribbean peoples is not a new concept, "having begun five centuries ago when the region was absorbed into the orbit of global capital accumulation," but is instead connected to a long-standing legacy of movement (Ho 112).

Notes

CHAPTER ONE: The Immigrant Experience: Trauma, Folklore, and Migration in Danticat's *Breath, Eyes, Memory* and *Krik? Krak!*

1. This chapter applies Donald Hill's understanding of folklore as the "traditional beliefs and behaviors that circulate within a group of people in different versions based on a perceived model" (9). While Hill notes that folklore is "learned and transmitted verbally or by example within a 'face-to-face' setting," Danticat uses the medium of fiction to transform and transmit folklore for a wider audience (9).

2. As Melissa Farley, Colin Ross, and Harvey Schwartz explain, "Dissociation is an elaborate escape and avoidance strategy in which overwhelming human cruelty results in fragmentation of the mind into different parts of the self that observe, experience, react, as well as those that do not know about the harm" (quoted in Sullivan 322).

3. The soucouyant is a shapeshifter who "creeps into homes through cracks and sucks the blood or 'life-blood' (human life essence, or soul) of unsuspecting neighbors" (Anatol 45).

4. Subsequent references to *Breath, Eyes, Memory* will refer to the text as *BEM*.

5. Jana Evans Braziel notes that Dédée Bazile, a revolutionary figure, was known as Défilée-la-folle, or Défilée the Madwoman (59).

6. The text draws its significance from the Parsley Massacre of 1937, which resulted in the persecution and death of thousands of Haitians. "It earned the name the Parsley Massacre because Dominican soldiers carried a sprig of parsley and would ask people suspected of being Haitian to pronounce the Spanish word for it: 'perejil.' . . . Historians estimate that anywhere between 9,000 and 20,000 Haitians were killed in the Dominican Republic on the orders of the Dominican dictator Rafael Trujillo" (Davis).

7. Subsequent references to *Krik? Krak!* will refer to the text as *KK*.

8. While the term is "often translated 'werewolf,' Haitian stories concerning lougarous have nothing to do with the European werewolf" (N'Zengou-Tayo par. 15). The term is known in the "English Eastern Caribbean as 'sukuyan' or 'soucouyant' . . . an old woman who removes her skin at night to fly like a ball of fire . . . drink[ing] young children's blood or eat[ing] human flesh" (N'Zengou-Tayo par. 15).

9. Here, Danticat refers to the Massacre river. "Bodies were dumped in the Massacre River, ominously named after an earlier colonial struggle between the Spanish and French" (Davis).

10. Emphasis original.

11. Emphasis original.

CHAPTER TWO: Divided Allegiances and Alternative Histories: Michelle Cliff's and Margaret Cezair-Thompson's Focus on Psychological Exile

1. As Jenny Sharpe notes in *Ghosts of Slavery: A Literary Archaeology of Black Women's Lives*, "the term *maroon* is believed to be derived from *cimarrón*, a Spanish term for 'wild' or 'untamed' originally used for domestic cattle that had escaped into the bush. . . . The original

maroons were Spanish-owned slaves who escaped to the inaccessible recesses of Jamaica when England captured the island from Spain in 1655. They inhabited two regions that were separated from each other by a strip of white settlements: the Cockpit Country on the leeward side of the island and the Blue Mountains on the windward side" (4–5).

2. In the narrative, creolization functions as an "ongoing and ever-changing process," and transculturation generates a "ceaseless creation of new cultures" (Olmos and Paravisini-Gebert 3–6). Kamau Brathwaite sheds light on the genesis of the term. He writes, "The word itself appears to have originated from a combination of the two Spanish words *criar* (to create, to imagine, to establish, to found, to settle) and *colono* (a colonist, a founder, a settler) into *criollo*: a committed settler, one identified with the area of settlement, one native to the settlement though not ancestrally indigenous to it" (xxx).

3. Red is a term that, in Jamaica, signifies a degree of whiteness. Someone as light as Michelle Cliff, for instance, is considered "local white" (Palmer 275).

4. Cliff joins efforts that reach at least as far back as 1930s with the Negritude movement. As Denis Ekpo notes on Negritude, "African emotion or African participatory cosmology were seen as the intellectual foundation" (178). Also influential was the work of scholars such as C. L. R. James and historians including Eric Williams, as well as Sylvia Wynter and Kamau Brathwaite, who started the journal *Savacou* in 1970. *Savacou* ran until 1979 and came out of the Caribbean Artist Movement, a force that was concerned with "Caribbean artistic production and with consolidating a broad alliance between all 'Third World' peoples" ("Savacou").

5. As O. Nigel Bolland notes, "By the late eighteenth and early nineteenth centuries this creative process of adaptation, transformation, and synthesis had laid the groundwork of a Caribbean culture that was neither African nor European, though it had developed out of the interaction between African, European, and Amerindian peoples. In the Caribbean most people who participated in this process were of African descent and it was largely through their struggle against the double domination of enslavement and colonialism that an Afro-Creole culture developed" ("Reconsidering Creolization" 10). Bolland concludes by proclaiming that "when we think of the creole civilization of the Caribbean we should be considering it in all its diversity, with its various peoples 'constantly producing themselves anew' in 'an incredible explosion of cultures'" ("Reconsidering Creolization" 12).

6. I understand cultural hybridity as referring to the result of interactions between colonized and colonizers. With regard to race, specifically, hybridity indicates "the integration of two races which are assumed to be distinct and separate entities" (Yazdiha 32). In writing on racial creolization specifically, Haj Yazdiha notes that the "freedom to move between identities carries its own power in defying the claims of essentialized racial identity" (33).

7. In *Ghosts of Slavery*, Jenny Sharpe discusses Nanny, the legendary Maroon leader. She writes of an oral story that "presents Nanny as an originary ancestress of the maroon people. The story tells of two sisters, Nanny and Sekesu, who were captured and brought to the New World as slaves. Although there are several versions to the story, they all speak of how Nanny, unlike her sister, decided to fight for her freedom. The maroons are Nanny's *yoyo* or children, while the rest of Jamaicans are the descendants of Sekesu, who remained a slave until *backra* (the white man) decided to free her" (6).

8. As Cliff writes, "In 1733, Nanny, the sorceress, the *obeah*-woman, was killed by a *quashee*—a slave faithful to the white planters—at the height of the War of the Maroons. . . . Her Nanny Town, hidden in the crevices of the Blue Mountains, was the headquarters of the Windward Maroons—who held out against the forces of the white men longer than any rebel troops. They waged war from 1655–1740" (14).

9. *The True History of Paradise* focuses on the violence following Edward Seaga's election. At play in this turmoil was the international oil crisis, food shortages, and the "announcement of the intended construction of a Democratic Socialist State in October 1974. . . . Later in 1980, the Michael Manley government cancelled the IMF agreement after an all-night meeting of the PNP National Executive Council" (Burke).

10. Norman Washington Manley "founded the moderately socialist People's National party in 1938, and, with his cousin, Alexander Bustamante, dominated Jamaican politics for several decades. He served as chief minister of Jamaica (1955–59) before being designated prime minister (1959–62). He pushed land reform and encouraged economic growth, especially in the bauxite and tourist industries" ("Norman Washington Manley").

11. Michael Norman Manley, "Prime minister of Jamaica (1972–80, 1989–92); son of Norman Manley. A leader of the socialist People's National party, he was first elected to parliament in 1967. Winning a landslide victory in 1972, he shifted Jamaican politics to the left, establishing close relations to Cuba, nationalizing industry, and denouncing U.S. imperialism. He was reelected in 1976, but in 1980 lost to conservative Edward Seaga. Manley was returned to power in 1989, this time leading a more moderate government and encouraging foreign investment. Following serious illness, he resigned in 1992" ("Michael Norman Manley").

12. Edward Seaga "became leader of the conservative Jamaican Labor party (JLP) in 1974, and in 1980 the JLP won the elections and he became prime minister. Seaga severed relations with Cuba, promoted close ties with the United States, and emphasized free-market policies. In 1989 the JLP lost to the People's National party in a landslide and Michael Manley became prime minister. Seaga retired from parliament and as JLP leader in 2005. Served as Prime Minister from 1980–89" ("Edward Seaga").

13. Sir Alexander Bustamante was Prime Minister of Jamaica from 1962–67. "He became active in the labor movement, gaining prominence with his flaming oratory, and founded the country's largest trade union. After being jailed (1941–42) as a rabble-rouser, he formed (1943) the Jamaica Labour party, a relatively conservative group that attracted right-wing support. A flamboyant leader, he maintained close relations with the United States and launched an ambitious five-year program of public works and land reform. Illness caused him to retire from politics in 1967. He was knighted by Queen Elizabeth II in 1955" ("Sir Alexander Bustamante").

14. As Colin Clarke notes, in 1980 the CIA "allegedly supported Seaga's JLP, which confronted the Cuban-backed PNP government of Michael Manley in an essentially Cold War election . . . about 500 people were killed in Kingston during these elections and the violence and mayhem almost destroyed the democratic process" (430–31). From a historical standpoint, Clarke reminds us that "party-political violence in Kingston clearly dates back to the colonial period. . . . The use of violence was ratcheted up after independence in the

1960s. . . . Party-political violence was 'professionalised' by the recruitment of gangs to become electoral enforcers for the politicians during the 1960s and 1970s, and dons emerged as community leaders and drug dealers" (436).

15. At the same time, though, it must be remembered that "historically, the Jamaican people have a tradition of rebellion and resistance to oppression dating back to the Maroons in the 1600s . . . by the 1960s a new phenomenon had emerged, a pattern of internal violence which stemmed from a number of conditions. Economic and social frustrations had developed in the 1950s . . . we find in Kingston in the mid-1960s the development of open political warfare" (Kitson 171).

16. As Sam Vásquez writes, "Jamaica is the most violent country. Jamaica is a homophobic place. Jamaica is an underdeveloped space. Jamaica is the ideal locale for hedonistic fun. Jamaica is a paradise. Variations of these stereotypes appear continually in the foreign media" (43). Vásquez also notes that "in Jamaica, a country generally understood as being virulently opposed to same-sex relationships, homosexuality has fallen under the problematic rubric of hypersexuality" (48).

17. "On the main island, Spanish Town was also demolished. Even the north side of the island experienced great tragedy. Fifty people were killed in a landslide. In all, about 3,000 people lost their lives on June 7. There was little respite in the aftermath—widespread looting began that evening and thousands more died in the following weeks due to sickness and injury. Aftershocks discouraged the survivors from rebuilding Port Royal. Instead, the city of Kingston was built and remains to this day the largest city in Jamaica" ("Earthquake").

18. Emphasis original

CHAPTER THREE: Traversing the Triangular Road: Retrieving the Past and Reconsidering Cultural Identity in *Praisesong for the Widow* and *Small Island*

1. In the works, transnationalism operates as the "multiple ties and interactions linking people or institutions across the borders of nation-states" (Vertovec preface).

2. The Oxford English Dictionary defines mystical as "having a spiritual character or significance by virtue of a connection or union with God which transcends human understanding."

3. This chapter understands doubling to be a form of dissociation that allows "women to detach themselves from incidents that inflict bodily pain" (Francis 87). Doubling operates literally and figuratively in the text. Drawing from W. E. B. Du Bois's concepts of the veil and double-consciousness, which Marshall appears to be in conversation with, doubling indicates a separation of body and soul as well as a feeling of "twoness." While dissociation references a state of altered consciousness, it is not automatically attributed to the mystical or supernatural.

4. "For Africans, a praisesong is a particular kind of traditional heroic poem. Sung in various communities over the entire continent, praisesongs embody all manner of elaborate poetic form, but are always specifically ceremonial social poems, intended to be recited or sung in public at anniversaries and other celebrations, including funerals of the great. . . .

Important for its use here, they can also be sung to mark social transition. Sung as a part of rites of passage, they mark the upward movement of a person from one group to the next. The novel therefore celebrates for the widow her coming to terms with her widowhood—a reconciliation that has greater implications than a coming to terms with the loss of an individual husband only" (Busia 198).

5. The island of Carriacou is one of the "most easterly of the Caribbean Islands. That is, it is closest, physically, to the home continent of Africa. The physical closeness is simply a physical representation of the spiritual proximity that the widow is to see manifest" (Busia 201).

6. In reading Marshall's text in this way, I draw on the pre-Enlightenment definition of travel meaning "to labor" instead of the post-Enlightenment understanding as leisure (OED).

7. This line harkens back to Judith Butler's assertion that the matrixial borderspace prompts us to see "the space in which we are not one, cannot be, and yet we are not without the capacity to see" with the eyes of a child ("Forward: Bracha's Eurydice" xii).

8. The Kongo Cosmogram is a "'cross' inscribed in a circle or reclining oval, with the horizontal east-west line representing the *kalunga* interface and the vertical north-south line connecting the high noon (masculine power) of this life, above, with the midnight (feminine power) of the other world, below. In this symbol of the cosmos, the outer circle or oval described the counterclockwise movement of the sun, when seen from the southern hemisphere. Ritual kick fighters, within their moving circle, purposely adopted inverted positions—supporting their weight on their hands, with their feet in the air—thereby symbolically mirroring *kalunga* to draw on its power" (Slenes).

9. As a Smithsonian Institution article notes, "the Big Drum Dance is one of the most significant musical rituals on the island of Carriacou in the Grenadines. Really a long series of dances, the Big Drum Dance is prepared for special festivals such as marriage ceremonies, tombstone raisings, fishing boat launchings and in the case of ill-health or ill-fortune. In each occasion, the main focus is twofold: remembering lineage and respecting ancestors. The music consists of singing and chanting typically joined by three drums, shakers and maracas" ("The Big Drum").

10. In *Diaspora and Transnationalism*, Rainer Baubock and Thomas Faist define diaspora as "religious or national groups living outside an (imagined) homeland, whereas transnationalism is often used both more narrowly—to refer to migrants' durable ties across countries" (9).

11. James Hall notes that "stories about Africans who could fly have been recorded throughout the Americas for the past 200 years. . . . The tales of flying Africans, whether or not they focus on injustice, are always closely connected to the history of slavery. Sometimes these tales involve an individual or a group of slaves resisting forced work or feeling homesick for a homeland. On other occasions, they are just forceful and disruptive acts carried out by extraordinary people. In all versions, the main theme is one of 'escape.' . . . Many historians suspect that this particular version of the story is related to a real event. In 1803, a group of Igbo slaves arrived in the United States from the western coast of Africa (in the area of present-day Nigeria). Immediately upon delivery to Saint Simons Island in

Georgia, they fled their owners and captors and ran to certain death in Dunbar Creek. To commemorate the incident, this area of Saint Simons is called Ebos Landing—after the Igbo people who bravely resisted their fate."

12. In her article on black British fiction of the 1950s and 1960s, Roxy Harris notes that Britain became a multicultural society in the 1950, but that this development did not extend to black authors. As Harris states, "The 'colour problem' was debated in parliament, on television, in newspapers, magazines, on the radio. It was the big story of the 50s" (484). From a historical standpoint, Harris reminds readers that "the end of World War II marked a distinctive moment for black and brown people in the British empire. Having for the most part supported Britain during the war, they were no longer willing to return to pre-war subjugations and humiliations" (486). While Levy situates her text in the years following World War II, her discussion of race comments on the "deeply felt sense of incompatibility between Englishness/Britishness and being black or brown skinned" (Harris 488).

13. As the British Library Board notes, "When the Empire Windrush passenger ship docked at Tilbury from Jamaica on 22 June 1948, it marked the start of the postwar immigration boom which was to change British society.... After WWII, Britain encouraged immigration from Commonwealth countries. To a large extent this was to help rebuild the country as there was a shortage of labour at the time. Windrush carried 492 migrants who were coming to a country promising prosperity and employment" ("Windrush").

14. As Douglas Haynes notes, "Some 230,000 migrants entered Britain during the eighteen-month period before the Commonwealth Immigration Act (1962) went into effect. By 1965, some 50,000 a year arrived" (142). Also writing on the immigration of colonial citizens, Venetia Newall states, "In 1968 there were an estimated 1 million Commonwealth immigrants resident in Britain; half of these were West Indian and 60 per cent of the same number originated from Jamaica ... their position as an ethnic minority is somewhat unusual in that they tend, initially, to identify culturally with Britain" (25).

CHAPTER FOUR: Redefining Beauty: Elizabeth Nunez's and Pauline Melville's Exploration of Illness, Migration, and Transformation

1. Kathleen Fitzpatrick and James Lock find that anorexia nervosa is "characterized by a low body mass index (BMI), fear of gaining weight, denial of current low weight and its impact on health, and amenorrhoea. Estimated prevalence is highest in teenage girls, and up to 0.7% of this age group may be affected.... Most people with anorexia nervosa recover completely or partially, but about 5% die from the condition and 20% develop a chronic eating disorder" (1).

2. In *The Migration of Ghosts*, *Anna In-Between*, and *Boundaries* (2011), exile operates as a condition of displacement that functions as a "mechanism for liberation" (Chancy 14).

3. Kathleen Renk explains that "while some critics conflate magical and marvellous realism, it is important to distinguish the terms from one another. An international style found in literature and film, magical realism combines realism and the fantastic so that the marvellous seems to grow organically within the ordinary.... It was Alejo Carpentier who

first referred to 'lo real maravilloso americano.' In the 1940s, after spending time among the Surrealists in Europe, Carpentier reacted to their style, particularly noting the 'melting clocks' in Salvador Dali's 'The Persistence of Memory' and finding the strangeness and mystery of the Surrealists to be 'premeditated' and 'manufactured' rather than authentic" (103).

4. Approximately eighty-five pounds.

5. Kenneth Bilby and Jerome Handler describe obeah as a "catch-all term that encompasses a wide variety and range of beliefs and practices related to the control or channeling of supernatural/spiritual forces by particular individuals or groups for their own needs" (154).

6. Subsequent references will refer to *Anna In-Between* as *AIB*.

CHAPTER FIVE: Consuming the Caribbean: Sexuality, Social Norms, and Belonging in *Here Comes the Sun* and *Land of Love and Drowning*

1. Also reflecting on the construction of paradise, Mimi Sheller finds that "contemporary views of tropical island landscapes are highly over-determined by the long history of literary and visual representations of the tropical island as Paradise" (37). Sheller argues that "the picturesque vision of the Caribbean continues to be a form of world-making which allows tourists to move through the Caribbean, and to see Caribbean people simply as scenery" (62). For more on how a series of imaginaries informs more contemporary representations of the Caribbean, see Sheller's *Consuming the Caribbean*.

2. This chapter understands landscape as an instrument of power as well as a "cultural image that structures or symbolizes surroundings" (Daniels and Cosgrove 1).

3. In *Tourism Mobilities*, Mimi Sheller and John Urry make the point that the Caribbean has "been repeatedly imagined as a tropical paradise in which the land, plants, resources, bodies, and cultures of its inhabitants are open to be invaded, occupied, bought, moved, used, viewed, and consumed in various ways" (13). Sheller and Urry note that the construction of paradise is "performed through mobilizations of capital, demobilizations of labour, and remobilizations of colonial narratives, heritage, and built environments" (18).

4. As Phyllis Chesler explains, "Female children turn to their fathers for physical affection, nurturance, or pleasurable emotional intensity—a turning that is experienced as 'sexual' by the adult male, precisely because it is predicated on the female's (his daughter's) innocence, helplessness, youthfulness, and monogamous idolatry" (59).

5. Carole Pateman defines the sexual contract as a "socio-sexual pact . . . about political right as *patriarchal right* or sex-right, the power that men exercise over women." The missing half of the story tells how a specifically modern form of patriarchy is established. The new civil society created through the original contract is a patriarchal social order (1). Diane Richardson finds that Pateman's definition of the sexual contract highlights the "significance of a married heterosexual context as the norm for full citizen status" (210).

6. For more on the relationship between sexuality and violence, see Evelyn O'Callaghan's chapter in Faith Smith's edited collection *Sex and the Citizen*. O'Callaghan observes that "women and men whose sexuality does not conform to the moral norm of the patriarchal model are feared, hated, and targeted for discrimination, if not violence" (133).

7. In *Pathologies of Paradise*, Supriya Nair notes that "the incest taboo as explained by Claude Lévi-Strauss is the necessary prohibition that marks the evolution of culture (from an original state of nature) and the institution of kinship through the patriarchal gift exchange of women between men . . . the presence of the daughter in the family is a sexual threat and the object of desire must be safely 'given away' by the father to avoid the temptation of incest" (40). Nair later asserts that "one of the most damaging aspects of surviving incest is not the taboo itself but the taboo against naming it, against acknowledging that it even exists" (42).

8. Erica Johnson and Patricia Moran note that "men [often] commit violence against others in order to alleviate feelings of shame whereas women turn their feelings of shame inward" (16). For more on shame, see Johnson and Moran's *The Female Face of Shame* and J. Brooks Bouson's *Embodied Shame*.

9. In *Sister Citizen*, Melissa Harris-Perry explains that "individuals who do not conform to social norms are subject to frequent and enduring experiences of shame.... shame works through real or anticipated social sanctions that punish violations of group rules and thus helps us stay within the lines of acceptable behavior and thought" (106, 107).

10. As Laurie Vickroy writes in *Trauma and Survival in Contemporary Fiction*, "Traumatic experiences can produce a sometimes indelible effect on the human psyche that can change the nature of an individual's memory, self-recognition, and relational life" (11). Cathy Caruth describes trauma as "the story of a wound that cries out, that addresses us in the attempt to tell us of a reality or truth that is not otherwise available" (4).

11. In the Virgin Islands, known by the moniker "America's paradise," beach privatization led to a "national beach access movement, which tried to protect and expand the public's ability to gain physical access to the shoreline" (Felix 421). This movement is fictionalized in Yanique's *Land of Love and Drowning*.

12. Sam Vásquez observes that in Jamaica, "a country generally understood as being virulently opposed to same-sex relationships, homosexuality has also fallen under the problematic rubric of hypersexuality, enacting yet another level of violence against historically marginalized bodies" (48).

13. In "Rethinking Sexual Citizenship," Diane Richardson observes that "constructions of sexual citizenship constitute neo-orientalist and colonial practices" (209).

BIBLIOGRAPHY

PRIMARY SOURCES

Cezair-Thompson, Margaret. *The True History of Paradise*. Random House, 1999.
Cliff, Michelle. *Abeng*. Penguin Books, 1984.
Danticat, Edwidge. *Breath, Eyes, Memory*. Vintage Contemporaries, 1994.
Danticat, Edwidge. *Krik? Krak!* Vintage Contemporaries, 1995.
Dennis-Benn, Nicole. *Here Comes the Sun*. Liveright, 2016.
Levy, Andrea. *Small Island*. Picador, 2004.
Marshall, Paule. *Praisesong for the Widow*. Plume, 1983.
Melville, Pauline. *The Migration of Ghosts*. Bloomsbury, 1998.
Nunez, Elizabeth. *Anna In-Between*. Akashic Books, 2009.
Nunez, Elizabeth. *Boundaries*. Akashic Books, 2011.
Yanique, Tiphanie. *Land of Love and Drowning*. Riverhead Books, 2014.

SECONDARY SOURCES

Adisa, Opal Palmer. "Journey into Speech—A Writer Between Two Worlds: An Interview with Michelle Cliff." *African American Review*, vol. 28, no. 2, 1994, pp. 273–81.
Adjarian, M. M. *Allegories of Desire: Body, Nation, and Empire in Modern Caribbean Literature by Women*. Praeger, 2004.
Ajagunna, Ibrahim A., and Ann P. Crick. "Managing Interactions in the Tourism Industry—a Strategic Tool for Success." *Worldwide Hospitality and Tourism Themes*, vol. 6, no. 2, 2014, pp. 179–90.
Alayarian, Aida. *Trauma, Torture and Dissociation: A Psychoanalytic View*. Karnac Books, 2011.
Alexander, Simone A. *Mother Imagery in the Novels of Afro-Caribbean Women*. University of Missouri Press, 2001.
Alexandre, Sandy, and Ravi Y. Howard. "My Turn in the Fire: A Conversation with Edwidge Danticat." *Transition*, vol. 12, no. 3, 2002, pp. 110–28.
@Alyssa_Milano. "If you've been sexually harassed or assaulted write 'me too' as a reply to this tweet." *Twitter*, 15 Oct. 2017, 1:21 p.m., https://twitter.com/Alyssa_Milano/status/919659438700670976.

Amato, Toni. "Shame Is the First Betrayer." *Yes Means Yes! Visions of Female Sexual Power and a World Without Rape*, edited by Jaclyn Friedman and Jessica Valenti. Seal Press, 2008, pp. 221–26.

Anatol, Gisele. "Transforming the Skin-Shedding Soucouyant: Using Folklore to Reclaim Female Agency in Caribbean Literature." *Small Axe*, 7, 2000, pp. 44–59.

Balaev, Michelle. "Trends in Literary Trauma Theory." *Mosaic: A Journal for the Interdisciplinary Study of Literature*, vol. 41, no. 2, 2008, pp. 149–66.

Barnes, Fiona R., and Catherine Wiley. *Homemaking: Women Writers and the Politics and Poetics of Home*. Garland Pub., 1996.

Barnwell, Kattian. "Motherlands and Other Lands: Home and Exile in Jamaica Kincaid's *Lucy* and Paule Marshall's *Praisesong for the Widow*." *Caribbean Studies*, vol. 27, no. 3, 1994, pp. 451–54.

Baubock, Rainer, and Thomas Faist, eds. *Diaspora and Transnationalism: Concepts, Theories and Methods*. Amsterdam University Press, 2010.

Bauer, Ralph. "The Hemispheric Genealogies of 'Race': Creolization and the Cultural Geography of Colonial Difference across the Eighteenth-Century Americas." *Hemispheric American Studies*, edited by Caroline F. Levander and Robert S. Levine. Rutgers University Press, 2008, pp. 36–56.

Benjamin, Shanna G. "Weaving the Web of Reintegration: Locating Aunt Nancy in *Praisesong for the Widow*." *MELUS*, vol. 30, no. 1, 2005, pp. 49–67.

Bhabha, Homi K. *The Location of Culture*. Routledge, 1994.

"The Big Drum Dance of Carriacou." *Smithsonian Folkways*.

Bilby, Kenneth M., and Jerome S. Handler. "Obeah: Healing and Protection in West Indian Slave Life." *Journal of Caribbean History*, vol. 38, no. 2, 2004, pp. 153–83.

Bolland, O. Nigel. "Reconsidering Creolization and Creole Societies." *Shibboleths: Journal of Comparative Theory*, vo. 1, no. 1, 2006, pp. 1–14.

Bolland, O. Nigel. "Creolisation and Creole Societies: A Cultural Nationalist View of Caribbean Social History." *Caribbean Quarterly*, vol. 44, no. 1, 1998, pp. 1–32.

Booker, M. Keith, and Dubravka Juraga. *The Caribbean Novel in English: An Introduction*. Ian Randle Publishers, 2001.

Bordo, Susan. *Unbearable Weight: Feminism, Western Culture, and the Body*. University of California Press, 2003.

Bouson, J. Brooks. *Embodied Shame: Uncovering Female Shame in Contemporary Women's Writings*. State University of New York Press, 2009.

Boyce-Davies, Carole. *Black Women, Writing and Identity: Migrations of the Subject*. Routledge, 1994.

Brah, Avtar. *Cartographies of Diaspora: Contesting Identities*. Routledge, 1996.

Brathwaite, Kamau. *The Development of Creole Society in Jamaica 1770–1820*. Ian Randle Publishers, 2005.

Braziel, Jana Evans. "Re-membering Défilée: Dédée Bazile as Revolutionary *Lieu de Mémoire*." *Small Axe*, vol. 18, 2005, pp. 57–85.

Brown-Guillory, Elizabeth. *Middle Passages and the Healing Place of History: Migration and Identity in Black Women's Literature*. Ohio State University Press, 2006.

Burke, Michael. "30 Years after 1980 Election." *Jamaica Observer*, 28 Oct. 2010.

Bush, Barbara. "Sable Venus, 'She Devil' or 'Drudge?' British Slavery and the 'Fabulous Fiction' of Black Women's Identities, c. 1650–1838." *Women's History Review*, vol. 9, no. 4, 2000, pp. 761–89.

Busia, Abena P. A. "What Is Your Nation?: Reconnecting Africa and Her Diaspora through Paule Marshall's *Praisesong for the Widow*." *Changing Our Own Words: Essays on Criticism, Theory, and Writing by Black Women*, edited by Cheryl A. Wall. Rutgers University Press, 1989, pp. 196–212.

Butler, Judith. "Forward: Bracha's Eurydice." *The Matrixial Borderspace*, edited by Bracha L. Ettinger. University of Minnesota Press, 2006, pp. vi–xii.

Butler, Judith. *Gender Trouble: Feminism and the Subversion of Identity*. Routledge, 1990.

Butler, Judith. *Undoing Gender*. New York: Routledge, 2004. Print.

"Caribbean Cruises Leave Wave of Bitter Merchants." *Cleveland.com*, 10 Oct. 2012.

Caruth, Cathy. *Unclaimed Experience: Trauma, Narrative, and History*. The Johns Hopkins University Press, 1996.

Chakrabarty, Dipesh. *Provincializing Europe: Postcolonial Thought and Historical Difference*. Princeton University Press, 2000.

Chancy, Myriam J. A. *Framing Silence: Revolutionary Novels by Haitian Women*. Rutgers University Press, 1997.

Chesler, Phyllis. *Women and Madness*. Four Walls Eight Windows, 1997.

Christian, Barbara T. "Ritualistic Process and the Structure of Paule Marshall's *Praisesong for the Widow*." *Callaloo*, vol. 18, 1983, 74–84.

Clarke, Colin. "Politics, Violence and Drugs in Kingston, Jamaica." *Bulletin of Latin American Research*, vol. 25, no. 3, 2006, pp. 420–40.

Crowder, Kyle D. "Residential Segregation of West Indians in the New York/New Jersey Metropolitan Area: The Roles of Race and Ethnicity." *International Migration Review*, vol. 33, no. 1, 1999, pp. 79–113.

Daniels, Stephen, and Denis Cosgrove. *The Iconography of Landscape: Essays on the Symbolic Representation, Design and Use of Past Environments*. Cambridge University Press, 1994.

Davis, Nick. "The Massacre That Marked Haitian-Dominican Republic Ties." *BBC News*, 12 Oct. 2012.

DeLoughrey, Elizabeth. "Quantum Landscapes: A 'Ventriloquism of Spirit.'" *Interventions*, vol. 9, no. 1, 2007, pp. 62–82.

Diedrich, Maria, et al. *Black Imagination and the Middle Passage*. Oxford University Press, 1999.

"Earthquake Destroys Jamaican Pirate Haven." *History*, 13 Nov. 2009, https://www.history.com/this-day-in-history/earthquake-destroys-jamaican-pirate-haven. Accessed 26 Feb. 2019.

Edmondson, Belinda. *Making Men: Gender, Literary Authority, and Women's Writing in Caribbean Narrative*. Duke University Press, 1999.

Edmondson, Belinda. "Public Spectacle: Caribbean Women and the Politics of Public Performance." *Small Axe*, vol. 13, 2013, pp. 1–16.

"Edward Seaga." *Columbia Electronic Encyclopedia*, Sep. 2013.

Edwards, Justin. *Postcolonial Literature*. Palgrave Macmillan, 2008.

Ekpo, Denis. "Introduction: From Negritude to Post-Africanism." *Third Text*, vol. 24, no. 2, 2010, pp. 177–87.

Fanon, Frantz. *The Wretched of the Earth*. Grove Press, 2004.

Felix, Aliya T. "*Take Back the Beach!*" *An Analysis of the Need for Enforcement of Beach Access Rights for U.S. Virgin Islanders*, 10 Fla. A&M U. L. Rev. (2015).

Fernandez, Irene P. "Representing Third Spaces, Fluid Identities and Contested Spaces in Contemporary British Literature." *Atlantis*, vol. 31, no. 2, 2009, pp. 143–60.

Fitzpatrick, Kathleen K., and James Lock. "Anorexia Nervosa." *Clinical Evidence*, 2011, pp. 1–36.

Foucault, Michel. *The History of Sexuality: Volume I: An Introduction*. Pantheon Books, 1978.

Francis, Donette A. "'Silences Too Horrific to Disturb': Writing Sexual Histories in Edwidge Danticat's *Breath, Eyes, Memory*." *Research in African Literatures*, vol. 35, no. 2, 2004, pp. 75–90.

Francois, Pierre. "Incest and the Ontology of Memory in Pauline Melville's *The Ventriloquist's Tale*." *Commonwealth Essays and Studies*, vol. 21, no. 2, 1999, pp. 37–48.

Friedman, Susan S. "Bodies on the Move: A Poetics of Home and Diaspora." *Tulsa Studies in Women's Literature*, vol. 23, no. 2, 2004, pp. 189–212.

Gikandi, Simon. *Writing in Limbo: Modernism and Caribbean Literature*. Cornell University Press, 1992.

Gillespie, Carmen. "Past as Prologue: Rewriting and Reclaiming the Marked Body in Michelle Cliff's *Abeng* and Margaret Cezair-Thompson's *The True History of Paradise*." *Color, Hair, and Bone: Race in the Twenty-First Century*, edited by Linden Lewis and Glyne Griffith. Bucknell University Press, 2008, pp. 147–60.

Gourdine, Angeletta K. M. *The Difference Place Makes: Gender, Sexuality, and Diaspora Identity*. Ohio State University Press, 2002.

Gowricharn, Ruben S. *Caribbean Transnationalism: Migration, Pluralism, and Social Cohesion*. Lexington Books, 2006.

Griffin, Farah J. "Textual Healing: Claiming Black Women's Bodies, the Erotic and Resistance in Contemporary Novels of Slavery." *Callaloo*, vol. 19, no. 2, 1996, pp. 519–36.

Hall, Anthony. "The Response of the Tourism Industry in Jamaica to Crime and the Threat of Terrorism." *Worldwide Hospitality and Tourism Themes*, vol.6, no. 2, 2014, pp. 59–72.

Hall, James C. "Flying Africans." *Footsteps: The Young Person's African American History Magazine*, May–June 2006, *General OneFile*.

Handley, George, and Elizabeth M. DeLoughrey. "Introduction." *Postcolonial Ecologies: Literatures of the Environment*, edited by George Handley and Elizabeth M. DeLoughrey. Oxford University Press, 2011, pp. 3–39.

Harris, Roxy. "Black British, Brown British and British Cultural Studies." *Cultural Studies*, vol. 23, no. 4, 2009, pp. 483–512.

Harris-Perry, Melissa V. *Sister Citizen: Shame, Stereotypes, and Black Women in America*. Yale University Press, 2011.

Haynes, Douglas M. "Teaching Twentieth-Century Black Britain." *Radical History Review*, vol. 87, 2003, pp. 139–45.

Herman, Judith Lewis, and Lisa Hirschman. *Father-Daughter Incest*. Harvard University Press, 2000.

Hill, Donald R. *Caribbean Folklore: A Handbook*. Greenwood Press, 2007.

Ho, Christine G. T. "Caribbean Transnationalism as a Gendered Process." *Reading Women in Latin America and the Caribbean: The Political Economy of Gender*, edited by Jennifer Abbassi and Sheryl L. Lutjens. Rowman and Littlefield, 2002, pp. 112–30.

Huggan, Graham, and Helen Tiffin. *Postcolonial Ecocriticism: Literature, Animals, Environment*. Routledge, 2015.

Ippolito, Emilia. *Caribbean Women Writers: Identity and Gender*. Camden House, 2000.

Johnson, Erica L., and Patricia Moran. "Introduction." *The Female Face of Shame*, edited by Erica L. Johnson and Patricia Moran. Indiana University Press, 2013, pp. 1–22.

Johnston, Barbara R. "'Save Our Beach Dem and Our Land Too!' The Problems of Tourism in America's Paradise." *Cultural Survival*, vol. 14, no. 2, 1990.

Johnston, Lynda, and Gill Valentine. "Wherever I Lay My Girlfriend, That's My Home: The Performance and Surveillance of Lesbian Identities in Domestic Environments." *Mapping Desire: Geographies of Sexualities*, edited by David Bell and Gill Valentine. Routledge, 1995, pp. 99–113.

Kaplan, Sara. "Souls at the Crossroads, Africans on the Water: The Politics of Diasporic Melancholia." *Callaloo*, vol. 30, no. 2, 2007, pp. 511–26.

Katrak, Ketu H. *Politics of the Female Body: Postcolonial Women Writers of the Third World*. Rutgers University Press, 2006.

Kemp, Yakini B., and Janice Liddell. *Arms Akimbo: Africana Women in Contemporary Literature*. University Press of Florida, 1999.

Kempadoo, Kamala. *Sexing the Caribbean: Gender, Race, and Sexual Labor*. Routledge, 2004.

Kenan, Randall, and Margaret Cezair-Thompson. "Margaret Cezair-Thompson." *BOMB*, vol. 69, 1999, pp. 54–59.

Kitson, Doris. "Jamaica and the Electoral Coup of 1980." *Race Class*, vol. 24, 1982, pp. 169–78.

LaCapra, Dominick. *Writing History, Writing Trauma*. Johns Hopkins University Press, 2014.

Lewis, Barbara. "Negotiating Multiple Worlds: A Public Interview with Elizabeth Nunez." *Black Renaissance*, vol. 4, no. 2, 2002, pp. 202–13.

MacDonald-Smythe, Antonia. "Macotte: An Exploration of Same-Sex Friendship in Selected Caribbean Novels." *Sex and the Citizen: Interrogating the Caribbean*, edited by Faith Smith. University of Virginia Press, 2011, pp. 224–40.

Mahler, Sarah J. "Theoretical and Empirical Contributions toward a Research Agenda for Transnationalism." *Transnationalism from Below*, edited by Michael P. Smith and Luis E. Guarnizo. Transaction Publishers, 1998, pp. 64–100.

Manley, Rachel. "Thoughts on Writing from Exile." *Small Axe*, vol. 12, no. 6, 2002, pp. 201–8.

Mardorossian, Carine. *Reclaiming Difference: Caribbean Women Rewrite Postcolonialism*. University of Virginia Press, 2005.

Marshall, Paule. *Triangular Road*. Basic Cevitas Books, 2009.

McNeil, Elizabeth. "The Gullah Seeker's Journey in Paule Marshall's *Praisesong for the Widow*." *MELUS*, vol. 34, no. 1, 2009, pp. 185–209.

"Michael Norman Manley." *Columbia Electronic Encyclopedia*, Sep. 2013.

Mohanty, Chandra T. *Feminism without Borders: Decolonizing Theory, Practicing Solidarity.* Duke University Press, 2003.

Moynagh, Maureen. "The Ethical Turn in Postcolonial Theory and Narrative: Michelle Cliff's *No Telephone to Heaven.*" *ARIEL: A Review of International English Literature*, vol. 30, no. 4, 1999, pp. 109–33.

Munoz-Valdivieso, Sofia. "Africa in Europe: Narrating Black British History in Contemporary Fiction." *Journal of European Studies*, vol. 40, no. 2, 2010, pp 159–74.

Murdoch, H. Adlai. "A Legacy of Trauma: Caribbean Slavery, Race, Class, and Contemporary Slavery in *Abeng*." *Research in African Literatures*, vol. 40, no. 4, 2009, pp. 65–88.

Nair, Supriya. *Pathologies of Paradise: Caribbean Detours.* University of Virginia Press, 2013.

National Park Service. "Magic Bowls." https://www.nps.gov/ethnography/aah/aaheritage/lowCountry_furthRdg4.htm. Accessed 20 Sept. 2019.

Newall, Venetia. "Black Britain: The Jamaicans and Their Folklore." *Folklore*, vol. 86, no. 1, 1975, pp. 25–41.

"Norman Washington Manley." *Columbia Electronic Encyclopedia*, Sep. 2013.

Nunez, Elizabeth. "How I Came to America." *Changing English*, vol. 12, no. 3, 2005, pp. 373–76.

N'Zengou-Tayo, Marie-José. "Rewriting Folklore: Traditional Beliefs and Popular Culture in Edwidge Danticat's *Breath, Eyes, Memory* and *Krik? Krak!*" *MaComère*, vol. 3, 2000 pp. 123–40.

O'Callaghan, Evelyn. "Caribbean Migrations: Negotiating Borders." *Sex and the Citizen: Interrogating the Caribbean*, edited by Faith Smith. University of Virginia Press, 2011, pp. 125–35.

Olmos, Margarite F., and Lizabeth Paravisini-Gebert. *Creole Religions of the Caribbean: An Introduction from Voudou and Santería to Obeah and Espiritismo.* New York University Press, 2003.

Page, Kezia. *Transnational Negotiations in Caribbean Diasporic Literature: Remitting the Text.* Routledge, 2011.

Papastergiadis, Nikos. *The Turbulence of Migration: Globalization, Deterritorialization and Hybridity.* Blackwell Publishers Inc., 2000.

Paravisini-Gebert, Lizabeth. *Literature of the Caribbean.* Greenwood Press, 2008.

Pateman, Carole. *The Sexual Contract.* Stanford University Press, 1988.

Raiskin, Judith L. "The Art of History: An Interview with Michelle Cliff." *Kenyon Review*, vol. 15, no. 1, 1993, pp. 57–71.

Renk, Kathleen W. "Magic That Battles Death: Pauline Melville's *Marvelous Realism.*" *Journal of Commonwealth Literature*, vol. 44, no. 1, 2009, pp. 101–15.

Richardson, Diane. "Rethinking Sexual Citizenship." *Sociology*, vol. 51, no. 2, 2017, pp. 208–24.

Robinson-Walcott, Kim. "Claiming an Identity We Thought They Despised: Contemporary White West Indian Writers and Their Negotiation of Race." *Small Axe*, vol. 14, no. 7, 2003, pp. 93–110.

Rodriguez, Maria C. *What Women Lose: Exile and Construction of Imaginary Homelands in Novels by Caribbean Writers.* Peter Lang Publishing, 2005.

Rody, Caroline. *The Daughter's Return: African-American and Caribbean Women's Fictions of History.* Oxford University Press, 2001.

Rogers, Susan. "Embodying Cultural Memory in Paule Marshall's *Praisesong for the Widow*." *African American Review*, vol. 34, no. 1, 2000, pp. 77–93.

Rosello, Mireille. "Marasa with a Difference: Danticat's *Breath, Eyes, Memory*." *Edwidge Danticat: A Reader's Guide*, edited by Martin Munro. University of Virginia Press, 2010, pp. 117–29.

Rubenstein, Roberta. *Home Matters: Longing and Belonging, Nostalgia and Mourning in Women's Fiction*. Palgrave, 2001.

Said, Edward. *Reflections on Exile and Other Essays*. Harvard University Press, 2002.

Sarthou, Sharrón E. "Unsilencing Defile's Daughters: Overcoming Silence in Edwidge Danticat's *Breath, Eyes, Memory* and *Krik? Krak!*" *Global South*, vol. 4, no. 2, 2010, pp. 99–123.

"Savacou." *Chimurenga Library*, 2008. http://chimurengachronic.co.za/periodicals_posts/savacou/. Accessed 25 Jan. 2014

Savory, Elaine. "Mathematical Limbs and Other Eventualities: Translocation of the Body in Pauline Melville's *Shape-Shifter*." *New Literatures Review*, vol. 30, 2005, pp. 47–57.

Seidman, Steven. *The Social Construction of Sexuality*. Norton, 2003.

Sharpe, Jenny. *Ghosts of Slavery: A Literary Archaeology of Black Women's Lives*. University of Minnesota Press, 2003.

Sheller, Mimi. *Consuming the Caribbean: From Arawaks to Zombies*. Taylor and Francis, 2003.

Sheller, Mimi, and John Urry. *Tourism Mobilities: Places to Play, Places in Play*. Taylor and Francis, 2004.

Siegel, Kristi. *Gender, Genre and Identity in Women's Travel Writing*. University of Michigan, 2004.

"Sir Alexander Bustamante." *Columbia Electronic Encyclopedia*, Sep. 2013.

Slenes, Robert W. "Central African Religions and Culture in the Americas." *Encyclopedia of African-American Culture and History*, 2006. https://www.encyclopedia.com/history/encyclopedias-almanacs-transcripts-and-maps/central-african-religions-and-culture-americas. Accessed 7 Feb. 2019.

Strachan, Ian G. *Paradise and Plantation: Tourism and Culture in the Anglophone Caribbean*. University of Virginia Press, 2002.

Sullivan, Mary L. *Making Sex Work: A Failed Experiment of Legalized Prostitution*, Spinifex Press, 2007.

Tobin, Beth Fowkes. "Caribbean Subjectivity and the Colonial Archive." *Small Axe*, vol. 25, 2008, pp. 145–56.

Thomas-Hope, Elizabeth, and Adonna Jardine-Comrie. "Valuation of Environmental Resources of Tourism in Small Island Developing States." *International Development Planning Review*, vol. 29, no. 1, 2007, pp. 93–112.

Torregrosa, Luisita L. "Jamaica, Beyond the Beach." *New York Times*, 31 Mar. 2016.

Vásquez, Sam. "Violent Liaisons: Historical Crossings and the Negotiation of Sex, Sexuality, and Race in *The Book of Night Women* and *The True History of Paradise*." *Small Axe*, vol. 16, no. 2, 2012, pp. 43–59.

Vertovec, Steven. *Transnationalism*. Routledge, 2009.

Vickroy, Laurie. *Trauma and Survival in Contemporary Fiction*. University of Virginia Press, 2002.

Wahab, Amar. *Colonial Inventions: Landscape, Power and Representation in Nineteenth-Century Trinidad*. Cambridge Scholars Publishing, 2010.

Walters, Wendy W. *At Home in Diaspora: Black International Writing*. University of Minnesota Press, 2005.

Weitz, Rose. *The Politics of Women's Bodies: Sexuality, Appearance, and Behavior*. Oxford University Press, 1998.

White, E. Frances. *Dark Continent of Our Bodies: Black Feminism and the Politics of Respectability*. Temple University Press, 2001.

Wieringa, Saskia, and Horacio Sívori. "Sexual Politics in the Global South: Framing the Discourse." *The Sexual History of the Global South: Sexual Politics in Africa, Asia, and Latin America*, edited by Saskia Wieringa and Horacio Sívori. Zed Books, 2013, pp. 1–21.

Williams, Dana A. "Introduction." *Contemporary African American Fiction*, edited by Dana A. Williams. Ohio State University Press, 2009, pp. 1–9.

"Windrush: Post-War Immigration 1948." *British Library Board*. https://www.bl.uk/learning/timeline/item107829.html. Accessed 25 Jan. 2014

Wolf, Naomi. *The Beauty Myth: How Images of Beauty Are Used Against Women*. Harper Collins, 1991.

Yancy, George. *Black Bodies, White Gazes: The Continuing Significance of Race*. Rowman & Littlefield, 2008.

Yazdiha, Haj. "Conceptualizing Hybridity: Deconstructing Boundaries through the Hybrid." *Formations*, vol.1, no. 1, 2010, pp. 31–38.

INDEX

Abeng, 8, 36–49, 50, 53–54, 59, 61
Africa, 60, 65, 70, 71, 77, 140
Ajagunna, Ibrahim, 118
Alan, 55, 57, 59
Alayarian, Aida, 8, 135
Alexander, Simone, 6, 70
Alexandre, Sandy, 13
American Psychological Association, 5
Anatol, Gisele, 31
Anna In-Between, 7, 12, 84, 95–103, 106, 141
anorexia nervosa, 12, 84, 90–94, 141
At Home in Diaspora, 44
Atie, 15, 17, 21–22, 25–26
Azile, Défilée, 27–31

Balaev, Michelle, 8, 26, 125
Barbados, 12, 60, 63
Barnes, Fiona, 133
Barnwell, Kattian, 81
Baubock, Rainer, 140
Bazile, Dédée, 27–28, 136
beach access movement, 117, 127, 129–30, 143
beach privatization, 116–17, 143
Beauty Myth, The, 109
belonging, 6, 11, 24–25, 33, 60, 61–62, 69, 72, 83, 85, 112, 123–24, 128, 134
Bhabha, Homi, 38
Bilby, Kenneth, 142
bildungsroman, 5–6, 38, 44, 63
Bligh, Bernard, 73, 75, 78–79, 81–82
Bligh, Queenie, 61, 73–75, 78–83
Bolland, O. Nigel, 43, 137
BOMB movement, 117
Booker, M. Keith, 40

Bordo, Susan, 86, 88, 97, 99
Boundaries, 7, 12, 84, 95–96, 98, 100–106, 141
Bouson, J. Brooks, 3, 22–23, 94, 143
Boyce-Davies, Carole, 62, 71
Bradshaw, Antoinette, 109–11, 114
Bradshaw, Eeona, 108–16
Bradshaw, Owen Arthur, 109–16, 132
Brathwaite, Kamau, 39, 137
Braziel, Jana Evans, 136
Breath, Eyes, Memory, 6, 9, 12, 13–26, 34–35, 45, 67, 79, 84
Brown-Guillory, Elizabeth, 65
Burke, Tarana, 3
Busia, Abena, 62
Bustamante, Alexander, 138
Butler, Judith, 122, 140

Caco, Martine, 15–25
Caco, Sophie, 14–26, 45
cancer, 12, 84, 86–90, 95–97, 98–106. *See also* illness
Caribbean, 62–66, 71–72, 83, 107–8, 116, 118, 125, 130–32, 133–34, 137, 142
Caribbean Artist Movement, 137
Caribbean Women Writers, 36
Caroline, 14, 31–34
"Caroline's Wedding," 13, 14, 27, 31–34
Carpentier, Alejo, 141–42
Carriacou, 65–70, 140
Caruth, Cathy, 8, 143
cauls, 68–69
Cezair-Thompson, Margaret, 3, 7, 12, 36–37, 49–59
Chakrabarty, Dipesh, 57

Chancy, Myriam, 135
Chesler, Phyllis, 142
Clarke, Colin, 138
Cliff, Michelle, 3, 7, 8, 10, 12, 36–49, 53–54, 59, 133–34, 137, 138
Colonial Inventions, 127
Commonwealth Immigration Act, 141
community, 21–22, 25, 29, 31, 44, 70, 78, 80, 101, 120, 123–25, 127, 139
Consuming the Caribbean, 107, 142
corruption, 86, 90, 92–93, 120
Crawford, Susannah, 58
creolization, 39–40, 43–46, 49, 137
Crick, Ann, 118
cultural connection, 12, 31, 60, 62–64
cultural heritage, 12, 54, 60, 62, 64, 66, 69–71
cultural hybridity, 7, 23, 137
cultural reclamation, 44, 65–66
cultural reconciliation, 63, 83
cultural reconnection, 7, 62–63, 67–68, 70
Cuney, Aunt, 61, 64–71, 75

Dali, Salvador, 142
Dante Alighieri, 87, 89
Danticat, Edwidge, 3, 6, 9–10, 12, 13–35, 67, 79, 133–34, 136
Dennis-Benn, Nicole, 3, 7, 10, 12, 107–8, 118–32, 133
Diagnostic and Statistical Manual of Mental Disorders (DSM-III), 5
Diaspora and Transnationalism, 140
Difference Place Makes, The, 37, 107
discrimination, 61, 71, 75–76, 85, 143. *See also* race and racism
dissociation, 5, 9–10, 12, 14, 18–21, 26, 29, 45, 61, 64–67, 70, 79, 133, 135, 136, 139
dissociative disorders, 5
Dolores, 125–26
Dominican Republic, 30, 136
Dorothy, Aunt, 75
doubling. *See* dissociation
Du Bois, W. E. B., 68, 139
Duvalier, François, 16, 30

Edmondson, Belinda, 71, 118
education, 5, 44–45, 104, 120
Ellie, 84–91, 94–95, 103–5
Ekpo, Denis, 137
Embodied Shame, 94, 143
England, 38, 43, 45–50, 54–55, 57–59, 61, 71–83, 86, 90, 124, 135, 137, 141. *See also* London, England
"Erzulie," 86
exclusion, 4, 7, 62, 95, 131, 133
exile, 5, 7, 11, 12, 22, 26, 31, 36, 40, 43–44, 59–60, 72, 76, 80–81, 83, 85–86, 90, 95, 123, 126, 132, 133, 135, 141; cultural, 64; emotional, 42; psychological, 36–59, 61; social, 59
exploitation, 3, 6, 11, 12, 73, 86, 90, 92–93, 107–8, 118–19, 121, 125–28, 131–32

Faist, Thomas, 140
Fanon, Frantz, 129
Farley, Melissa, 136
Faye, 51–52, 56
Female Face of Shame, The, 143
Fitzpatrick, Kathleen, 141
folklore, 6, 12, 13–35, 64, 70, 136
Foucault, Michel, 123
Freud, Sigmund, 8, 63
Friedman, Susan, 11

gender, 6, 8, 10, 12, 14, 18, 24, 28, 34, 40–41, 86, 119–20, 131, 135
Gender Trouble, 122
Ghosts of Slavery, 136, 137
Gikandi, Simon, 46, 48–49
Glissant, Edouard, 127
Gourdine, Angeletta, 37, 107–8
Grace, 14, 31–34
Grandmè Ifé, 20, 24–25
Grenada, 65–66, 68, 70
Griffin, Farrah, 39
Guyana, 12, 85–86

Haiti, 12, 14–18, 20–33, 35, 64, 86, 136
Hall, James, 140
Handler, Jerome, 142

Harris, Roxy, 141
Harris-Perry, Melissa, 4, 9, 114, 135, 143
Hay, Charles, 85–86, 90–94
Hay, Susan, 8, 84–86, 90–95
Haynes, Douglas, 141
Here Comes the Sun, 12, 107–8, 118–32
Herman, Judith, 110
Hill, Donald, 6, 135, 136
Hirschman, Lisa, 110
History of Sexuality, The, 123
home, 3–4, 6–7, 9–11, 14, 15, 17–27, 31, 36–37, 42, 48–50, 54, 56–58, 60–63, 65, 70–75, 81–83, 85, 95–96, 98, 106, 108, 120, 132, 133, 140
Homemaking, 133
homophobia, 5, 10, 11, 51, 120, 124, 139. *See also* sexual orientation
Howard, Ravi, 13
Huggan, Graham, 118

identity, 4, 6, 7, 9, 10–12, 20–21, 23–26, 31, 37–38, 40, 46–50, 53, 60–67, 71–72, 118, 120, 124, 126, 128; African, 60, 61; African American, 63, 65, 67; American, 60; black, 40; Caribbean, 60; class, 41; creole, 49; cultural, 37–38, 41–42, 44–45, 60–83; development, 24; gender, 44; hybrid, 42, 47, 48; immigrant, 35; nationalistic, 83; pan-Caribbean, 11; personal, 11, 22, 61; politics, 134; racial, 12, 39, 41–44, 137; sexual, 41, 44; transnational, 12, 26; West Indian, 63; white, 42–43
illness, 12, 84–106, 133–34. *See also* cancer
immigrants, 4, 11, 13–35, 36, 42, 60, 62–63, 72–73, 76, 78–79, 83, 95–96; second-generation, 32, 60, 61–62, 72, 83, 129
incest, 12, 14, 32, 108–17, 143
Inferno, 87, 89
Ippolito, Emilia, 36
Is Nothing Sacred?, 89

Jamaica, 12, 36–38, 42–44, 46, 48–51, 54–59, 61, 72–74, 77–78, 81, 107, 118–21, 123–29, 132, 137, 138, 139, 141, 143
James, C. L. R., 137

Johnson, Avey, 11, 61–71, 73, 75, 83
Johnson, Erica, 4, 143
Johnston, Lynda, 120
Joseph, 17–20, 22, 23–24
Joseph, Gilbert, 72–78, 81–83
Joseph, Lebert, 65, 67–70
Josephine, 28, 30
Juraga, Dubravka, 40

Kaplan, Sara, 63
Katrak, Ketu, 112, 135
Kempadoo, Kamala, 118
Kenan, Randall, 53
Kincaid, Jamaica, 126
Kongo Cosmogram, 69, 140
Krik? Krak!, 6, 9, 12, 13, 14, 26–29, 34–35, 134

land development, 12, 107–8, 119, 126, 129–32, 138
Landing, Jean, 11, 12, 37, 49–59, 61
Landing, Lana, 53–54, 56, 58
Landing, Monica, 50, 53–54, 57
Landing, Moses, 55–56
Landing, Rebecca, 55, 57
Landing, Roy, 53–54, 58
Land of Love and Drowning, 9–10, 12, 107–17, 131–32, 143
Langley, Celia, 72, 74
language, 15, 25, 30, 36, 45, 47–48, 65–66, 69, 127
Lévi-Strauss, Claude, 143
Levy, Andrea, 6, 12, 60–62, 71–83, 133, 141
Lewis, Barbara, 95
Lock, James, 141
London, England, 61, 74, 78–79, 86, 90, 92. *See also* England
lougarous, 28, 136
Lovelace, Earl, 5
"Lucifer's Shank," 84, 86–91, 94, 100, 103–4, 106

MacDonald-Smythe, Antonia, 41
Making Men, 71
Manley, Michael Norman, 50, 138
Manley, Norman Washington, 138

Manley, Rachel, 59
Manman. *See* Azile, Défilée
Mardorossian, Carine, 5
Margot, 108, 118–26, 130, 132
Maroons, 37–40, 42–43, 45–49, 136–37, 138, 139
Marshall, Paule, 6, 7, 9, 11, 12, 60–71, 75, 83, 134, 139, 140
Martinique, 65–66
Massacre River, 29–30, 136
materialism, 70, 90, 94
Mattie, Miss, 42
McKay, Claude, 5
Melville, Pauline, 7, 8, 12, 84–95, 100, 105–6
Michael (soldier), 79–82
Michael (child), 80–83
Middle Passage, 65–66, 71
Middle Passages and the Healing Place of History, 65
migration, 3–7, 9–12, 13–35, 36, 38, 51–52, 57–59, 61–62, 71, 73–74, 76–79, 83, 84–106, 124, 133, 135
Migration of Ghosts, The, 6, 7, 12, 84–85, 90, 95, 141
Milano, Alyssa, 3
Mohanty, Chandra, 6
Moore, Verdene, 120–21, 123–24, 126, 132
Moran, Patricia, 4, 143
Moreau, Louis, 111–12
"Motherlands and Other Lands," 81
Murdoch, H. Adlai, 37–38, 49
mysticism, 25, 29–30, 32, 34, 61, 64, 66–67, 69–70, 75, 85–87, 90–93, 139

Naipaul, V. S., 5
Nair, Supriya, 46, 107–8, 143
Nationality Act, 78
Newall, Venetia, 141
New York City, 15–16, 20, 22, 25, 31, 62, 71
Nigeria, 84–85, 90–92, 94–95
"Nineteen Thirty-Seven," 13, 14, 27–31
Norman, Lyonel, 115
No Telephone to Heaven, 37, 40
Nunez, Elizabeth, 6, 7, 12, 84–85, 87, 95–106

obeah, 92, 131, 138, 142
O'Callaghan, Evelyn, 142–43
Ogun, 92, 93–94
Open Beaches Committee, 117
Open Shorelines Act, 117
oral lore, 14–15, 18, 26–28, 34–35, 63, 66–67, 70, 137

Page, Kezia, 135
Papa Legba, 64, 67
Papastergiadis, Nikos, 10
Paradise and Plantation, 58, 83
Paravisini-Gebert, Lizabeth, 46
"Parrot and Descartes, The," 86
Parsley Massacre, 136
Pat, 51–52, 56
Pateman, Carole, 111, 142
Pathologies of Paradise, 143
Paul, 56, 58–59
Paul (doctor), 102–3, 106
"Persistence of Memory, The," 142
Phillips, Mrs., 42–43
politics, 14; body, 4; identity, 134; power, 12, 112; racial, 39, 53–54, 62; sexual, 4, 8
Politics of the Female Body, 135
post-traumatic stress disorder, 5
poverty, 90, 93, 108, 117
Praisesong for the Widow, 7, 9, 11, 12, 60–71, 75–76, 140
praisesongs, 139–40
prostitution. *See* sex work
Provincializing Europe, 57
public trust doctrine, 117

race and racism, 3, 5, 7, 10, 11, 37–39, 43, 48, 61, 72, 75–76, 78–83, 86, 120, 127, 129, 137, 141. *See also* discrimination
Raiskin, Judith, 133
rape, 15–22, 25–26, 35, 43, 51. *See also* sexual abuse
Reflections on Exile and Other Essays, 61
religion, 37, 46–47, 64, 89, 92, 93–94, 113, 123, 140
Renk, Kathleen, 141

resistance, 5, 12, 27–32, 36–37, 46–48, 57, 86, 116, 120, 130–31, 139
"Rethinking Sexual Citizenship," 143
Richardson, Diane, 111, 125, 142, 143
Roberts, Hortense, 61–62, 72–83
Robertson, George, 67
Rosello, Mireille, 18
Ross, Colin, 136
Rubenstein, Roberta, 64
Rushdie, Salman, 89

Said, Edward, 36, 58, 61
Sarthou, Sharron, 60
Savacou, 137
Savage, Boy, 38, 43–48, 53
Savage, Clare, 8, 12, 37–49, 50, 53–54, 59, 61
Savage, Kitty, 38, 42–44, 46–48
Savory, Elaine, 89
Schwartz, Harvey, 136
Seaga, Edward, 49–50, 138
Searching for Safe Spaces, 135
Seidman, Steven, 111, 123
Sex and the Citizen, 142
sexual abuse, 3–4, 5, 9, 11, 18, 20–26, 84, 114, 134. *See also* rape
sexuality, 8, 12, 79, 86, 107–32, 119, 122–26, 132, 139, 142, 143
sexual orientation, 40–41, 52, 118–19, 123–26, 132, 143. *See also* homophobia
sex work, 12, 108, 118–22, 126, 130
shame, 3–4, 7, 8–12, 18, 22–23, 43, 54, 80, 86, 94, 97, 104, 114–15, 133, 135, 143
shapeshifting, 14, 26, 90–91, 136
Sharpe, Jenny, 136, 137
Sheller, Mimi, 11, 107, 120, 125, 128, 142
Sinclair, Anna, 7, 95–105
Sinclair, Beatrice, 84–85, 95–106
Sinclair, John, 97, 101, 103, 105
Sister Citizen, 9, 135, 143
Sívori, Horacio, 112
slavery, 10, 25, 37–39, 46–49, 52, 54, 56, 137, 138, 140–41
Small Island, 6, 12, 60–62, 71–83
Small Place, A, 126
Smith, Faith, 142

social class, 6, 37, 39, 41, 44, 47, 68, 74, 77, 82, 97–98, 101–2, 118–19, 125, 129
Social Construction of Sexuality, The, 111
social norms, 4, 8–12, 14, 18, 27, 31, 43–44, 54, 80, 110–13, 115, 123, 125, 131–32, 133, 143
soucouyants, 14, 27–29, 31, 136
"Sparkling Bitch, The," 8, 84–86, 88, 90–95, 106
stereotypes, 73, 119, 131, 139
Strachan, Ian, 58, 83

Tatem, GA, 64–65, 69–70
Tiffin, Helen, 118
Tobin, Beth, 7
Tourism Mobilities, 11, 142
tourists and tourism, 51, 68, 107–8, 116–17, 124, 126–32, 138, 142; sex tourism, 107, 118–23
transformation, 10, 12, 34, 64, 66–68, 70, 79, 84–106, 137
transnationalism, 6, 12, 23, 38, 48, 60, 64, 72, 76, 135, 139, 140
trauma, 5–7, 8–12, 13–35, 60, 65, 83, 126, 133, 143; collective, 7, 108, 116; definition, 5, 8; emotional, 135; gender-based, 3, 18; historical, 4; individual, 7, 125; inherited, 21; race-based, 3; sexual, 3, 13–14, 18, 22; site rejection, 4
Trauma, Torture and Dissociation, 135
Trauma and Survival in Contemporary Fiction, 143
travel, 14, 23, 32–33, 49, 60, 62–71, 74, 76–77, 84–86, 104, 128, 140
Triangular Road, 60, 83
Trinidad, 95, 127
True History of Paradise, The, 7, 11, 36–37, 49–59, 61, 138
Trujillo, Rafael, 14, 29, 30, 136

Unbearable Weight, 86, 97
Urry, John, 11, 142

Valentine, Gill, 120
Vásquez, Sam, 52, 55, 139, 143
Vickroy, Laurie, 114, 143

violence, 3–4, 5, 6, 7, 11, 18, 21, 26, 29, 30–31, 36–37, 40–41, 49–52, 55–57, 59, 109, 123, 131–32, 133–34, 138, 139, 142, 143
Virgin Islands, 12, 107–8, 111, 115–18, 132, 143
virginity testing, 14, 17–20, 22–23
Vodou, 64, 86

Wahab, Amar, 107, 127
Walters, Wendy, 44
war, 5, 50–52, 57, 61, 72–73, 75, 77–78, 81–82, 135. *See also* World War II
Wellington, Alphonso, 118, 121–22, 129–31
West Indies, 60, 71–72, 74, 76–83, 141
Wieringa, Saskia, 112
Wiley, Catherine, 133
Williams, Dana, 24
Williams, Eric, 137
Wolf, Naomi, 109
World War II, 61, 71–73, 75–82, 141. *See also* war
Writing in Limbo, 48–49
Wynter, Sylvia, 137

Yancy, George, 79
Yanique, Tiphanie, 3, 9–10, 12, 107–17, 131–32, 133, 143
Yazdiha, Haj, 137

Zoe, 40–41, 45–47

ABOUT THE AUTHOR

Photo by Thomas Donahue

Dr. Jennifer Donahue specializes in Caribbean literature with a focus on the relationship between narrative, trauma, and sexual politics. Her teaching and research interests include Caribbean and postcolonial literature, Anglophone African literature, and women's and gender studies. Her work has appeared in *A Review of International English Literature*, the *Journal of Commonwealth Literature*, *Studies in Gothic Fiction*, and *Restoration and Eighteenth-Century Theatre Research*.